LATINOS UNIDOS

Critical Perspectives Series
General Editor, Donaldo Macedo, University of Massachusetts, Boston
A book series dedicated to Paulo Freire

Debatable Diversity: Critical Dialogues on Change in American Universities, by Raymond V. Padilla and Miguel Montiel

Pedagogy of Freedom: Ethics, Democracy, and Civic Courage, by Paulo Freire

Critical Education in the New Information Age, by Manuel Castells, Ramón Flecha, Paulo Freire, Henry A. Giroux, Donaldo Macedo, and Paul Willis

Latinos Unidos: From Cultural Diversity to the Politics of Solidarity, by Enrique (Henry) T. Trueba

Forthcoming:

Ideology Matters, by Paulo Freire and Donaldo Macedo

Paulo Freire and the Social Imagination, by Maxine Greene

LATINOS UNIDOS

From Cultural Diversity to the Politics of Solidarity

Enrique (Henry) T. Trueba

ROWMAN & LITTLEFIELD PUBLISHERS, INC.
Lanham • Boulder • New York • Oxford

ROWMAN & LITTLEFIELD PUBLISHERS, INC.

Published in the United States of America
by Rowman & Littlefield Publishers, Inc.
4720 Boston Way, Lanham, Maryland 20706

12 Hid's Copse Road
Cumnor Hill, Oxford OX2 9JJ, England

British Library Cataloguing in Publication Information Available

Library of Congress Cataloging-in-Publication Data
Trueba, Enrique T., 1931–
    Latinos unidos : from cultural diversity to the politics of
solidarity / Enrique T. Trueba.
        p.   cm.
    Includes bibliographical references and index.
    ISBN 0-8476-8728-7 (alk. paper)—ISBN 0-8476-8729-5 (pbk. alk. paper)
    1. Hispanic Americans—Ethnic identity.   2. Hispanic Americans—
Social conditions.   3. Hispanic Americans—Education.   I. Title.
E184.S75T78   1999
305.868—dc21   98-8617
                                                           CIP

Printed in the United States of America

♾ ™ The paper used in this publication meets the minimum requirements of
American National Standard for Information Sciences—Permanence of Paper
for Printed Library Materials, ANSI Z39.48-1984.

Estas páginas están dedicadas a ustedes, a los niños Latinos de los Estados Unidos del Norte que forman la generación más importante para el futuro del mundo occidental y su democracia. Cada letra ha sido escrita con profundo amor y completa fé en un futuro brillante para cada uno de ustedes. Mi deseo más ferviente es que la vida les traiga muchas sonrisas y mucho aliento para realizar su potential total y llevar a cabo grandes obras en el mundo de las artes, las letras, la ciencia, y la tecnología. Que Dios les de la fuerza y el talento para enfrentarse a los retos que les esperan en este país.

Lo que ustedes necesitan es una confianza suprema en sus talentos y su capacidad de sacrificio. Si algún día se encuentran a personas que no los aprecien, que los vean con desdén, o no los acepten porque ustedes pertenecen a otra cultura y poseen otra lengua (además del Inglés), no se entristezcan, ni se enojen, ni se acobarden. Enséñenles con su vida, con sus logros y su dedicación que ustedes son mejores y que merecen el respeto y apoyo de esta nación. **Sí se puede**, y no hagan caso as los que dicen que no se puede. ¡Que Dios los bendiga!

Contents

Tables and Figures

Tables

Figures

Foreword

Donaldo Macedo, Series Editor

Enrique Trueba's book, *Latinos Unidos: From Cultural Diversity to the Politics of Solidarity,* is not only timely, but it is also a brilliant response to the unrelenting assaults on Latinos in the United States that are forcing most of them to live under a permanent state of siege. By strategically using the mass media to demonize and devalue Latinos via sound bites in the form of empty slogans and clichés, the cultural commissars have successfully prevented a rigorous analysis that accurately points to the colonizer-colonized context that has historically informed, and still informs, the relationship between the United States, Mexico, and other Latin American countries and that is "inextricably intertwined by a complex history of militarily, politically, and economically oppressive relationships over the last two hundred years. Latinos have, generation after generation, at times through enormous personal sacrifices and working in subhuman conditions, made significant contributions to this country's cultural life and to its economic and democratic institutions." Unfortunately, the present-day assaults on Latinos, in general, and on Mexican-Americans in particular, demonstrate, once more, that the more things change, the more they stay the same. In other words, the passage of Proposition 187 in California has unleashed a systematic demonization of Latinos such that even the border patrol supervisors seem to encourage beatings of suspects who run away from agents: " 'Thump 'em' " and " 'catch as many tonks as you guys can. Safely. An alien is not worth busting a leg.' Tonk, the sound made as an agent's flashlight strikes the head of a suspect, is now used to refer to an undocumented worker."

However, we should not be terribly surprised with present-day dehumanization of Mexican Americans, because according to Trueba, violence against Mexicans of the Southwest "was justified on the basis of Manifest Destiny, that is, the presumed will of God to have Anglo-Saxon people christianize the savage Mexican folks deemed unworthy of keeping their land [as] T. J. Farhan, for example, writes in his travel journal of 1855."

> Californians [Mexicans] are an imbecile, pusillanimous, race of men, and unfit to control the destinies of that beautiful country. . . . The Old Saxon blood must stride the continent, must command all its northern shores . . . and in their own unaided might, erect the altar of civil and religious freedom on the plains of the Californias. (Cited by Menchaca and Valencia, 1990, 229)

Central to the present-day demonization of Latinos is the creation of an ideologically coded language that serves at least two fundamental functions: On the one hand, this language veils the racism that characterizes U.S. society, and on the other hand, it insidiously perpetuates both ethnic and racial stereotypes that devalue identities of resistance and struggle. I want to argue that although the present assault on Latinos is mostly characterized by a form of racism at the level of language, it is important to differentiate between language as racism and the experience of racism. For example, former presidential candidate Patrick Buchanan's call for the end of illegal immigration "even if it means putting the National Guard all along the Southern frontier" constitutes a form of racism at the level of language.[1] This language-based racism has had the effect of licensing institutional discrimination, whereby both documented and undocumented immigrants materially experience the loss of their dignity, the denial of their humanity, and, in many cases, outright violence, as witnessed by the recent cruel beatings of a Mexican man and woman by the border patrol. This incident was captured on videotape and outraged the Latino/Mexicano communities in the United States, as well as in Mexico, leading to a number of demonstrations in Los Angeles. Language such as "border rats," "wetbacks," "aliens," "illegals," "welfare queens," and "non-White hordes" used by the popular press not only dehumanizes other cultural beings but also serves to justify the violence perpetuated against subordinated groups.

Language as racism is one example of what Pierre Bourdieu refers to as the "hegemony of the symbolic violence."[2] As educators, we need to understand fully the interrelationship between symbolic violence produced through language and the essence of the experience of racism. Although the two are not mutually exclusive, "language also constitutes and mediates the multiple experiences of identity by both historicizing it and revealing its partiality and incompleteness, its limits are realized in the material nature of experience as it names the body through the specificity of place, space, and history.[3] This is very much in line with John Fiske's notion that "there is a material experience of homelessness . . . but the boundary between the two cannot be drawn sharply. Material conditions are inescapably saturated with culture and, equally, cultural conditions are inescapably experienced as material."[4]

By deconstructing the cultural conditions that give rise to the present violent assault on undocumented immigrants, affirmative action, African Americans, and other racial and ethnic groups, we can single out those ideological factors that enable even highly educated individuals to embrace blindly, for example, conservative radio talk-show host Rush Limbaugh's racist tirades designed to demonize and dehumanize ethnic and cultural identities other than his own.

- "There are more American Indians alive today than there were when Columbus arrived or at any other time in history. Does that sound like a record of genocide?"
- "Taxpaying citizens are not being given access to these welfare and health services that they deserve and desire. But if you're an illegal immigrant and cross the border, you get everything you want."[5]

The racism and high level of xenophobia we are witnessing in our society today are not caused by isolated acts of individuals such as Limbaugh or one-time Louisiana gubernatorial candidate David Duke. Rather, these individuals are representatives of an orchestrated effort by segments of the dominant society to wage a war on the poor and on people who, by virtue of their race, ethnicity, language, and class, are reduced, at best, to half citizens and, at worst, to a national enemy responsible for all the ills afflicting our society. We need to understand the cultural and historical context that gives rise to over twenty million Limbaugh "ditto heads" who tune in to his weekly radio and television programs.

We need also to understand those ideological elements that inform our policymakers and those individuals who shape public opinion by supporting and rewarding Limbaugh's unapologetic demonizing of other cultural subjects. For example, television commentator Ted Koppel considers Limbaugh "very smart. He does his homework. He is well informed." Syndicated columnist George Will considers him the "fourth branch of government," and former Secretary of Education William Bennett—the virtue man—describes Limbaugh as "possibly our greatest living American."[6] What remains incomprehensible is why highly educated individuals like Koppel, Will, and Bennett cannot see through Limbaugh's obvious distortions of history and falsification of reality. I posit that the inability to perceive distinctions and falsifications of reality is partly because of the hegemonic forces that promote an acritical education via the fragmentation of bodies of knowledge. Such a process makes it very difficult for students (and the general population) to make connections among historical events so as to gain a more critical understanding of reality. The promotion of an acritical education was evident when David Spritzler, a twelve-year-old student at Boston Latin School, faced disciplinary action for his refusal to recite the Pledge of Allegiance, which he considered "a hypocritical exhortation to patriotism" in that there is not "liberty and justice for all." According to Spritzler, the pledge is an attempt to unite "[the] oppressed and oppressors. You have people who drive nice cars, live in nice houses and they don't have to worry about money. Then you have the poor people, living in bad neighborhoods and going to bad schools. Somehow the Pledge makes it seem like everybody's equal when that's not happening. There is no justice for everybody."[7] Spritzler's teachers' and administrators' inability to see the obvious hypocrisy contained in the Pledge of Allegiance represents what Noam Chomsky calls a "real sign of deep indoctrination [in] that you can't understand elementary thoughts that any ten-year-old can understand. That's real indoctrination. So for him [the indoctrinated individual], it's kind of like a theological truth, a truth of received religion."[8]

Against these cruel and racist cultural conditions, we can begin to understand that it is not a coincidence that Patrick Buchanan reiterated in his first presidential campaign platform that his fellow Americans should "wage a cultural revolution in the nineties as sweeping as the political revolution of the eighties."[9] In fact, this cultural revolution is indeed moving forward with rapid speed, from the onslaught on cultural diversity and multicultural education to Patrick Buchanan's call to U.S. national and patriotic sense to build a large wall to keep the "illegals" in Mexico. Some might claim that Patrick Buchanan's vicious attack on immigrants could be interpreted in ways other than racism. If that were the case, how could we explain his unfortunate testament: "I think God made all people good, but if we had to take a million immigrants in—say Zulus next year or Englishmen—and put them in Virginia, what group would be easier to assimilate and would cause less problems for the people of Virginia?"[10]

It is the same U.S. national and patriotic sense that allowed President Clinton not to be outdone by the extreme Right's forcing him to announce in his 1995 state of the union address that:

All Americans, not only in the states most heavily affected, but in every place in this country, are rightly disturbed by the large numbers of illegal aliens entering our country. The jobs they hold might otherwise be held by citizens or legal immigrants. The public services they use impose burdens on our taxpayers. That's why our administration has moved aggressively to secure our borders more by hiring a record number of new border guards, by deporting twice as many criminal aliens as ever before, by cracking down on illegal hiring, by barring welfare benefits to illegal aliens.[11]

A close analysis of the Republican attack on immigrants and cultural groups and of our liberal Democratic president's remarks during his state of the union address confirms what has been for decades the United States's best-kept secret: There is no critical ideological difference between the Republican and Democratic Parties. Ideologically speaking, in the United States we have a one-party system of government represented by two branches with only cosmetic differences, cloaked in the guise of Republicans and Democrats.

Although these examples point to racism at the level of language, the relationship between racist statements and their effects on people's lives is direct. For example, although California Governor Pete Wilson and other politicians made speeches using a kind of language that demonized so-called illegal immigrants, the actual experience of racism became immeasurably worse with the passage of Proposition 187 in California. In fact, Proposition 187 can be viewed as a precursor to a pattern of assault on subordinated groups that culminated with the passage in November 1996 of Proposition 209, which proposed to end affirmative action in California. The cultural condition that led to the passage of these laws, which were designed to control the flow of illegal immigrants and to end affirmative action in California, has had the effect of licensing institutional discrimination whereby both legal and illegal immigrants materially experience the loss of their dignity, the denial of human citizenship, and, in many cases, outright violent and criminal acts committed by those institutions responsible for implementing the law. According to Human Rights Watch/Americas, "the politically charged drive to curb illegal immigration may be coming at a serious price: beatings, shootings, rapes and death of aliens at the hand of the U.S. Border Patrol."[12]

As anti-immigrant sentiment grows stronger, the Immigration and Naturalization Service (INS) plans to increase its force from 4,200 to 7,000 by the end of 1998, with few safeguards in place to ensure that the new hires will not continue to increase the human rights abuses perpetrated along the U.S.-Mexican border. As Allyson Collins of

Human Rights Watch/Americas notes, the "anti-immigrant sentiment dims the hope of safeguarding aliens as the United States fortifies its border. These are very unpopular victims."[13] Not only is there no guarantee that the INS will protect the rights of human beings who have already been dehumanized as "aliens" or "illegals," but this dehumanizing process has also been met by an unsettling silence, even among liberals. This is not entirely surprising, given the liberals' paradoxical posture with respect to race issues. On the one hand, liberals progressively idealize "principles of liberty, equality, and fraternity [while insisting] upon the moral irrelevance of race. Race is irrelevant, but all is race."[14] On the other hand, some liberals accept the notion of difference and call for ways in which difference is tolerated. For example, there is a rapid growth of textbooks ostensibly designed to teach racial and multicultural tolerance. But, what these texts in fact do is hide the asymmetrical distribution of power and cultural capital through a form of paternalism that promises to the other a dose of tolerance. In other words, because we coexist and must find ways to get along, I will tolerate you. Missing from this posture is the ethical position that calls for mutual respect and even racial and cultural solidarity. As David Goldberg argues, tolerance "presupposes that its object is morally repugnant, that it really needs to be reformed, that is, altered."[15] Accordingly, the racial and cultural tolerance practiced by the dominant sectors within U.S. society may be viewed as a process through which the different "other" is permitted to think, or at least hope, that through this so-called tolerance, the intolerable features that characterize the different "other" will be eliminated or repressed. Thus, Goldberg is correct in pointing out that

> liberals are moved to overcome the racial differences they tolerate and have been so instrumental in fabricating by diluting them, by bleaching them out through assimilation or integration. The liberal would assume away the difference in otherness, maintaining thereby the dominance of a presumed sameness, the universally imposed similarity in identity. The paradox is perpetrated: the commitment to tolerance turns only on modernity's natural inclination to intolerance; acceptance of otherness presupposes as it at once necessitates delegitimization of the other.[16]

Tolerance for different racial and ethnic groups as proposed by some White liberals not only constitutes a veil behind which they hide their racism, it also puts them in a compromising racial position. While calling for *racial tolerance,* a paternalistic term, they often maintain the privilege that is complicit with the dominant ideology. In other words, the call for tolerance never questions the asymmetrical power relations that give them their privilege. Thus, many White liberals willingly call and work for cultural tolerance but are reluctant to confront issues of inequality, power, ethics, race, and ethnicity in a way that could actually lead to social transformation that would make society more democratic and humane and less racist and discriminatory. This form of racism is readily understood by its victims, as observed by Carol Swain, an African American professor at Princeton University: "White liberals are among the most racist people I know; they're so patronizing towards blacks."[17]

It is against this landscape of cruel racism that Enrique Trueba, in his book *Latinos Unidos*, forcibly brings to light the complex neocolonized status of Latinos who find themselves relegated to a bittersweet existence at the periphery of our so-called democracy. *Latinos Unidos* is not another multicultural book that teaches us how to tolerate Latinos. And it is not a book that entertains us through an anthropological discussion of how Chicanos, for example, celebrate "Cinco de Mayo." Although the knowledge of such cultural traits is useful, I do not think it prepares us to deal with the tensions and contradictions generated by the coexistence of multicultural groups in a racist society. Instead, Enrique Trueba challenges us in *Latinos Unidos* to deconstruct the neocolonial reality that has colonized the minds of even some Mexican Americans themselves who work against the interest of their own people. For example, Richard Estrada, whose grandfather immigrated to El Paso, Texas, in 1916, declared that "illegal immigration threatens our national security,"[18] substantiating his claim by stating that Americans in Los Angeles cannot find jobs because of immigrants. Therefore, he argued that we need to militarize the border in order to protect the spirit of Proposition 187 and take our country back. Estrada's reference to "taking our country back" means keeping Mexicans from their own land in much the same way as Native Americans have been kept from theirs, because Mexicans inhabited the land until the U.S. government legitimized the expropriation of almost half of Mexico through the Mexican–American War, which it intentionally provoked. This expropriation was justified through the idea that if you fight for it and you win, you deserve the land. The attempt to use war for land expropriation is eloquently captured in Carl Sandburg's poem, "The People, Yes":

> "Get off this estate."
> "What for?"
> "Because it's mine."
> "Where did you get it?"

"From my father."
"Where did he get it?"
"From his father."

"And where did he get it?"
"He fought for it."
"Well, I'll fight you for it"[19]

   If we critically deconstruct our seemingly democratic society, we begin to understand how the ideological construction of ethnicity and race has played an important role in the reproduction and reinscription of undemocratic structures and power relations along racial, ethnic, cultural, class, and linguistic lines. Thus, *Latinos Unidos* demonstrates how imperative it is that we describe and analyze the historical and social conditions of the United States in order to understand how this ideology produces and reproduces inequalities through invisible institutional mechanisms. Central to these hidden mechanisms, language has played a pivotal role in the production and reproduction of distorted realities. The distortion of realities further demonizes Latinos so as to also rob them of their citizenship as human beings who participate and contribute immensely in our society. The dehumanization of Latinos is painfully captured in the following poem that was distributed to Republican legislators in California by State Assemblyman William Knight:

"Ode to the New California"

I come for visit, get treated regal,
So I stay, who care illegal.

Cross the border poor and broke,
Take the bus, see customs bloke.

Welfare say come down no more,
We send cash right to your door.

Welfare checks they make you wealthy,
Medi-Cal it keep you healthy.

By and by, I got plenty money,
Thanks, American working dummy.

Write to friends in mother land,
Tell them come as fast as can.

They come in rags and Chebby trucks,
I buy big house with welfare bucks.

Fourteen families all move in,
Neighbor's patience growing thin.

Finally, white guy moves away,
I buy his house and then I say,

Send for family, they just trash,
But they draw more welfare cash.

Everything is much good,
Soon we own the neighborhood.

We have hobby, it's called "breeding,"
Welfare pay for baby feeding.

Kids need dentist? Wife need pills?
We get free, we got no bills.

We think America damn good place,
Too damn good for white man's race.

If they no like us, they can go,
Got lots of room in Mexico.[20]

When the legislators' Latino caucus complained that the poem was racist, Knight explained without apologizing that he thought the poem was "clever" and "funny," adding that it was not intended to offend anyone.

In the United States, how can we honestly speak of human freedom in a society that generates and yet ignores ghettos, reservations, human misery, and savage inequalities, and then has the audacity to joke about it? How can we honestly speak of human freedom when the state of California passes Proposition 187, which robs millions of children of their human citizenship? The law proposes to

1. refuse citizenship to children born on U.S. soil to illegal parents,
2. end the legal requirement that the state provide emergency health care to illegal immigrants,
3. deny public education to children of illegal immigrants, and
4. create tamper-proof identification cards for legal immigrants so they can receive benefits.[21]

What becomes clear through *Latinos Unidos* is that our "democracy" remains paralyzed by a historical legacy that has bequeathed to us rampant social inequality along the lines of ethnicity and race. Instead of allowing ourselves to be paralyzed by a historical legacy that dehumanizes, we should pay heed to the humanity of the "other," as eloquently written by Carlos Fuentes, a Mexican writer and social critic. "People and their cultures perish in isolation, but they are born or reborn in contact with other men and women, with men and women of another culture, another creed, another race. If we do not recognize our humanity in others, we shall not recognize it in ourselves."[22]

Notes

1. Michael Rezendes, "Declaring 'Cultural War': Buchanan Opens '96 Run," *Boston Globe*, March 21, 1995, 1.
2. Cited in Henry Giroux, *Border Crossings: Cultural Workers and the Politics of Education* (New York: Routledge, 1992), 20.
3. Henry A. Giroux, "Transgression of Difference," in *Culture and Difference: Critical Perspectives on Bicultural Experiences* (Westport, Conn.: Bergin and Garvey, 1995).
4. John Fiske, *Power Plays, Power Works* (London: Verso Press, 1994), 13.
5. Steven Rendall, Jim Naureckas, and Jeff Cohen, *The Way Things Aren't: Rush Limbaugh's Reign of Error* (New York: New Press, 1995), 47–54.
6. Ibid., 10.
7. Donaldo Macedo, *Literacies of Power: What Americans Are Not Allowed to Know* (Boulder, Colo.: Westview Press, 1994), 10.
8. C. P. Otero, ed., *Language and Politics* (New York: Black Rose Books, 1988), 681.
9. Cited in Giroux, *Border Crossings*, 230.
10. Adam Pertman, "Buchanan Announces Presidential Candidacy," *Boston Globe*, December 15, 1991, 13.
11. William Clinton, "Clinton Speech Envisions Local Empowerment," in *Congressional Quarterly*, January 28, 1995, 303.
12. "Trouble on the Mexican Border," *U.S. News and World Report*, April 24, 1995, 10.
13. Ibid.
14. David T. Goldberg, *Racist Culture* (Oxford: Blackwell, 1993), 6.
15. Ibid., 7.
16. Ibid.
17. Peter Applebone, "Goals Unmet, Duke Reveals the Perils in Effort to Increase Black Faculty," *New York Times*, September 19, 1993, 1.
18. Richard Estrada, "Immigration: Setting the Context." Paper presented at "In or Out? Immigration and Proposition 187," conference held at Harvard Graduate School of Education, February 15, 1995.

19. Carl Sandburg, *The People, Yes* (New York: Harcourt, Brace and World, 1964), 75.

20. From "I Love America!" a poem distributed in May 1995 to California legislators by State Assemblyman William J. Knight. Quoted in Dan Morain and Hank Gladstone, "Racist Verse Stirs up Anger in Assembly," *Los Angeles Times,* May 19, 1993, 3. *The California Journal* 24, no. 7 (1993).

21. Proposition 187 text approved by California voters on November 8, 1994.

22. Carlos Fuentes, "The Mirror of the Other," *The Nation,* March 30, 1992, 411.

Foreword

George Spindler

I have known Henry Trueba since he was a graduate student at Stanford University in the early 1960s.

We did not have much contact, and as far as I know, he did not take any of my courses. In fact my first reminder of his sojourn as a Stanford student was when I glimpsed the master's degree placard on the wall of his study during a visit in 1986, when Louise Spindler and I were visiting his home during our stay as visiting professors at the University of California at Santa Barbara. He had invited us to come, but he had not mentioned that he had been a Stanford student. Now I regret not knowing him during this interesting period of his life. I had heard about him now and then, as a Catholic priest who had dropped out of the priesthood, as an interesting person who had made a decisive career change, and as a good student with some original ideas, and had shaken hands with him, but I didn't know him personally at all. During the ensuing years I have had many and prolonged contacts with him and have come to respect his scholarship and dedication to anthropology and its uses in the betterment of the human condition.

Latinos Unidos is no exception. It is a book clearly written from direct experience and from passion. Trueba's heart is in his writing, as he discusses the travails of being Latino in the United States, and as he discusses the triumphs of the Latinos in the United States. Latinos are not seen as one homogeneous mass of immigrants subject to the same experiences in making adaptations to the exigencies of life in the United States. Many are poor and undereducated. Some are doctors or lawyers or field-workers. There are professors and graduate students and even more undergraduates. There are legions of dropouts. But all of these diverse elements share a heritage of language and culture that acts as a unifying force. The potential is great for social and political action.

Many White mainstreamers are frightened by the "browning" of America. In no place in the United States is this more apparent than in California. The governor of the state and its legislators try to avert what they see as a threat to their supremacy in politics, law, and in the economy by repealing laws benefiting minorities and enacting new ones that restrict and oppress minorities. Inevitably much of this action is directed at Latinos, because they are the largest minority in the state and the fastest growing one. Apparently they do not understand that oppression and limitations will only serve to reinforce the growing solidarity of Latinos. Instead, their policies should be aimed at helping minorities to achieve in schools, in occupations, and in their general participation in the broad middle-class mainstream. Why is it important that they are brown-skinned (but many are not) or that they originally came from Mexico (but many did not)? The hidden racism of the U.S. mainstream is revealed.

Enrique Trueba treats all of these problems and many more in *Latinos Unidos*. It is a book that no one interested in the future of California and in the United States of America, as a holding company for unified diversity, can afford to miss.

George Spindler
Stanford University

Acknowledgments

When you reach your early sixties your intellectual debts are often great and hidden like subterranean rivers that continue to bring life to the large trees that provide shade and permit the life of many other creatures. I could never list all the people whose words, guidance, and writings have inspired my efforts. Some of the earliest scholars that impacted my life, such as George Peter Murdock, George and Louise Spindler, Paulo Freire, and George De Vos, are giant trees that facilitated and nurtured the growth of many of us. There are, however, a number of younger scholars who have made very significant contributions to my intellectual development, and I want to express to them my sincere gratitude. The important work of Carola and Marcelo Suárez-Orozco and their friendship, support, and affection over the years come to mind first. I am grateful for the work and extraordinary insights of Gary Orfield and his continued support and the nurturing soul that makes him one of the persons most loved in academia and most respected by colleagues and students. His assistance, honest response, and friendship are deeply appreciated and have marked one of the most productive years of my life, the 1996–1997 academic year at Harvard University. Also, the stimulating and genuinely challenging views of Donaldo Macedo and Lilia Bartolomé have forced me to engage in a literature not well known before; their ideas have brought home many experiences as an immigrant that had been buried over the years of academic work as a formal member of the institution, of the academy. I appreciate the extraordinary work of Jorge González with an entirely fresh view of culture in action, of communication, and of communities in Mexico.

This volume was greatly improved by the penetrating analytical remarks of Walter Secada, who made me think twice about the relationship between my religious and academic experiences. His questions forced me to recognize the need to articulate in a clearer way the relationships between the parts of the whole, between the various segments of chapters and the overall flow of ideas. I am deeply grateful for his help and support. I also want to acknowledge a debt of gratitude to a loyal friend who has helped me a great deal in my writing. She has intuitively read my mind and analyzed possible ways to reconstruct sentences, chapters, paragraphs, and ways of putting complex thoughts into words. This woman, Jackie Captain, is still today the most honest, efficient, and bright editor I have ever met. This and other books would have never come to exist without her patient and determined hand, which leaves no stone unturned. Along with her and other colleagues, friends, and extraordinary minds that I have been fortunate to encounter, I want to thank my students and dear friends from Harvard University; the young promising scholars of tomorrow whose work I admire and whose views influenced my views and stimulated my thinking in many ways. Their remarks invited reflection and demanded from me a new and honest analysis of myself as an ethnographer, Latino, professor, and a human being. I will never be able to mention all of them, but I must at least thank Mariela Páez, Norma Jiménez, Daniel Bekeli, Guiomar García, Corinne Varon, Peggy Freedson, Julie Pulerwitz, Amy Emura, Maria Martinelli, Bill Tsang, Nurit Sheiberg, Erik Jacobson, and many other outstanding students.

Chapter 2 will include small portions that appear in the digest of the ERIC Clearinghouse on Urban Education (Teachers College, Columbia University) entitled *Latinos in the United States: The Emerging Majority in Our Schools and Society* (with L. Bartolomé). Some examples of equity problems mentioned in chapter 3 are taken from a chapter entitled "Race and Ethnicity in Academia," to appear in L. Valverde and L. A. Castanell (eds.) (in press), *The Multicultural Campus: Strategies for Transforming Higher Education*, Walnut Creek, Calif.: Altamira Press. Portions of chapters 4 and 5 may appear in another publication (under negotiation at this point).

My hope is that these brief and simple pages may invite reflection and bring educators to their senses in the face of one of the most rapid and overwhelming changes in the ethnic and racial composition of American society and more importantly in the cultural fabric of this nation of immigrants. This is an optimistic book, but it calls for a realistic assessment of our priorities and perspectives on the education of the next generation. It will be a brown generation, multiracial and multilingual, but a generation as competent and patriotic as any of the previous generations of immigrants.

Introduction: The Genesis of This Volume and Its Author

In the most secret compartment of our souls, each of us seeks a legitimate reason to express our ideas and share our experiences with other humans. As other people reflect on their interactional patterns and their perception of us, they help us define our self-identity. As we grow older and interact with different groups, we tend to look into our isolated selves and discover multiple layers of our personality and multiple identities developed in response to our engagement in making meaning with peoples from diverse cultures, languages, and social strata. Our outlook on life, however, seems to change with the audience we engage, and making sense of life becomes a priority. Making sense of our own personal life is the first step in a series of efforts to articulate meaningfully our existence and define ourselves, our quintessence, and our raison d'être. I cannot detach issues of my personal identity from issues of Latino solidarity, cultural hegemony in America, and the terrifying experience of discovering that our enduring self is gone or is a stranger from our past; so distant from our *situated self* (or our *situated selves*) that a major reconstruction job becomes essential. Let me explain. Contrary to a simple theory of adaptive strategies that mark in our lives a sequence of "situated selves," a chain of consecutive identities modifying the original enduring self, formed and nursed by our family of origin, through the early years of our life in the company of our parents and other adults, my identities (and probably those of many Latinos) seem to coexist and remain vital throughout my entire life. Each identity becomes dominant vis-à-vis the group I interact with and the topic or focus of our interaction. I then can code-switch and take another identity, deal with another group, manage other matters, and move on to a third or fourth. The addition of several identities throughout my life seems to complicate matters and make it harder to totally integrate them all into a single set of values, lifestyles, or coherent set of personal characteristics. I may be wrong in my attempt to link my previous religious life with my current academic life. Yet, I see a continuity of intellectual effort, analytical strategies, daily habits associated both with religion and thought processes, and, most of all, a profound commitment to the world of ideas that was nourished within the peculiar lifestyle into which I was socialized as a Jesuit. To me, it makes sense. My academic life would have never existed, at least the type of academic life I have lived, without my religious experiences. This chapter attempts to illuminate this connection. Let me explain the relationship of my religious and academic experiences by describing my life first.

I am a Latino, and I share much of my identity with groups that are very different from me but with whom I have interacted meaningfully and intensively. When I ask myself why I have been in the United States since 1962, I realize that there have been many unexpected events and turns in my life that somehow placed me in this country. If I ask who I was before I came to this country, I can assure myself that I am still the same, and because I return to Mexico occasionally, I recover my own sense of the person I was when I lived there. Of course, I have changed a great deal; as the years have gone by I have lost some hair, and what is left is turning white. I lost part of my home language and may even have an accent in Spanish (in addition to the accent I have in English). I am still a person of Mexican descent (a Chicano, Mexican, or Mexican American—depending on who wants to know). But I have added a number of identities to that one. Therefore, answering the question of who I was (as briefly as I can) may not still explain why I am, who I am, or why I have different identities; my experiences in this country are a continuation of my previous experiences, yet critically important, and such that they helped shape my life and self-concept radically.

I was born on October 29, 1931, in Mixcoac, a small *colonia* (neighborhood) fifteen miles south of downtown Mexico City. We had a very large Catholic family, twelve children—I was number ten and one of seven boys. Although my father was not always a regular practicing Catholic, he believed in God and died a fervent Catholic in 1950 when I was nineteen years old. Although my childhood in Mexico during the depression was marked by some memories of hunger and lack of clothes, overall I was not fully aware of our poverty. As a young child I sometimes wondered why we enjoyed so many toys of paper and games at home or a good meal at Christmas and a few gifts (mostly clothes), without feeling deprived. I do remember, however, that every so often, after we were in bed, my mother would cry for hours. She was worried about the next day's meals. Watery oatmeal with sugar, a bit of milk, and a piece of bread would carry us until the afternoon. A good meal would consist of tortilla soup, rice, and once in a while, a piece of chicken so tender that we would carefully chew all the little bones. I do not recall ever having a new pair of pants or a new pair of shoes during the first twelve years of my life. I always wore my older brothers' old pants and shoes until they fell apart. My bed was an old crib we had used for many years; I inherited it when I was five; by the time I was ten, my legs were sticking out the slats to the knees. I recall that when I was about five, my brothers were already organized into a sort of gang, and there were fights in the street very frequently. I had my share of fights and was often pushed into them and rescued if I was losing. One of my older brothers was good with knives and guns, and my father finally kicked him out of the house when he was sixteen. Eventually, he would become an entrepreneur, who did very well economically but died in his forties of a heart attack (after having been a heavy smoker).

As happened often among large immigrant families (especially those coming from Spain), I was carefully groomed and socialized into the church and gradually became one of two children designated to enter the seminary. To prepare for life in the seminary, at the age of twelve I was sent to a special Jesuit boarding school called Escuela Apostólica de San José. The discipline and supervision were unbearable; I felt as if I lived in a correctional school except for the obligatory prayers several times a day and the silence or readings during the meals (except on holidays). I hated the place so much that I went through all kinds of sneaky plans to escape at times for days. I would get out of the dorms (after going to the bathroom) and jump over a high wall that gave access to the playground of a military academy next door. It was not easy; at times the black dog guarding the academy was nearby and I felt very scared. Eventually I saved enough money (from gifts from uncles and my godfather) to escape from Mexico City and go to Guadalajara to visit with some cousins. I was suspended, kicked out of the school, and later readmitted. I returned home for less than a year when I was almost sixteen, and at that point I decided to give in, made good grades, and entered the seminary. It made some sense at the time because life at home was not only crowded but conflictive in many ways, and I could not stand seeing the economic troubles my parents were going through. Besides, my oldest brother and I never got along well.

On December 31, 1947, two years after my parents had celebrated their twenty-fifth wedding anniversary, I entered the Jesuit seminary. I was not allowed to see my family for an entire year and was permitted to see them only twice a year thereafter. My immersion into the religious experience was total. I prayed intensively every day, practiced self-discipline, castigated my body with chains of sharp wire tied around my legs and whipping instruments (*la disciplina*) that left marks on my back for life. I fasted and prayed for thirty days and nights at the beginning of my career as a Jesuit and again at the very end after my ordination into the priesthood. I worked as a missionary among the Tzeltal Indians in Chiapas and taught in the Jesuit colleges of Puebla and Mexico. In brief, I lived with the Jesuits for eighteen years, until December 25, 1965! The many experiences of my Jesuit life shaped my life and values beyond measure. I am who I am in my way of thinking, daily routines, views of life, and values as a result of training with the Jesuits, in spite of the fact that I left the Jesuit order and reclaimed my autonomy, stopped practicing the Catholic religion, and even became quite skeptical about some of the religious dogmas and practices. The reason why I bring all this up is that my *enduring self* has indeed endured, and I have finally accepted the fact that it left a more profound mark on me than I ever wanted to acknowledge. Even the things I did to dramatize my independence and change my life have been pretty much acts of rebellion against Jesuit dogma. But even my own righteousness in rejecting certain liberal practices in daily life, in personal relationships, sexual practices, and so on, are ways of getting back at the Jesuits, those I knew were less than moral in their daily lives (or, if you want, just human and weak). One of the last important jobs I had as a Jesuit was to become the special confessor of priests for a year. They would come to my private room (where I had a confession box with foolproof privacy for anybody coming in any time day or night) and confess again and again the same "sins." They all sounded so confused, humiliated, disturbed, and obsessed with their sexual experiences—at times so absurd that I promised myself I would never become one of them, and I would expedite my departure from the order. On the other hand, my profound love of the ritual (the Mass, the choir, the *Kyrie Eleison,* and the *Oremus* with the appropriate Gregorian tones, especially during Holy Week and Easter) can bring instantly to mind moments lived thirty years ago. The tendency to give generously, to help others, and to assist in any way I can betrays my common sense and sets me up to be used again and again by people who smell a free ride and crave personal attention. That is me, for better or for worse. All other identities have found a corner and fit one way or another. Even the "other" identities in personal relationships, in intellectual endeavors, in political struggles, in status changes as a married person, a lover, a father, a friend, a professor, a boss, and so on, all take a slight overtone of priestly love and tender care that are normally absent in those roles.

The religious socialization was so powerful that it was almost impossible to think about leaving the Jesuit order, and any attempt to do so was met with such resistance on the part of the superiors that one would not dare try again for several years. Many of my attempts to leave were silenced by my spiritual directors as "a temptation" that should be dismissed. Many sleepless nights (at one point, I spent over a month with insomnia) and profound anxiety caused me to have an ulcer before I was twenty-five years old, convinced that in the short range there was nothing I could do to leave, to regain my freedom, or to find another life. The systematic and daily *examination of conscience*, the careful writing of journals, recording my reflections on my spiritual life and how I resolved my crises, the encounters with real-life persons, and the enormous longing for my freedom became both a treasure and a trap. I kept a little black book in which I had underlined many passages that I would read and reread during difficult crises. When one day I read the book for the last time, I realized I was trapped, paralyzed, and unable to detach myself from a very profound engagement in a spiritual dead end. I then decided that the time had come for me to leave the order forever. Therefore, I finally decided that I would wait to leave until after my ordination to the priesthood. I could not bring myself to tell my family the truth, especially my mother, who was sixty-six years old when I was ordained as a priest on June 17, 1962. It was then that the idea of going to the United States occurred. My superiors felt that being a good student I would gain from going to the United States to study theology; furthermore, they hoped that the trip might help me forget the idea of leaving the Jesuit order. Actually I was determined to leave and leave with permission from Rome, and I spent a number of years writing to the Roman Curia and the general of the Jesuit order until I received permission to leave.

Fortunately for my future life as an academician, while I was working in Chiapas as a missionary (as a sort of paramedical expert in parasites and lung problems but willing to try to cure anybody with any problems), I met some anthropologists from Stanford (and assisted them to get out of town safely after they had taken blood samples and made the town angry). Eventually this contact would bring me to Stanford as a student in anthropology. This was an important incident that linked my life with the United States permanently. Because I was determined to request permission to leave the Jesuit order (having finished theology and been ordained into the priesthood), I was called to Mexico City to face my superior in the fall of 1965. I had a long talk with him, and he asked me to return the next morning. As I left his office, I met an old friend and classmate of mine who worked with the provincial. He asked me what the provincial had said; when I mentioned I was coming back the next morning for a final word with the provincial, my friend promptly changed his tone and in a confidential and delicate manner begged me to go back to the United States immediately and not to come the next morning. He explained that several other Jesuits who had the intention of leaving had been confined to a mental hospital from which they could not get out. I was alarmed. I followed his advice and went straight to the airport to return to California, where I was finishing my master's degree in anthropology. I sent a letter to the Jesuit superiors announcing that if I did not receive the dispensation of my vows by the end of December, I would leave without permission and make it public. This ultimatum worked. By Christmas of 1965, I actually received permission to leave the Jesuit order, said my last Mass, and announced my decision to everyone. Several years later in the streets of Mexico City I met two of my former ex-Jesuit friends; they were begging in the street, toothless, and most likely suffering dementia. I thought to myself, "That would have been me if I had kept my appointment with the superior." I felt sad, angry, and sure I had made the right decision. This was a devastating experience. All this made me feel more secure in the United States away from the Jesuit order. In fact, as it was stipulated in the rules and contracts I had to sign to leave the order, I stopped all communication with persons who knew me as a priest and cut all my contacts with other Jesuits.

As I left behind one type of life and took another, I had to relearn how to behave, how to walk safely, and how to support myself economically. To complicate matters, as I was leaving the Jesuit order, I felt invincible and psychologically powerful. Stress, however, was so high that the very day I was going to drive from Palo Alto to Los Angeles in search of a summer job prior to beginning my doctoral program at the University of Pittsburgh, I began to lose my sight and had to pull over on the freeway. The police called a friend and I spent about a month recovering, until I could see well and read again. I began to write a few words at first, and several weeks later I could focus and read again. My friend thought I had tried to poison myself, but I don't recall having taken any medicine! With a five-hundred-dollar loan from my friend and a few books in my old car I drove to Los Angeles in May 1966. Having left the priesthood I had to earn a living. Another friend at the University of California at Los Angeles was kind enough to hire me as a researcher for the School of Public Health in a project studying the heart conditions of African Americans in Venice, California (at that time a tough ghetto). From the altar to the ghetto! I had to learn fast. I had not been in Venice on Brook Street for more than ten minutes when, as I was looking for an apartment to rent, I was beaten up by a Black gang. They broke my nose and knocked me unconscious. When I woke up and spoke, they said, "This guy is not an American. Who are you?" Still bleeding, I calmly explained I was working with the physicians of UCLA. From that day on they called me "Doc" and escorted me every place I went. No problem. In fact, I became the private consultant for the head of the gang and a sort of friend. I could date Black girls without any repercussions. This experience in Venice woke me up to the reality of a life in America quite different from that of the priests and scholars. Furthermore, for the first time in my life I had the freedom to talk to women, to visit with them, and to be intimate. I had much to learn, of course, and I was already thirty-four years old.

My identity as an anthropologist doing fieldwork in the ghetto did not interfere with my priestly concerns about people. I had to divide my time between gathering data for the project and taking people to the hospital, helping them learn to write, purchasing and bringing food for some families, and keeping safe (especially on the weekends). The shootings on Saturday nights were frightening. Fortunately for me, Mrs. Chávez, one of the wisest persons I ever met in the ghetto, became my guardian angel, and she coached me during difficult moments. That woman, part Indian, married to a Latino, was the only one respected by opposite gangs any time day or night. She knew everybody in the streets by name and would not hesitate to shout out her name and walk through during the shootings. I learned a great deal from her, and I learned more about myself than I ever expected. As I became aware of the drug activity in the area, I set my clock to be awake from 3:00 A.M. on and drive around or observe from my apartment. My neighbors had upper-class young people (some were UCLA students) coming to their homes to use cocaine or marijuana, and I was often invited. Of course, I never felt I could try, but I was curious about them and visited their parties. I was more curious about what was going on in the nightclubs. One day I discovered that a Latino girl I had met was being sexually abused by a strong Latino man in his fifties when she was drunk. I tried to help (my priestly instinct), and this man pulled out a knife and put it to my neck. I left very angry, went to one of my neighbors, and borrowed a gun with the intention of "getting this guy." I returned to the club and found the man very drunk, lying on the floor with his wife and child. The wife read my intentions and pleaded, *"Por favor, no lo mate"* ("Please, don't kill him"). That was a rapid change of identity for me. Was I capable of killing someone? Could I do it? I think I was very close. So close that I changed entirely my strategies and fieldwork activities. I concentrated on families and left the nightlife. I worked with Latinos who had just arrived from Mexico, and I saw a misery that I had never seen in Mexico (not even in the dump areas around Mexico City). I recall that an eighteen-year-old Mexican kid who looked pretty peaceful and normal killed his father with an ax. Weekends were the most dangerous. Black and Latino gangs would continue to fight in the streets, and the weekends would often end with one or two youngsters having been killed. I was glad to end my fieldwork and go to Pittsburgh with a few bucks, my own car (an old Volvo I bought in Los Angeles), my books in the backseat, and fresh memories of intense experiences. I drove across the country with the girl who had been raped in the nightclub, with the mission to take her to her family in Texas. I remember the heat of the summer, the confusion in her face, and her shy request for a "loan." I left her in Uvalde, and when I arrived at El Paso and parked in a shopping mall, my car was stolen. It took the police several days to find it. The windows were broken, but the books were intact! I fixed the car and left for Pittsburgh, broke again but ready to study.

I began to realize that this period of my life marked a drastic transition from my comfortable life as a priest where I was rich, with money both in my pocket and in the bank, despite my vow of poverty, to a life as a poor student. I had been a member of the clergy for so long that I had no idea of how difficult it was to get money, to buy a car, to buy food, and to keep finances straight. Now that I was really poor—actually permanently broke because I had to send money to my mother from the fellowship I obtained—I felt happy and accepted the challenge. I had survived in Chiapas, why couldn't I survive in Pittsburgh? I knew by now about ghettos and could sense danger in advance; I knew when to get out quickly, when to stay inside the car, and when to walk and on what side of the street. I loved anthropology and was truly honored to be a doctoral student. Pittsburgh was the best experience in my life. I could work in the library all day long. In a sense, it was a backdoor entrance to a regular life as a Jesuit, meaning a Jesuit intellectual accustomed to reading and writing all day long, without having the constraints and mental struggles of Catholic dogmas, theology, and dual standards regarding women, families, rituals, and so on. Furthermore, I was learning so much so fast about everything, including intimate relationships and friendships with women. It was so wonderful! Why was this wonderful? Primarily because I was free! I felt responsible for myself; I was really an adult for the first time in my life, responsible for my acts out in the world. But was I? In some sense I was reliving my adolescent life and trying to become an adult, always aware of my handicaps and my priestly generosity, often mistaken for ingenuity or even stupidity by some, but also attracting many others, especially younger women, thus creating for me conflicting obligations and strange relationships. This time of my life was definitely marking another drastic change and new self-identity as an adult male in relationships with women. Amazing how much one needs to learn to play those roles!

Now I could speak to women and visit them and learn about that world I had fantasized and dreamed about for so many years! Was it true that . . . ? How does one . . . ? Who would teach me? Actually, I found women who were extraordinarily generous, kind, intriguing, intellectually challenging, and totally enchanting. The problem was that I found all women that way, and I could not disentangle my adolescent growth from genuine lasting relationships. During this period of transition, my *situated self* and my other identities were undergoing transformation and were somewhat confused; what was clear to me and consistent from the previous twenty years was my commitment to learn, to read and write, to grow, and to cross disciplinary boundaries. I had left theology and philosophy behind; in fact, I had burned my books in anger when I left the priesthood. I was now reading everything I could in anthropology and linguistics, and I was taking courses on many regions, such as Mesoamerica, Micronesia, the Americas, and Africa. I had hardly any contact with Latinos because there were none in my department, and the few women I encountered at parties or at other meetings would have nothing to do with an ex-priest. So I found friends among Anglo-Americans, especially Protestants, agnostics, and Jewish people.

I was lucky to get an Andrew Mellon Fellowship (not lucky, but fortunate to have mentors and supporters; the chair of the department and his wife had been so kind and generous—both were Jewish). I sent money to my mother every month, was intellectually productive, and began to feel profoundly patriotic in this country. I was truly grateful to be given a chance and to study at a major university. So many people, bright professors and students, were willing to help my professional development that I was overwhelmed with gratitude. One of the "Jesuit" traits is a philosophy and theology of self-degradation whereby we must believe we are worthless, and whatever we have must be given in return for having been forgiven by God and helped by others. That sense of obligation to each and every person who helped me became an obsession and was often the reason why I organized parties for faculty members and students, offered any help I could in any possible way, and spent much of my time trying to help others. At the same time, I was never sure I was good enough, and I was willing to remain quiet to come across as less competitive. But when my papers were finished and the professors realized how much effort I had put into them and became aware of the ideas I presented, they got curious and helped me more. Peter Murdock, an extraordinary intellectual and a savvy politician (feared by many of his colleagues), took an interest in me and hired me as one of his assistants. His direction, demands (at times unrestrained and even demeaning), his genuine care, and his mentoring changed my life and opened opportunities I would never have had without his intervention. I was always somewhat frightened by his intellect, and even my expressions of gratitude were always formal and distant. When he died, my deepest regret was never having had the courage to tell him how much I loved him and how much his support meant to me. Murdock loved to verbally attack a student and kick him out of class or to take the Jesuits to task and then ask me embarrassing questions. He never tolerated a job half done or a poor excuse. But he recognized excellence. He asked me, "How did you learn English so fast?" meaning how could I write so well (I knew I had syntactic problems but could manage the content). I was ranked his second-best student in my cohort, and I still treasure that honor. It was Murdock who gave me detailed feedback on my data and analysis, and he was the only one who could place a single phone call and get me an interview and a job. He did more to help me succeed than anybody else in academia I can think of.

By the time I was a doctoral student at the University of Pittsburgh in the fall of 1966, I had been in the country for four years and felt confident in the language (at least in the written language). I knew I could never go back to Mexico because I did not want to face the Jesuits and my family, who never forgave me for leaving the Jesuit order. I appreciated my freedom, the university libraries, and the quality of my life. As I discuss the research projects and intellectual struggles in which I have participated, the components of my various identities will become clearer. In fact, my very choice of intellectual endeavors, theoretical arguments, research projects, personal relationships, and professional affiliations are integral components of those identities and often permitted the coexistence of seemingly contradictory or at least divergent self-identities. I don't think these various directions are either contradictory or divergent, but to understand them I need to draw from a much deeper set of experiences in my life. As I reflect on my personal life and examine the transition from an intensively religious Jesuit life to that of an anthropology student and later a professor, I can see the continuity in my daily routines and the uninterrupted intellectual life of reading, writing, teaching, and thinking. My academic life did not end with theology, and it did not begin with anthropology. Yet, the kind of academic life I have had is uniquely marked by my religious life. I have used my personal experience in an attempt to understand the phenomenon of apparent multiple identities intertwined in a single life of an immigrant. I am speculating that perhaps other

Latino immigrants may go through similar experiences of overlapping identities and personal lives.

I suspect that much of what happens today to Latinos and a fair analysis of their many identities and their resiliency are connected with experiences that, like mine, have forced them to survive in entirely different worlds; not only different intellectual and disciplinary worlds (from philosophy and theology to anthropology, psychology, and linguistics) but from one set of intimate friends to another, from one set of cultural norms to another, and from one set of political principles to another. Resiliency and the emerging collective identity of Latinos are better understood in the larger context of the rapid sociocultural change and adaptation of most Latinos in the United States.

Personal Resilience and Self-Identities

Resiliency does not completely explain the ontological need for hope and the investment of our lives in pedagogical activities, but it is a beginning in the right direction:

> Hope is an ontological need. Hopelessness is but hope that has lost its bearings, and become a distortion of that ontological need. . . . Hope, as it happens, is so important for our existence, individual and social, that we must take every care not to experience it in a mistaken form, and thereby allow it to slip toward hopelessness and despair. Hoplessness and despair are both the consequence and the cause of inaction and immobilism. . . . One of the tasks of the progressive educator, through a serious, correct political analysis, is to unveil opportunities for hope, no matter what the obstacles may be. (Freire 1995, 8–9)

Latinos in this country have consistently found themselves in settings and circumstances that seem at times opposite and even contradictory. Paulo Freire understands this. He himself has been there during his exile experiences, and he has been able to hold to two opposite extremes, one of absolute and honest realism about the oppression of many in our world, and the other, of indestructible hope and a visionary utopia in which there is a world of peace and equity for all. In confronting a daily reality of pain and frustration, hope becomes a necessary condition to continue life; hope becomes an "ontological need" because we cannot exist without it. Slipping into any form of hopelessness and despair is giving up life; it is suicide. Perhaps what characterizes Latino populations is their skill in survival in the most trying circumstances. Prior to arriving in the United States, many Latinos have experienced terrorism, poverty, political and religious persecution, hunger, extended periods of high stress, arduous physical activities, the bureaucratic nightmare of standing in daily lines to obtain legal documents, physical danger, and other tests of mental endurance. Their histories are as diverse as their physical, socioeconomic, and cultural characteristics.

There is a popular saying that characterizes the resiliency of Latinos, which has become the title of a Mexican telenovela, *"esperar contra toda esperanza,"* which means to hope against all hope. Latinos are undoubtedly one of the most resourceful groups of immigrants of the twentieth century. Their creativity, insistence, and perseverance in penetrating through any borders to this country are only matched by their capacity to survive under the most adverse circumstances. The experiences of the *mojados* has always amazed growers, politicians, law-enforcement and immigration officers, and members of other immigrant groups. I interviewed a Mexican in his seventies who shined shoes in Brownsville, Texas. He was proud to say that before he became an American citizen, he had crossed the border more than twenty times and had worked all over this country. He had clear memories of Midwest winters and agricultural labor in Texas, Oklahoma, Ohio, and even Wisconsin. The woman who cleaned my apartment in Cambridge, Massachusetts, came from Central America without documents and witnessed the brutal rape of young women traveling with their father. They had only one meal in six days and traveled lying on top of each other, twelve people in the trunk and on the floor of an old station wagon in the winter.

Latinos don't fit any traditional category. They can be as white as Caucasians from mainstream America and Europe, as black as native Africans and African Americans, as Asian as native Japanese, Chinese, or Asian Americans; or they can look like Indians, Canadian Indians, Native Americans, Indians from Mexico and Latin America, or like mestizos, because most Mexicans and many Latin Americans are of mixed Indian-European descent. Their lifestyles, social backgrounds, and experiences in their home countries are so distant and diverse that some may know more about the middle class in America and be more comfortable living in a large American city than they would be in a small rural town in their country of origin. Economically, Latino immigrants come from the richest families as well as from the poorest; educationally, Latinos may come from the most sophisticated intellectual groups of university professors who are closely associated with the best European institutions, or from the illiterate peasant villages in Sonora, Oaxaca, or Chiapas. As far as religious affiliation is concerned, immigrants range from practicing devote traditional Catholics to skeptical atheists; many are still nature-worshiping Indians from animistic religions and non-Western religions, and many have recently become converts to Protestant denominations such as Baptists, Seventh-Day Adventists, Pentecostals, and Presbyterians. We can also find converts to the Mormon religion and to almost any other religious group. The enormous flexibility of Latinos in their ability to accommodate and bend in order to survive has been the most instrumental characteristic of their spread throughout the entire hemisphere, including to Canada and Alaska. Mexicans joke about *"la reconquista pacífica del Suroeste"* ("the peaceful reconquest of the territories of the Southwest" that were taken away from Mexico during the mid-nineteenth century).

Dealing with Latinos is not easy for the press, the law-enforcement agencies, the government, or for mainstream populations. I can see the terror in the eyes of senior citizens in central California as they see their towns becoming brown. The mere presence of large brown-skinned families walking in the supermarket, in public parks, and shopping malls raises high levels of anxiety among some Whites. They are not quite sure how to take this peaceful invasion. When the press discusses racial issues, often the discourse is dichotomized into Black and White; they have no racial category into which Latinos fit. To complicate matters further, white-looking Latinos (racially of light complexion) can pass for either European, if they have a noticeable accent, or for American, if they speak English without a heavy accent. To add to the confusion, many Latino women marry into non-Latino families and take Anglo last names, further camouflaging their ethnic identity as Latinas. In this complex context of racial, cultural, social, and economic diversity, the multiple phenotypic characteristics of Latinos and Latinas mislead many into believing that there is no cultural cohesiveness within any given ethnic subgroup (Mexican, Cuban, or Puerto Rican), much less across groups. The fact is, there is a strong cultural affinity among Latinos within and across ethnic subgroups. How do we explain the increasing cultural and political solidarity of Latinos in the United States? Why do so many Latinos show their determination to maintain a distinct ethnic identity (or identities) without necessarily giving up their position in American society (often within the mainstream society)? How do they manage to walk the fine cultural line between the various subcultures in American society? The terms *multiple identities* and *multiple affiliations* allude to a unique characteristic of Latinos. One could argue that people of color have a difficult time passing for, or crossing racial, ethnic, and cultural lines because of the phenotypical characteristics that mark and separate them. Yet, in my limited experience, I have seen Black Latinos straddle between African American groups and racially mixed Latino groups (such as Cubans or Puerto Ricans). Many other Latinos cross racial and cultural lines between mainstream Anglos and the Latino community at work, in school, and in a variety of public institutions and settings on a daily basis. I suggest that it is precisely in this phenotypic ambiguity and cultural flexibility of Latinos that their strength lies; they can code-switch (linguistically and culturally), pass for members of many groups, reproduce interactional styles, and function comfortably across social strata of different ethnic groups in ways that no other immigrants have managed to do. Their accommodation goes beyond their skills in using their phenotypic characteristics and is more about developing flexible, adaptive strategies and the ability to handle stress. Latinos have managed to survive the most oppressive situations across borders in this hemisphere, and they have adapted to the American lifestyle through multiple strategies. Some Latinos have established a genuine bicultural existence of frequent social intercourse with their home culture and mainstream America; others have re-created their home culture in this country and have recruited their *paisanos* (country-men) to rebuild a series of networks that provide them with an informal social security system. Others have a very utilitarian view of the United States; they see it first, from a nativistic perspective, as a place to work without becoming attached to it, and they state their firm commitment to never learn English; but later they change, and as they see their children grow competent in English, learn the American way of life, and get an education, they change their minds and begin to resign themselves to stay in this country.

Latinos, in spite of their diversity in terms of ethnic affiliations, social class, race, religion, educational level, language, and culture, demonstrated a unique political cohesiveness for the first time in this country during the 1996 presidential elections. The percentage of votes more than doubled that of the previous elections. A few days after Tuesday, November 5, 1996, presidential election day, the papers began to publish articles about the unexpected show of force by Hispanic voters in southern California. The *New York Times* published the following statement on the front page:

> The results of Tuesday's balloting around the country made clear that the Democratic-leaning Hispanic vote is becoming an ever larger factor in American politics, nowhere more so than here in Orange County, the sprawling suburb south of Los Angeles that has traditionally been an icon of conservative Republicanism. In Orange County, as elsewhere in California, and in states like Arizona, Texas, and Florida, Hispanic voters showed up at the polls in record numbers, giving President Clinton 72 percent of their ballots. They also gave many other Democratic candidates in federal, state and local races major support and, in some cases, the edge

needed for victory. (B. Drummond Ayres Jr., *New York Times*, Sunday, November 10, 1996, 1)

Also in Orange County Loretta Sanchez, a Hispanic Democrat, unseated Representative Robert K. Dornan, one of the most vocal conservative Republicans, who had clearly expressed his anti-immigrant sentiments. Dornan bitterly complained that he had lost because "illegals" had voted against him. Despite the apparent victory of a stronger Latino political presence at the polls, there was also the failure to persuade the public that Proposition 209 was xenophobic and unconstitutional; the vote was 54 percent in favor of Proposition 209 (46 percent against). The text of the proposition, somewhat misleading to the public, demanded that the state should not discriminate against, or grant preferential treatment to any person or group in public employment, education, or contracting. Governor Pete Wilson's strong support of this proposition profoundly alienated Latinos. This proposition threatened to end affirmative action in California as we knew it. However, on December 7, 1996, the *New York Times* stated that the previous week, Chief Judge Thelton E. Henderson of the Federal District Court in San Francisco had ordered the university system to retain affirmative action programs and had issued a temporary restraining order against Governor Pete Wilson and Attorney General Daniel E. Lungren until the public hearings of December 16, when the court would consider the arguments for a preliminary injunction against the enforcement of the new initiative. The grounds were that Proposition 209 had a "strong probability" of being unconstitutional (*New York Times*, December 7, 1996, 10). Although Latinos were not alone in building opposition to Proposition 209, they were a major force. African American students were also deeply affected by the initiative. For better or for worse, the time has come for Latinos to establish a strong political affiliation with groups that will decide the future of ethnically, culturally, and economically diverse populations in the country. The attacks against the multicultural fabric of American society have been coming nonstop through many channels.

The contemporary history of Latinos in the United States is intriguing and unpredictable. The accommodation and survival of the population to public policies, xenophobic backlash, and the increasing lack of tolerance for cultural difference will trigger a number of responses among Latino populations. Yet the reality of a demographic explosion among Latino groups and their rise to political power are here to stay. This volume will look at some of the current attempts in the social sciences to conceptualize and rationalize the limited knowledge and bias about the Latinos in the United States; for example, their characterization as *castelike minorities* (to use the term popularized by Ogbu 1974, 1978). It will describe the demographic trends and unique economic characteristics of the various Latino groups along with their various sociocultural traits and occupational profiles. The book will discuss the victimization of Latino immigrants and the current abuses by law enforcement agencies of undocumented workers. I will describe the binational existence of many farmworkers and their ability to survive psychologically and culturally by commuting between Mexico and the United States to endure employment instability. I will describe the pockets of Latino intelligentsia in American universities and other institutions. In the end, the question of how to explain the cultural and political cohesiveness of Latinos in this country is faced with several hypotheses. The book concludes with a second look at critical pedagogy as a means to analytically examine the situation of Latinos and the importance of their education for the future of this society and its democratic structures.

References

Freire, P. *Pedagogy of Hope: Reliving Pedagogy of the Oppressed.* New York: Continuum, 1974.

New York Times. "On Proposition 209." December 7, 1996, 10.

Ogbu, J. *The Next Generation: An Ethnography of Education in an Urban Neighborhood.* New York: Academic Press, 1974.

Ogbu, J. *Minority Education and Caste: The American System in Cross-Cultural Perspective.* New York: Academic Press, 1978.

1

The Politics of Latino Self-Identity

To be Chicana in the myriad and infinite ways there are of being, to come as we are poses a threat to integrated schools and to mainstream society. In the absence of collectivity in my graduate seminar, I could not be true to my vision as a Chicana. . . . As I look back, describe, and theorize about my seminar experience, I can articulate the elements that constituted my marginalization and my complicity in the discourses of difference and "othering." The power of the dominant discourse of "other," the objectification of my experiences as the "other" through detached, rational argumentation, and the severing of a collective vision and memory that disabled me and rendered me voiceless, all constituted marginalization and complicity. These elements resurfaced when I started the process of conducting qualitative research with the Latino community in Hope City, North Carolina. There my dilemma of being a Chicana and a researcher became problematic in ways similar to my experiences in the seminar, that is, as an accomplice to the marginalization and objectification of my identity and experiences as a Chicana, which became embedded in the power structure of the dominant and the disenfranchised. (Villenas 1996, 718–719)

Wrestling with our ethnic identity is a daily event that takes many forms. If we carry the language and ideology from one setting (our home) to another (school or work) we are in trouble. We readily see ourselves as unable to function and communicate. If we keep these worlds separate, we feel marginalized in all of them; not really belonging to any. Worse still, we feel we are betraying one cultural world or another any time we switch codes, cultural audiences, communicative styles, or patterns of behavior. In fact, for me, writing this book has been a struggle of inner feelings and a conflict of loyalties. Why should I tell the general public about some of my struggles and the struggles of my people? Should I paint them as exemplary and emphasize their virtues and accomplishments? In brief, I have experienced some of the

1

feelings described above by Sofía Villenas. Exposing my own life, a long journey of obstacles and personal encounters with my own ambiguities, insecurities, and undefined identities, feels like betraying my family and my people. Should they not always be strong, cohesive, and successful? When I look closely at "my heroes," the successful Latinos whom I admired as colleagues and friends, I notice the scars and hurts left by partial failures and rough encounters with prejudice because of their ethnicity: the hypersensitivity, defensiveness, rivalry, petty politics, depression in the face of opposition, and isolation (perhaps as a mechanism to find some safety). Then the question of who these successful Latinos really are and what the political contexts of their self-identity are becomes central.

A Brief Historical Perspective:
From a Colonized Mentality to Liberation

The United States, Mexico, and other Latin American countries are inextricably intertwined by a complex history of militarily, politically, and economically oppressive relationships over the last two hundred years. Latinos have, generation after generation, at times through enormous personal sacrifices and working in subhuman conditions, made significant contributions to this country's cultural life and to its economic and democratic institutions. In the Southwest, for example, Latinos built one of the most powerful agricultural industrial systems in the world. Those who lived in the Southwest before that territory belonged to the United States feel invaded and colonized. In a strict historical sense, however, the ancestors of the Latinos (the Spaniards) came to the Southwest area and colonized it. The Californias (the northern and southern portions) were not coveted immediately after Cortez's arrival, primarily because the Spaniards found no gold or any other attractive features there. But in the late 1600s and early 1700s a renewed interest attracted missionaries and soldiers. European colonizers came by the hundreds from the mid-1800s on (Thompson and West 1883).

Many Latinos whose families lived in the Southwest prior to the annexation of Mexican territory by the Guadalupe Hidalgo Treaty of 1848 have never accepted the status of "immigrant" or "newcomer" to this country. They feel they are the rightful owners of the land taken forcefully by the North Americans. They also refuse to be exploited as "inferior" people and resist the illegal deprivation of their civil rights (a practice ongoing since the nineteenth century).

According to the Black Legend, the annexation of the Southwest to

North America's territory was justified on the basis of Manifest Destiny, that is, the presumed will of God to have Anglo-Saxon people Christianize the "savage" Mexican people deemed unworthy of keeping their land. T. J. Farnham, for example, writes in his 1855 travel journal, "Californians [Mexicans] are an imbecile, pusillanimous, race of men, and unfit to control the destinies of that beautiful country. . . . The Old Saxon blood must stride the continent, must command all its northern shores . . . and in their own unaided might, erect the altar of civil and religious freedom on the plains of the Californias" (cited by Menchaca and Valencia 1990, 229).

The Civil Practice Act of 1850, which excluded the Chinese and Indians from testifying against Whites, was extended to Mexicans because they were partially Indian. The residential segregation of Mexicans, firmly established on the West Coast at the turn of the twentieth century, became the foundation for the widespread segregation of the 1920s and 1930s. Mexicans were not allowed in public facilities such as schools, restaurants, swimming pools, and theaters (Menchaca and Valencia 1990, 230). Mexicans who lived in the central and southern states had been coming to the United States to work in increasing numbers from the beginning of the twentieth century. The anxiety generated by the immigration waves at the end of the twentieth century, intimately related to the worldwide restructuring of the economy and global sociopolitical and economic changes, has resulted in the increased *demonizing* of immigrants as criminals. And although there are indeed no *guest* workers, there are *ghost* workers, who must be there to do the jobs no one else wants to do. And they must be voiceless and invisible.

The Latino people are racially, socially, and economically quite diversified, in spite of the fact that they share a culture, language, history, values, worldview, and ideals. Caribbean, Puerto Rican, and Cuban Latinos have common histories of slavery and oppression and share ethnoracial characteristics that tend to separate them further from other Latinos (especially those of European ancestry). Their upward mobility varies a great deal depending on their levels of literacy, bilingualism, and educational attainment. Latinos from Mexico, overrepresented by rural mestizos and Indians and less by European subgroups, have deep roots in diverse ethnolinguistic communities with native home languages other than Spanish and popular cultures unfamiliar to Mexicans from the middle and upper classes living in large cities. Their religious practices and rituals, their community and family social organization, and their home and village lifestyles are being transferred to the United States and may even shock other Latinos. Because of their different backgrounds, their reactions to urban America, to drugs, and to violence and poverty may also differ a great deal. If we compare rural Latinos with Latino metropolitan dwellers, the former may react to the urban environment with shock and isolation, whereas the latter may use successful adaptive mechanisms and survival strategies. We know that the early exposure of rural Mexican youth to urban problems often results in academic underachievement and gang activity (see Suárez-Orozco and Suárez-Orozco 1995a and 1995b; Vigil 1983, 1988, 1989, and 1997; and Moore, Vigil, and Garcia 1983).

Latinos (presumed undocumented workers and criminals) have become the victims of border patrol and police officers, vigilantes, coyotes, white supremacists, and other racist citizens committing repugnant acts of violence. Even border patrol supervisors seem to encourage beatings of suspects who run away from agents: "Thump'em" and "catch as many tonks as you guys can. Safely. An alien is not worth busting a leg." *Tonk*, the sound made as an agent's flashlight strikes the head of a suspect, is now used to refer to an undocumented worker. Paranoiac and hateful law enforcement officers portray undocumented workers as terrorizing gangs of aliens who invade our country and break our laws. Nothing is further from the truth. In fact, Mexican workers seek only a chance to work and survive; they are the true victims, as Suárez-Orozco and Suárez-Orozco have amply documented (Suárez-Orozco and Suárez-Orozco 1995a and 1995b; Suárez-Orozco 1996 and in press).

The North American People's View of Immigrants

A comparative study of governmental policies, ideologies, and reform efforts both in the United States and in Europe provides a macrostructural perspective for the study of racism and exclusion. J. Macias compares racial conflict in Germany (understandable in terms of a nationalistic ideology and social Darwinism that views German culture as superior to others and demands both biological and cultural purity of the presumed homogeneous "White" race) with the historical segregation and oppression of Mexicans in the Southwest and concludes the following:

> The abundance of uninformed, political, and emotionally charged solutions suggests the potential and critical role of education beyond school fences. Although Proposition 187 surfaced in the political arena, its ideas obviously found support in many other places, including families, the workplace, and the media. Parents and families must somehow be supported in their task of caring for and socializing their children and helped

to gain new understanding about human differences that should not matter, such as race, and actions that are unsupportable, such as negative stereotyping and discrimination. . . . The backlash against affirmative action policy reminds us that lasting social progress is ultimately dependent on popular understandings that support that change. (Macias 1996, 250)

As it happened in Europe, the United States has seen the most unlikely alliances join forces in political action against immigrants of color. The neoliberals and radical conservatives have discovered in their most profound fundamentalist religious beliefs enough common ground to pursue "patriotic" policies of puritanical procedures to curtail the presumed crime and immoral conduct of immigrants. Thus, the political pressures to increase border surveillance on the grounds that illegal immigrants are key agents in the drug traffic, the refusal of health and social services not only to undocumented immigrants but to all immigrants, and the recent initiatives behind Propositions 187 and 209 in California are clear examples of joint political actions of groups traditionally opposed to each other. As P. McLaren has eloquently pointed out:

> Young white males and females who may find these racist groups [the Ku Klux Klan, the Posse Comitatus, the Order, White Aryan Resistance, Christian Identity, National Alliance, Aryan Nations, American Front, Gun Owners of America, United Citizens of Justice, and other militia groups] unappealing can still find solace in politicians such as Pete Wilson and Bob Dole whose antiimmigrant and Latinophobic policies and practices deflect their racializing sentiments through flag waving, jingoism, and triumphalist acts of self-aggrandizement—such as the disguising of Proposition 209 as a civil rights initiative—designed to appeal to frightened white voters who feel that growing numbers of Spanish-speaking immigrants will soon outnumber them. Politicians have become white warriors in blue suits and red ties dedicated to taking back the country from the infidel. (McLaren 1997)

Europe and North America have been the theater of ethnic violence and trends to redefine *whiteness* in both racial and cultural terms as consisting primarily of Anglo-Saxon Whites, united by not only history, culture, and religion, but also by economic interests. In Europe the Basques, the colonized North Africans, and Asian and Latino immigrants do not belong within the presumed "homogeneous" European culture, in spite of the fact that many of them were born in Europe. In North America, the recent trends to exclude nonwhite citizens from our history, culture, and political life is not an accident. The linkages between European and North American groups can be documented. The debate over these issues in the United States has become a referendum on American democracy, and the emotions run high. The additional pressure of a changing demography plus the need for professionals, scientists, and laborers in certain fields increase the anxiety of many Whites. The politicization of senior America, a class whose membership is expanding rapidly, has paved the way for a number of political maneuvers passing for pure patriotism that prey on frightened senior citizens.

Fear in an Older and Impoverished America

The current historical period will test the strength of our democratic ideals. The stakes are high because traditionally what provided a rationale for unity during extraordinary national efforts associated with war and economic recovery was precisely the rhetoric of democracy and a bright future for all, including citizens of color. Public demoralization and the undermining of democratic values are not only feeding secret militias and frustrating common citizens, they are also destroying the very foundation of this country, that is, the faith of the youth in the nation, its government, its institutions, and its sociopolitical system. In the past, the youth generously sacrificed everything, including their lives, for this country. Nationalist views did not exclude Latino, Black, or Native Americans; they served in this country's wars and moved up the social ladder through education, federal support, and recognition. No group of young people is eager to sacrifice their lives for a country that rejects them. Senior citizens view with nostalgia the years of enthusiastic reconstruction of Germany and Japan after the victory of the allies in World War II. That era is gone, and respect for this country is shaky. The estimated U.S. population as of May 1, 1996, was 265,022,000 people. Race, ethnicity, and age trends show a dramatic change and a frightening contrast in the eyes of senior citizens. Of the population sixty-five years of age and over, Whites constitute 85 percent, and they make up only about 60 percent of the population under eighteen years of age (*Population Today: News, Numbers and Analysis* 24, no. 8, August 1996: 6). Senior citizens are also very concerned about the poverty and low educational levels of Black and Latino populations. The number of children and senior citizens considered "poor" has increased in the last five years (*Current Population Reports*, published by the U.S. Census Bureau, Department of Commerce, Economics, and Statistics Administration, June 1996: 2–5).

Economic crises affecting the United States have a devastating impact in Mexico and Latin America, and consequently, the increase in poverty among the rural population results in a larger number of immigrants searching for jobs and often displacing more established workers. The most recent arrivals are willing to take lower pay and less-stable jobs. The ultimate consequences have a ripple effect on the populations that have reached a measure of economic stability. This phenomenon has been interpreted as a myopic and selfish effort on the part of agricultural business people to exploit cheap labor and at the same time import "third-world" conditions (Martin and Taylor, 4). The interpretation of economic and political crises in this country plays a key role in (mis)informing politicians and policymakers. Suárez-Orozco (in press) argues that in this country a general discontent of the American people based primarily on economic and political crises and the resulting pervasive sense of anxiety about the future have contributed to the public xenophobia and anti-immigrant sentiment. The presidential campaign of 1996 raised the level of intolerance and immigrant-bashing attitudes when the Republican candidates "blamed illegal aliens for overcrowded public-school classrooms, bankrupt hospitals, crime, high taxes and even potential voter fraud" (Cornelius 1996, B4). Naturally the response by the current administration was equally vigorous promoting immigration control, increasing the Immigration and Naturalization Services budget in order to strengthen the southern border surveillance. The expression of these sentiments is nothing unusual in this country. What is unusual, however, is its occurrence during a period of economic recovery, as manifested by lower unemployment and a rise in productivity.

According to a number of polls cited by Cornelius (1996), including the General Social Survey conducted by the National Opinion Research Center at the University of Chicago, in the last three years we find a larger portion of the population demanding cuts in immigration and favoring the construction of a Berlin-like wall between Mexico and the United States. Other national surveys by political scientists seem to indicate that an individual's particular economic situation (income, type of employment, job loss, or other circumstances affecting the quality of work) has nothing to do with his or her position on immigration:

> Such findings may reflect the realities of a labor market in which fewer and fewer Americans—particularly white, middle-class voters—ever compete directly with immigrants for jobs or hold jobs whose wages have been depressed by large numbers of immigrants in a given company or industry. But the data also may indicate that non-economic factors, especially culture and ethnicity, have become more salient in shaping Americans' attitudes toward immigration. Survey respondents who have negative views on Hispanics and Asians as ethnic groups—not just as immigrants—are more likely to prefer a restrictive immigration policy than other people are. (Cornelius 1996, B4)

Other recent research seems to indicate that Anglos who see them-selves as "conservative" (particularly as fiscal conservatives) are op-posed to cultural diversity and the use of languages other than English in elementary education or on the ballots and favor restrictions on im-migration. Their main concerns seem to be a replication of those mani-fested by European populations: ethnic purity, a single national iden-tity, and pragmatic and conservative fiscal policies. Unfortunately, the general public seems to view Latinos as more likely to draw welfare benefits, to be less educated, and to contribute less to the general econ-omy of this country. The bizarre combination of cultural and ethnic purity with fiscal conservatism makes it very difficult for researchers to investigate in a tidy fashion. In previous decades, notably at the turn of the twentieth century, the public's racism, xenophobia, and intoler-ance were clearly identified and expressed. Scholars today have not been able to produce a clean set of data with which to inform policy-makers. Cornelius mentions the classic disagreement between fiscal conservatives, who variously calculate the percentage of immigrants using public assistance at 26.1 (George Borjas, a Harvard economist) and 5.1 (demographers Michael Fix and Jeffrey Passel of the Urban Institute). The disagreement ranges from the unit of analysis (whether they count immigrant households or individuals—documented and/ or undocumented; political refugees included or excluded) to the definition of *welfare* (food stamps, noncash assistance programs). Politi-cians then take the liberty of inflating the figures in order to support their political opinions. In the end, the benefits of immigration are rarely documented, because, with the exception of immigrants' contri-butions to state and federal taxes, the benefits come in the form of intangible, long-term developments. How does one measure, for exam-ple, the consumption of goods and services, the creation of jobs, the competitiveness of industries (agricultural, textile, etc.) in an interna-tional arena? The oversimplified notion (advocated by George Borjas 1985 and 1995) that this country is importing third-world poverty by bringing in uneducated immigrants has no empirical foundation. Ac-cording to Cornelius, demographer Dowell Myers of the University of Southern California "has found that Latino immigrants settling in southern California are becoming homeowners at a faster rate than native-born residents" (1996, B5).

The point that Cornelius raises consistently is that we have no empir-ical evidence, no substantive research to back up policies such as advo-cated by Proposition 187 (see Suárez-Orozco 1996) denying public edu-cation and other services to children of undocumented workers. In fact, it does not make economic sense to save a few dollars in the education of these children, when we consider the tax revenue losses resulting from the decrease in lifetime earnings and the cost of law enforcement, incarceration, emergency medical assistance, and other social problems related to uneducated youth (Cornelius, ibid.).

A New Collective Latino Identity: Unexpected High Political Profile

One of the most important clues to understanding the new, high political profile of certain Latino groups and the emergence of a new solidarity among young professional Latinos is to examine the extraordinary resiliency not of the individuals, but of families, binational organizations, networks, and other similar enclaves of survivors of the immigration experience. It is not a chain of clear successes in the history of one person but the collective survival and selective successes of members related to each other by blood, kin, friendship, *compadrazgo,* or other ties—very often ties that cross countries and continents. The phenomenon of resiliency is profoundly related to the construction of a new ethnicity and a new identity, without necessarily rejecting other identities. It is not only accommodation without acculturation (in the sense defined by Gibson in her study of the Punjabis) but a complex change of personal identities and collective identities over several generations for economic and political goals beyond the life of an individual or his or her nuclear family. Obviously, what we are facing is a new spiritual and social phenomenon that has taken more than a century to take shape and that could not have developed until there was a critical mass and a group of Latinos who occupied higher positions, knew the political and economic system well, and had retained their cultural and personal identities. It is a radical departure from the Richard Rodríguez types and from the nativistic efforts cyclically occurring among some Native Alaskan, Canadian, and American Indian groups.* Although I will deal with the issues of collective identity, solidarity, and the formation of the "new" self later on, suffice it to say that the transformation of religious beliefs and of religious organizations into "new" political, economic, and social organizations structured to advance the collective cause of Latinos represents a radical change from previous strategies for survival. The analysis of this phenomenon demands a profound understanding of the role of religion among Latinos and the

---

*"Rodríguez types" refers to Mexican or Mexican American people who, in order to survive psychologically, feel obligated to reject their own language, culture, and their own people (even their family). This was expressed in Rodríguez's book *Hunger of Memory* (1982).

nature of the quasi-religious relationships among Latinos as they support each other in the face of crises, racism, poverty, and rejection in a foreign country. I am convinced of the extraordinary spiritual strength of Latino families. I know they will continue to amaze us with their capacity to survive the subhuman working conditions of the jobs they take. One of the most enriching experiences in doing research with Latino families is witnessing their spiritual strength and commitment to each other when everything else goes wrong; Latino children often learn this resiliency and are becoming the most promising youth of America's twenty-first century. What I wrote in 1989 I strongly believe today. "The end of the twentieth century is rapidly approaching. The children who will crowd our schools are already among us. Minority children are rapidly becoming, or already have become, the majority in a number of cities and areas of this country. . . . Moral, humanitarian, and economic arguments can be made to motivate us to support minority education in our schools. The future of this country will be in good hands if we extend our support to minority children today" (Trueba 1989, 185–186). Latino children are indeed the hope of multicultural America. These children are deeply rooted in the mythical Aztlán, the land of Indian, mestizo, and European Latinos who recreate their ethnicity through social life, daily radio broadcasting with Latino music, and a rich binational and bicultural existence. Many Latinos, regardless of their place of origin, develop a new sense of identity and a strong esprit de corps. They share the importance of salient figures such as Cesar Chavez, the hero of farmworkers, who spent his life and gave his health to struggle for the rights and dignity of agricultural workers. National icons like Selena (the famous young singer who was killed in Texas, initially ridiculed by some radio deejay, and eventually recognized internationally through an extraordinary movie) created political and cultural rituals, blending music, art, and politics in ways never expected in Texas or California. Addressing Mexican Americans who were nostalgic about Mexico, Selena sings Cuco Sánchez's song entitled *"Siempre Hace Frío"*:

> Este corazón aún te quiere
> Ya está muriendo tarde con tarde
> Como se muere la luz del día
> Ya no puedo más, tu me haces falta
> Vuelve conmigo, alma de mi alma, vidita mía.
> [My heart still loves you
> It is dying every sunset
> As the daylight dies
> I cannot stand it, I need you
> Come back, soul of my soul, my sweet life].

Folklore, religion, and politics make a powerful combination on both sides of the border. Political action in Mexico by repatriated migrant workers (some with U.S. citizenship) is on the increase. All this seems to point to a new ethnic and political reality for Latinos in the United States. The formation of a new identity is clearly associated with successful political action and the recognition of the political, social, and economic importance of Latinos in this country. Latinos' new identity is bringing together individuals from very diverse backgrounds: Latinos who are Black, Latinos of European ancestry, mestizos, Indians, Spanish monolinguals, English-Spanish bilinguals, Spanish–Indian language bilinguals, upper-, middle-, and lower-class Latinos, recent arrivals and old-timers, religious conservatives and liberals, and so on. We are witnessing the formation of a new ethnic identity that transcends any previous ethnic definitions, an identity clearly associated with the increasing representation of Latinos in political and economic positions of power. Furthermore, in contrast with previous processes of ethnic identification for political power, Latinos are being recognized not only within the United States (as it became clear in the last presidential and local elections) but in Latin American countries. Mexico has declared that Mexican citizens who acquire U.S. citizenship will not lose their Mexican citizenship. In fact, Mexico will claim over six million U.S. citizens of Mexican ancestry as its own in order to enhance that country's political power in the United States. It is a clear recognition of the emergence of Latino political, economic, and cultural power across nations.

The global debates on immigrants, their assimilation or their resistance to assimilation, their contributions to the national economy or their reliance on public service, go beyond the traditional debates of tolerance and intolerance characteristic of similar cyclic crises since the nineteenth century in America. It is not simply a recurrent xenophobia or racism that becomes exacerbated when economic pressures grow or when national politics reduces public confidence in the government. It is a much stronger ideological current that pushes ethnic and cultural purity as a cult and defends it even through violent expressions of hatred for immigrants of color (whether legal or undocumented). Uncertainty about the future is no longer anchored in a poor economy but on the certainty of demographic trends, which show drastic and steady increases of Latino and Asian immigrant populations. This is not to say that xenophobia is the prerogative of American society; we see plenty of it in China, Japan, and especially Europe. It is only that American society had managed to welcome all kinds of immigrants with a high degree of confidence of turning them into good Americans, and now that confidence is shaking.

In the long term, attempts at curtailing the power, the visibility, and the active participation of ethnic minority groups in American democratic institutions, particularly schools, have the very detrimental consequence of destroying the democratic traditions of this country and its inherent strengths. But these efforts are particularly dysfunctional and irrational when we consider the demographic trends and the economic needs of American society in the next century. It would seem that rather than attempting to prevent the participation of minorities in academia, this should be the time to make extraordinary efforts to bring them into academia even in larger numbers, in order to prepare them for the difficult roles in the century that is fast approaching. More than ever, we will need intellectual leaders, teachers, doctors, engineers, professionals in all the fields, technical experts, researchers, and businesspeople with the academic and human abilities to interact with highly diversified populations both at home and abroad. This is the worst time to direct our hostility inward to our own people as they make their best efforts to belong in American society and become productive through gaining higher education. The ultimate outcome of anti-affirmative action policies would be to make this country's population less competitive in the business world, in the various technical fields, and in the professions that require special skills and serious interdisciplinary research approaches. It seems that the problem is not one of equity principles but an ideological problem tinted by racism, cultural/ethnic nativism, and simple myopia. We cannot turn the clock back; the reality of American society is that it is already diversified and in search of new frontiers in science and technology that will require a new ideology of tolerance and respect for cultural, gender, racial, and ethnic differences both at home and abroad.

Perhaps unlike other ethnic populations, Latinos are facing not a simple change in ethnic identity, a transition from the home culture identification to a new single identity as Americans from a specific Latino descent. Rather, it seems to be a complicated process whereby Latinos retain multiple identities, multiple interactional settings, and diverse "situated selves" at one point in time. They can code-switch from one ethnocultural setting to another and use different linguistic forms and nonverbal behaviors. Not unlike other persons from mainstream America, many Latinos can function effectively in standard English and several English varieties appropriate to specific work, school, or entertainment settings. But they can also switch entirely from standard to nonstandard varieties of Spanish in order to deal with sociocultural populations that live in separate socioeconomic camps, reflect diverse acculturation stages into the mainstream American lifestyle, or live in a binational world intermittently going from one country to another. The compatibility of Latino identity within modern America is only one of the new characteristics of Latinos today. Another important characteristic is the fact that Latinos can establish bridges between traditionally rival groupings to create politically powerful groups.

Cultural Roots of Resiliency

The unstoppable reality of Latinos in businesses and professions from which they had been excluded and their subsequent rise to political power are understandable if we look at the increasing collective strength and resiliency that has accompanied their demographic explosion. In this volume I will examine some of the theoretical currents in the social sciences that conceptualize and rationalize Latino performance in schools and society, often on the basis of limited knowledge and prejudice. Their characterization as "castelike minorities" and the overgeneralization of groups and subgroups with different histories, cultures, and achievements do not give justice to the Latinos. But even those "scientific" documents that attempt to portray Latinos have not captured the power of the communities, families, collective groups, or their ethos and cultural values, which explain seemingly irrational decisions on personal achievement. The new collective identity of Latinos brings up a number of related questions that we must confront in the face of the other multiple identities they display, of their communication skills and affiliation with many other groups in spite of an apparent geographical and socioeconomic segregation. What does happen inside of these individuals regarding their personal identity and their multiple memberships in different groups? Who do they really think they are? What is the nature and source of their resiliency, adaptive skills, and apparent economic success? In other words, to what extent are Latinos redefining themselves in solidarity as a common group that is now claiming to share linguistic and cultural roots? Or are Latinos, in fact, creating a new collective identity with new rituals, beliefs, and practices in North America? There are definitely unique new experiences that shape Latino identity. These experiences are not primarily gained through the cognitive and intellectual channels of formal education, but many of them start in educational institutions, bring about deep emotional and symbolic messages, and result in shared religious, musical, artistic, and other cultural capital. More importantly, the common experience of oppression, rejection, and exclusion (often shared vicariously more than personally) is redefined, reinterpreted, and used constructively to gain political power and collective recognition. It is precisely the feeling of exclusion and oppression that creates the need for developing a new ethnicity, a new kinship system, a new set of personal relationships, almost a new, larger family where we can all protect each other. Marbella, a young, rural Mexican girl who is now in California, says:

> It's like a bet that we ought to win because we need to demonstrate to other people that we indeed can make it. That it's not because we are Hispanic we can't make it. At times they [Americans] are treating you badly, right? Then you say to yourself "I am going to demonstrate to those people that I indeed can be something, and that I have the capability to be something. It's not because I'm Hispanic that I can't make it." At these times, they give you desire to study more and become someone more quickly, so as to demonstrate to all the world that it is not because you are Mexican you are going to stop below. (Davidson 1997, 22–23)

Going to school and graduating are seen as the first steps to becoming somebody, and Mexicans' need to demonstrate to others that they can achieve underlines their pride in their collective identity. In fact, many Latinos' motivation to achieve at Harvard and Stanford is precisely to show the others (the Whites, who have been traditionally the expected members of academic elite institutions) that Latinos can also do well and achieve excellence. The profound motivation to achieve under these circumstances goes beyond personal achievement and becomes a matter of loyalty to the entire ethnic group. I recall the story of a Mexican American doctoral student at Harvard. She was, by all counts, an outstanding woman (beautiful, articulate, fully bilingual, with the best political connections and the highest grades in a series of quantitative courses, even coteaching some of those courses with the best faculty). She was devastated when in another course a faculty member (known for not liking Latinos and for labeling plagiarism as a "foreign problem" by frequently singling out Latino and Asian students as plagiarists) told her that her paper was garbage and she did not deserve to be at Harvard. The paper dealt with Latino equity issues. After her initial pain and anger decreased, this young woman reworked her paper and consulted with other faculty members to finally produce a masterpiece. She knew she could do a good job and was not about to accept a self-definition of "incompetent" because an Anglo faculty member was demeaning and thought she couldn't make it at Harvard.

For many years Latinos were depicted as divided, engaged in rivalry and conflict. We permitted others to define our problems and maximize our differences as we struggled to belong in this society and to be permitted into the higher ranks of academia. The personal hope of being accepted in mainstream society and in academia has become a collective goal affecting not just the Latino elites but *Raza* across social classes and racial groups. Intellectual power and excellence in our professions have led us to believe that solidarity is not only possible but desirable. As the new generations have grown together in this country and compared their immigration experiences, they have established a number of cultural rituals and institutions that facilitate the creation of new ethnicity and solidarity, a new and larger umbrella for political, economic, and intellectual intercourse. We were so few in certain professions twenty years ago that we had to become eclectic and individualistic to survive. The younger generations of Latinos are bringing extraordinary energy and imagination to many arenas and professions in the most selected intellectual environments, such as Harvard, Yale, Stanford, and the University of Texas at Austin. New groups of lawyers, physicians, bankers, investment experts, communication experts, and political leaders get together to discuss their needs as Latinos. Their efforts are not the casual result of lucky strikes but the result of systematic development over the years based on well-organized social action. Sophisticated networks of Latino families share information, political support, expertise, monies, and other resources to pursue common ends and protect one another. They may help in practical matters, such as finding a reliable mechanic who won't cheat them or a lawyer to resolve a legal problem, a mentor in a specific subject matter to help a child in school, a loan, advice on personal matters, information on traveling, a baby-sitter, or even a good life companion. This form of comprehensive, informal social security is an institution that originated in Mexico City in the downtown low-income *colonias,* such as La Lagunilla or Tepito. Newcomers from rural areas organized themselves into neighborhood units, or *vecindades,* to help each other adapt to their difficult experience, by offering informal support, small amounts of cash for emergencies, and moral support in case of abuse by the police or robbers. The *vecindades* became a surrogate extended family that would keep an eye on young children and assist parents in disciplinary matters. Finally, *vecindades* provided incentives to combine small amounts of capital for new ventures, helped to recruit coworkers, and helped newcomers survive the cultural shock of the large city. This institution, as it was transplanted into the United States, became an entirely new one in which rapid transportation, technology, and larger capital offered listservs, E-mail, computer-assisted information services, and other modern means of facilitating communication across families and networks. Beyond the more daily practical assistance, the organization offers many opportunities for Latinos to continue their collective presence in formal festivities, to maintain their folklore, and create culturally and linguistically congruent environments for family entertainment, such as mariachi music, Mexican movies, Día de los Muertos marches, Cinco de Mayo parades, concerts and *tamalada** in the Día de la Virgen de Guadalupe, and many other celebrations. Anthropological studies of *cofradías* and religious cargo systems that include the cult of the saints with a substantial investment of cash by the wealthiest people (often described as a mechanism for equalization) suggest that the dividing line between religious and civil life is never clear in Mexican politics. The fact is, even during the difficult years of the persecution of Catholic church officials, their influence was never questioned. Today, one of the most powerful bishops in Mexico is Samuel Ruiz from Chiapas, who has consistently been an advocate for the Mayan Indians in their struggle for human rights and their association with Zapatistas (see Robert DeVillar in Zou and Trueba 1998).

Religious Foundations of Resiliency and Solidarity

The cult of the saints in Mexico symbolizes both solidarity in a political sense and spiritual togetherness in a profound cultural pre-Hispanic sense. See, for example, the work by Dr. Sarah LeVine from Harvard University:

> Millions of Mexicans from every walk of life look to the saints and most especially to the Virgin Mary, mother and intercessor, for companionship, solace and grace. To demonstrate their devotion, rural folk and city-dwellers alike, go on pilgrimage as individuals, as families, and in community and professional groups to hundreds of shrine houses in cathedrals and goldleafed basilicas, parish churches and humble wayside chapels which, from the U.S. border to Guatemala and from the Caribbean island of Cozumel to the Pacific Coast, are dedicated to them. (S. LeVine 1997, 1)

These pilgrimages, as do other important religious rituals in Mexico, often involve taking *santitos*† and the creation of a kinship of saints whereby people from different communities create new spiritual ties through their common religious experiences. During colonial times the missionaries' mission was to destroy the Indians' pagan religions in order to ensure Christianization and control of the Indians (Nutini

---

Tamalada refers to the collective efforts of making *tamales* in large amounts for the family or community, especially on the occasion of special holidays.

†*Santitos* refers to the various pictures and statues of patron saints, or saints canonized by the Catholic church, often placed in an altar for people to pray to them and ask for special favors.

1988; León-Portilla 1963 and 1995; S. LeVine 1997). The *cofradía* system in Chiapas and the many other examples of community-sponsored religious activities that are at the foundation of both political and economic stratification and the mechanism to retain an equalitarian character in the community are elements that continue to be important for Mexican immigrants. Naturally, the rituals change, and the religious and political meanings become functionally relevant to North American society.

Many of the processes associated with the formation of one's own self-identity are related to the acquisition of knowledge. But we are less aware of who chooses, what is taught, and why. Political action, especially as it develops in the context of educational institutions, is highly instrumental in making us aware of the real purpose and nature of schooling. One of the most reasonable explanations for the formation of a new ethnic identity among Latinos through political action—which often begins in schools—is based on the common experience that such action is inherently empowering, invites profound reflection, is transformative, and demands immediate change. Political action, if it is meaningful (congruent with the appropriate sociocultural codes), can indeed dramatically impact and change the self-perception of members of an ethnic group by leading the group into a new understanding of the interrelationships among ideology, power, and culture. If Latinos view their lives in the United States as representing experiences of unequal distribution of power on the basis of race, cultural origin, social class, or gender, they can logically search for a common culture based on a similar historical tradition and try to break the hegemony (or ideological domination) of mainstream American society by importing cultural traditions from their places of origin. There is a clear example of this in California:

> The organization of the *Comité Pro-Fiestas*, the *Comité de Guadalupanas* (originally a religious organization), and the Mexican cowboy *(charro)* associations, such as the *La Regional, Los Caporales* and the folkloric dance groups function as the larger umbrella within which Mexican families found the moral support and appropriate climate to maintain their cultural values, rituals, and the activities that enhanced their identity. The splendor and pleasure that cultural activities produced were the cement that bonded ethnic pride and a sense of belonging within the community. Under this general umbrella, newcomers found an opportunity to share important information about the resources available from the various members of the Mexican community, valuable in both practical terms to resolve daily problems and in symbolic terms to restore the psychological well-being often threatened by degrading experiences (racial prejudice,

economic exploitation, exclusion from services, and opportunities available to other citizens. (Trueba, Rodríguez, Zou, and Cintrón 1993, 134)

In the context of these and other cultural activities, new networks are formed, for example through the informal organization of *compadrazgo,* a civil and religious binding relationship between godparents and godchildren ensued through baptism or confirmation whereby a child's spiritual welfare is ritually and officially entrusted to a close friend or relative, the godfather or godmother. In the end, this network grows into viable political organizations that sponsor celebrations and foster a sense of ethnic community. Through the relationships and networks a number of reciprocal services are exchanged in the form of partnerships, collaborative efforts, loans, information and referral services, recommendations, and so on. A number of major celebrations are used to retain cohesive clusters of Latinos: Fiestas Patrias (October 12, Día de la Raza, May 5, or Cinco de Mayo, September 16, or Día de la Independencia, December 12, or Fiesta de la Virgen de Guadalupe, the Patron Saint of Latin America, November 2, Día de los Muertos, a traditional celebration with pre-Hispanic cultural meaning, and many others). The transition from merely social and cultural activities to political organizational meetings is quite natural. In the case of Woodland, for example (Trueba, Rodríguez, Zou, and Cintrón 1993), in a single generation a number of political groups were formed, such as the Mexican American Political Action, the Movimiento Estudiantil Chicano de Aztlán, the Brown Berets, and the Latinos Unidos para Mejor Educación.

According to Camarillo, Latino organizations have been the result of the dramatic increase in immigration that required fraternal organizations, mutual aid and insurance benefits, protection of people's rights and privileges as Mexicans, and promotion of cultural and recreational activities (1979, 148). Mario Garcia alludes to the development of a new political force composed of both middle-class and working-class Mexican American leaders committed to bringing about change in their communities and demanding a place in the political arena (1989). Latinos pursued their goals of participation in the political process in order to obtain a higher quality of life and greater dignity in our society without compromising their ethnic identity. This is still a matter of great preoccupation with recent immigrants from Mexico and Latin America (Trueba 1997).

The training ground for political organization in Latino communities was the Civil Rights Movement of the 1960s and 1970s. A clear example of this process was the organization of Chicano militant groups in California's university campuses. The Movimiento Estudiantil Chicano de Aztlán (MECHA) was one of the most important because of its large membership and significant accomplishment throughout the entire state. Other important national organizations were the Association of Mexican American Educators (AMAE) and the United Farm Workers of America. Without these organizations the political victories of Latinos in the West Coast struggle for equity in schools, in the agricultural fields, or in city government positions would not have been possible.

But even in Harvard, among the sophisticated (mostly upper-class) graduate students from Mexico, Central and South America, many of whom will become permanent immigrants in this country, the search for religious and political rituals to cement our solidarity is conspicuous. On the cold day of November 2, 1996, in ten- to fifteen-degree Fahrenheit temperatures, we watched some Latino students going from Harvard Square to the Divinity school (nearly two miles away). The ritual dancers, or *danzantes*, wearing very light clothing—the men in shorts, no shirts, and sandals, and the women in light white gowns—crossed the campus dancing the Deer Dance (or in Aztec, *Danza del Venado*) and entered the elegant chapel to the beat of drums, to create a new ritual of remembrance of our dead, and especially to find in each other and our ancestors the support, warmth, and affection that we crave in New England. This we could only find in La Raza, our own people, and the spiritual community that transcends generations and life boundaries. Next to one another, speaking Spanish, English, and Spanglish, praying, singing, and dancing together in any language variety we knew best, with a Spanish flavor in common, always free to change and search for the most functional sentence in any language and always with the clear accents of second-language learners or native speakers who had forgotten their native language, we poured our hearts out. In a very subtle way, we were reinventing our ethnic identity, creating a new tradition, and reenacting our commitment to remain Latinos, to support one another, strengthen our cultural ties, assist each other, and search for a new kinship, a new family with fresh kin roles and relationships. As we pronounced in clear voices the names of our dead, beloved teachers, friends, and family members that had passed away, a loud and powerful *"PRESENTE"* was shouted by the new community. Every *"PRESENTE"* acknowledged dramatically the existence of a new community in front of our dead as if they were physically alive with us; long pauses and short prayers, tears and genuine love were all revealed there in front of the *altarcito*, the sacred altar at the steps of the beautiful church, with our *santitos*, or spiritual icons, our pictures, souvenirs, and flowers reminding us of La Raza that was there spiritually. It was a nontrivial ritual. For several months after the ceremony we would meet on campus and remind each other of that day. Some of the students I met there for the first time, remained close to me for months, and we still greet each other as though we have been lifelong friends! The power of the ritual and its impact on Latino identity exists because it creates a close group, a moral and spiritual community that makes life more bearable and meaningful. Some students from the West Coast see themselves as being in exile; rituals give them a sense of belonging.

Beyond religious rituals, community ties are strengthened through enacting folklore and participating in entertainment. A welcome-ceremony for several hundred Latino students in the area, especially students from Harvard and the Massachusetts Institute of Technology, brought brown faces, music, Latino food, and genuine enjoyment to Latinos who rarely get together in large numbers. The Mexican dances, songs, folklore, hot food, and one another's company were all fine, but all that under an eighteenth-century baroque ceiling at Harvard looked and felt a little strange. The apparent incongruity between Mexican dances like the *Jarabe Tapatío* and *La Negra,* or mariachi music in the midst of the magnificent, wealthy, and revered cathedrals of learning at Harvard, served only to accentuate the new Latino identities, the bizarre combination of high status, power, and down-to-earth adherence to Latino culture, Indian folklore, and the food our parents and ancestors in precolonial Mesoamerica enjoyed. Why here? Why these young men and women whose parents or grandparents were perhaps farmworkers, low-income immigrants, or undocumented workers? In fact, I know that some of these students themselves had to work with their hands for a time during their youth. They still show in their rough hands the scars of agricultural labor. In their minds, the promise to honor their parents and make them proud is the key factor that motivates them to seek academic excellence. Rural families, parents from Tangancícuaro (Michoacán) sending their children to MIT and Harvard? This is unusual. Young men and women from such humble origins rubbing elbows with the upper classes and the most powerful elite of intellectuals and politicians in this country? Many of their peers will probably control some of the most important and wealthiest law firms, or handle the top corporations in the country, or engage in this country's most delicate economic and political transactions. So will the Latinos now at Harvard and MIT. The new identity of Latinos has amazingly become incongruent, if not contradictory, when compared with the identities of the adults in previous generations. And I have no doubt that these young men and women are comfortable holding their seemingly opposite identities. They don't see or feel any incongruity. During Christmas break they go home to rural California, make tamales, help with the field chores, drive a tractor, sell agricultural merchandise in the market, repair their parents' home, and then go back to

Harvard, or UCLA, or any other elite school and play the role of scholars, members of editorial boards, quantitative researchers, expert analysts, and so on. At Harvard they are happy to debate, write, conduct research, and plan an ambitious future with the support of high-ranking academicians; yet they code-switch, greet each other in Spanish, and share each other's goodies that have been sent from home (tortillas, tamales, salsa, etc.). This is a new and extraordinary phenomenon that could not have occurred when I was going to school at Stanford in 1964 because then there was no quorum or even the hope of finding such persons in the halls of Stanford. During the later decades of the 1970s and 1980s, most rural Latino folks who made it into academia worked quietly and inconspicuously in the background, at least until they became secure. It was taboo to speak about one's own background and to associate with the migrant workers.

Redefinition of the Self and New Leadership

Let me revisit the issue of what constitutes the cement of our common bond, our linking together as Latinos, the quintessence of our solidarity in modern times. The bond of solidarity is based on our shared common narratives of inequity, our accounts of experiencing conflict, dilemma, exclusion, and adaptation problems in our new country. This is what could be called the politics of survival, and beyond survival, the pain of self-definition or discovery of new identity, which often comes with a serious dilemma, the dilemma of cultural values vs. academic demands. The voices of Latinos and other silenced Americans, such as African Americans, Native Americans (who are culturally and linguistically the closest to Mexican Americans), and Asian Americans, begin to articulate narratives of inequity as they struggle to become bona fide members of the academy through the process of tenure and promotion. These narratives show how survival in academia requires a sophisticated knowledge of the politics of legitimacy, recognition, and funding for scholarly endeavors. The politics of exclusion creates mechanisms that channel information and decisions through paths inaccessible to underrepresented persons. Narratives describe the politics of exclusion and the resulting litany of failures that occur before Latinos finally catch up and learn. This conscious learning and catching up triggers the most profound redefinition of the self in academia as intellectuals with unique strengths and special needs, with emotional wounds and extraordinary resiliency, with a unique capacity for standing firm in the midst of conflict, and for finding strength in intellectual chores and scholarly ideals. What remains the most rewarding

experience of many of the Latino intellectuals I have met is their commitment to research and their allegiance to the Latino community. The
new generation of Latino intellectuals not only has resiliency and extraordinary resourcefulness, but these Latinos are aware of their role
in the future of America as a democracy, as an economic and military
power, and as a country of immigrants. The formation of ethnic identity is an ongoing process that responds to the new personal experiences of individuals as they undergo continuous social, political, and
educational change. George and Louise Spindler (1982, 1989, and 1994)
have described this process when they speak of an *enduring self* constructed during the formative years in which the most fundamental
human relationships are established and the basic norms of human
interaction are internalized. As we grow and mature, we form a new
self-concept, the *situated self* (or *situated selves*), which reflects successive and sequential adaptations of the person to the changing environment. New human experiences require changes in behavior and a
"new" presentation of the self. Physical and mental growth, rites of
passage, changes in lifestyle and personal relationships, and changes
in language and culture are often associated in modern mobility and
worldwide political and economic instability. Adequate coping with
these changes demands a reconceptualization of the self. However,
when the contrast between our enduring self and our situated self becomes conflictive and overwhelming to the point that we no longer
recognize ourselves and cannot reconcile our present behavior with
our original values, then we face an *endangered self*, or a state of confusion and turmoil that can result in "multiple incompatible selves," reflected in changing patterns of behavior as we interact with different
groups of people. Multiple identities, a common phenomenon observable in multicultural modern Western societies, do not reflect pathology but adaptive strategies to a changing world, a fast-changing world
that creates bizarre and complex interactional settings among people
from diverse cultural, linguistic, ethnic, social, economic, and educational backgrounds. Are these interactive arenas becoming closer to a
pathological pattern of "multiple personalities" in conflict? Are they
resulting in a lack of cohesive value systems and clear personal identities? Are Latinos falling into this pattern? No, Latinos, in fact, are creating a new identity on the basis of common cultural values and the
increasing advantages of political alliances for action presumed to benefit the diverse Latino ethnic subgroups. In some real sense, political
action seems to play an instrumental role in forming a new ethnic identity with new cultural ties and values among Latinos who have been
marginalized and isolated. What is the nature of this process of indi-

vidual and collective redefinition of the self, and what is the role of new leaders in promoting a new collective self-identity?

This chapter presents a series of dilemmas that forces us to reconceptualize Latino identities. How, for example, has political action contributed to opening doors in higher education for Latinos and to a new ethnic identity for them? In California and Texas, Latinos have successfully obtained a measure of political power. This new power is becoming an important element in the formation of new personal Latino identities as well as our collective identity at the national level. Thus, Chicanos, one of the largest Latino groups in this country, are discovering a new sense of self-esteem and collective political power through their participation in political action. The emergence of Chicano leaders involved in political action is significant at the end of a century that has been marked by drastic changes in traditional racial, class, and ethnic roles ascribed to Latinos within American democracy. The formation of a middle class of Latinos who are well educated, understand the American political system well, and function effectively within that system has significant consequences for the future of America in both domestic and foreign affairs. Thus, the emergence of a new ethnic leadership is linked to the education and mainstreaming of a large group of new immigrants of color. To use Freire's concepts in critical pedagogy, education and politics are not only inseparable in the context of political action, they are the necessary and sufficient condition for creating a genuine democracy. This means that political action has educated both Chicanos and the rest of society, has redefined them ethnically within the larger society, and has facilitated their own survival as well as the survival of American democratic structures in schools and society. The making of ethnicity, as it occurred in the example given here, brings together the fundamental role of culture in politics and use of community resources for purposes of self-identification precisely during political action. Most important, this example brings up issues of how new ethnic leadership is exercised by educated persons who not only understand well (through their personal experiences) the nature of hegemonic structures, poverty, oppression, and ignorance, but who know the importance of education as the key requirement for conscientization, participation in the democratic process, and ultimately, empowerment. Political action is presented as culturally and linguistically congruent with the new Latino self-definitions (the situated selves) by leaders who exemplify successful adaptation without losing their cultural identity. Political socialization is clearly embedded in the educational process, in teaching and learning. Attitudes about the social system, ethnic, cultural, and economic diversity, about exploitation and multicultural curricula, are an integral part of teaching. As Freire points out:

> There has never been, nor could there ever be, education without content, unless human beings were to be so transformed that the processes we know today as processes of knowing and formation were to lose their current meaning. The act of teaching and learning—which are dimensions of the larger process of knowing—are part of the nature of the educational process. There is no education without teaching, systematic or not, of a certain content. . . . The fundamental problem—a problem of a political nature, and colored by ideological hues—is who chooses the content, and on behalf of which persons and things the "chooser's" teaching will be performed—in favor of whom, against whom, in favor of what, against what. (Freire 1995, 109)

The emergence of "new" ethnic identities is not free from conflict and struggle for control among rival factions (at times racialized and dichotomized into gender camps). The increasing conflict between Latinos and Blacks, Latinos and Asians on university campuses, government agencies, public businesses, and political forums in the United States is a time bomb with serious nefarious consequences for all. It is precisely in this context of cultural conflict and struggle that the emancipation of ethnic persons and groups must take place. They are becoming conscious of and socialized into the politics of modern democracies with a clear distaste for hegemonic structures and no tolerance for the infringement of human rights. The debates in universities over ethnic rights, ethnic recognition, fair distribution of resources, adequate representation of ethnic intellectuals among the faculty, and recognition of the cultural and theoretical contributions by ethnic scholars to the curriculum are only small opportunities for developing a training ground for our democratic institutions of the next century. What is significant about these encounters and political debates is that they take place across ethnic groups and all over this country. That means that (1) democratic debate can take place in a country that is already multicultural, highly diversified, and highly tolerant of differences, in contrast with many other nations and (2) democratic debate must create cultural, political, and ideological flexibility among individuals who have different languages and cultures, and who belong to different nations. As ethnic persons redefine themselves through ideological struggles and political action, they help other individuals from different social and economic groups across countries discover their own identities and explore their own democracies.

Over a period of twenty-five years, generations of Latino students and faculty in the Southwest (for example, at UC Berkeley, UCLA,

Southern California, and other institutions) have fluctuated in their degree of political activism and participation in political debates. Their impact on state and national politics (for example, during Vietnam) was extraordinary. Yet, we have seen radical students become conservative faculty and conservative faculty become radical citizens. We have also seen activists become university intellectuals and administrators (relatively neutral politically), and we have seen intellectuals become radicalized as they defined faculty rights. Unfortunately, we have also seen a measure of cannibalistic, violent, and conflictive behavior dividing Latinos politically across generations on issues of academic tradition, power, ideology, and participation in the control of university functions, resources, visibility, and recognition. What we have not seen in academia is the creation of strong new political fronts across Latino rival groups in the pursuit of the political power at the state and national levels needed to help Latino students. Why are Latinos in academia less willing and capable to create solid fronts for action favoring common goals? New leaders who have a keen political vision and substantial following in their local communities are emerging often from the nonacademic ranks.

Concluding Reflections

Latinos are finding a national voice that permits them to create a new self-identity not in conflict with their other identities (ethnic, social, religious, etc.). This new identity is associated with education for political action and participation in the democratic processes of ideological debate and involvement with the political system at all levels. Finally, the ideological debate and involvement are guided by new leaders who possess specific qualities of vision, biculturalism, multiple identities, the ability to code-switch, and a profound commitment to democratic ideals of fair participation in the political and economic arenas for all Americans. How do we handle the ideological debate and political participation of students and faculty in universities? What should be the role of universities vis-à-vis "education" or instruction that can facilitate the role of leaders in the new multicultural world in which we live? As D. Macedo insightfully points out:

> Literacy for cultural reproduction uses institutional mechanisms to undermine independent thought, a prerequisite for the Orwellian "manufacture of consent" or "engineering of consent." In this light, schools are seen as ideological institutions designed to prevent the so-called crisis of democracy. . . . I analyze how the instrumentalist approach to literacy,

even at the highest level of specialism, functions to domesticate the consciousness via a constant disarticulation between the narrow reductionis-
tic reading of one's field of specialization and the reading of the universe
within which one specialism is situated. The inability to link the reading
of the word with the world, if not combated, will further exacerbate already feeble democratic institutions and the unjust, asymmetrical power
relations that characterize the hypocritical nature of contemporary democracies. (Macedo 1996, 35–36)

The development of new Latino identities is linked to the fight against
what Macedo has called "literacy for stupidification," which takes
place particularly in institutions of higher education when the university ruling elites pretend to offer an education totally divorced from
the politics of daily life, the reproduction of the social and economic
system, and the struggle for liberation on the part of unrepresented
groups. Political action in the educational (university) context has the
particular value of presenting intellectuals (potential leaders) with the
consequences of their ideology for real-life issues and real people, not
as an exercise in futility to debate purely academic content. One of the
main goals of the new Latino leadership in higher education is to open
up institutions that have been traditionally closed by increasing the
pool of qualified candidates for both student and faculty positions. In
fact, Harvard and the Massachusetts Institute of Technology now count
hundreds of Latino students who are functioning well and obtaining a
very intensive academic socialization in two of the most competitive
universities in the world. This is a new phenomenon. But increasing
the pool of candidates is only one of the requirements for successfully
hiring, promoting, and retaining persons from underrepresented racial
or ethnic groups. A more serious challenge is to provide these persons
with adequate mentoring and guidance. We need to create new support systems, a combination of partnerships, state and federal grants,
and support from private agencies in order to identify and nurture the
new generation of Latino intellectual leaders.

Senior scholars should take young Latino researchers under their
supervision (with the necessary financial support), mentoring them
through an extended period (several years) and exposing them to participation in seminars, conferences, and research across institutions.
An important part of this process should concentrate on providing
young Latino intellectuals with an intense socialization in conducting
research and writing, in acquiring additional methodological and analytical skills, and in developing a broad network with peers and senior
scholars. Follow-up of these new intellectual leaders must take the
form of periodical conferences to provide them with specific profes-

sional advice in their professional careers. I believe that the time for seriously investing in Latinos is here. The social and intellectual implications of such a movement toward minority excellence and the development of leadership will certainly have an impact at all levels of education and will prepare this country for the challenges of a multicultural America in the next century.

There are at least two parallel processes taking place among ethnic communities in the United States. One affects each individual at a different pace and is primarily a psychological process that permits an ethnic person to redefine the self in adaptation to new social, economic, educational, and political surroundings; thus personal experiences can bring a person to a new understanding of the space he or she occupies and the need to find a voice in a competitive multicultural world. Another process is political, collective, and public; it strikes groups of individuals having a shared ethnicity with the realization that they can have power through political action and that this power dramatically alters their collective and personal identities in the public arena. What characterizes a new collective identity is the emergence of leadership and representation of common interests in the political arena.

The next chapter will describe the demographic trends and the unique economic characteristics of the various Latino groups with their various sociocultural traits and occupational profiles. One of the greatest enigmas that is keeping Americans in suspense is the Latino population. They don't seem to fit any particular category; they are multiracial, multilingual (including Latinos who speak European languages, as well as Indian languages), multiethnic, with local cultural traditions and literacy backgrounds in contrast. Despite all these profound differences, Latinos have a unique quality to accommodate to different settings and take over the linguistic forms and etiquette of different socioeconomic strata within their ethnic subgroup. It is not uncommon for a Mexican from an Indian and rural background to move up to high political and economic levels of power, return to his or her village of origin, and command the respect of the entire community, without having lost the Indian language and culture, the Spanish language and Mexican culture, while at the same time having acquired communicative competence in English.

References

Borjas, G. J. "Assimilation, Changes in Cohort Quality, and the Earnings of Immigrants," *Journal of Labor Economics* 3 (1985): 463–489.
———. "Assimilation and Changes in Cohort Quality Revisited: What Hap-

pened to Immigrant Earnings in the 1980s?" *Journal of Labor Economics* 13, no. 2 (1995): 201–245.

Bureau of the Census. *Current Population Reports.* Published by the U.S. Department of Commerce, Economics and Statistics Administration, June 1996.

Camarillo, A. *Chicanos in a Changing Society.* Cambridge, Mass.: Harvard University Press, 1979.

Cornelius, W. "Economics, Culture, and the Politics of Restricting Immigration." *The Chronicle of Higher Education* 43, no. 12 (Nov. 15, 1996): B4–B5.

Davidson, A. L. "Marbella Sanchez: On Marginalization and Silencing." In M. Seller and L. Weis (eds.), *Beyond Black and White: New Faces and Voices in U.S. Schools.* New York: State University of New York Press, 1997, 15–44.

DeVillar, R. "Indigenous Images and Identity in Pluricultural Mexico: Media as Official Apologist and Catalyst for Democratic Action." In H. Trueba and Y. Zou (eds.), *Ethnic Identity and Power: Cultural Contexts of Political Action in School and Society.* New York: State University of New York Press, in press.

Freire, P. *Pedagogy of Hope: Reliving Pedagogy of the Oppressed.* Translated by Robert R. Barr. New York: Continuum, 1995.

Garcia, M. *Mexican Americans.* New Haven, Conn.: Yale University Press, 1989.

Gibson, M. *Accommodation without Assimilation: Sikh Immigrants in an American High School.* Ithaca, New York: Cornell University Press, 1988.

Hayes-Bautista, D. E., W. O. Schink, and J. Chapa. *The Burden of Support: Young Latinos in an Aging Society.* Stanford, Calif.: Stanford University Press, 1988.

León-Portilla, M. *Aztec Thought and Culture.* Norman: University of Oklahoma Press, 1963.

———. *La Flecha en el Blanco: Francisco Tenamaztle y Bartolomé de las Casas en Lucha por los Derechos de los Indígenas 1541–1556.* Mexico: Editorial Diana, 1995.

LeVine, S. "Pilgrim Saints in Mexico." Unpublished manuscript. Department of Human Development and Psychology, Harvard University, 1997.

Macedo, D. "Literacy for Stupidification: The Pedagogy of Big Lies." In P. Leistyna, A. Woodrum, and S. Sherblom (eds.), *Breaking Free: The Transformative Power of Critical Pedagogy. Harvard Education Review, Reprint Series no. 27,* 1966, 31–57.

Macias, J. "Resurgence of Ethnic Nationalism in California and Germany: The Impact on Recent Progress in Education." *Anthropology and Education Quarterly* 27, no. 2 (1996): 232–252.

Martin, P., and E. Taylor. "Immigration and the Changing Face of Rural California: Summary Report of the Conference Held at Asilomar, June 12–14, 1995." Unpublished manuscript.

McLaren, P. "Unthinking Whiteness, Rethinking Democracy: Or Farewell to the Blong Beast; Toward a Revolutionary Multiculturalism." *Educational Foundations* spring 1997.

Menchaca, M., and R. R. Valencia. "Anglo-Saxon Ideologies in the 1920s–1930s: Their Impact on the Segregation of Mexican Students in California." *Anthropology and Education Quarterly* 21, no. 3 (1990): 222–249.

Moore, J., D. Vigil, and R. Garcia. "Residence and Territoriality in Chicano Gangs." *Social Problems* 31, no. 2 (1983): 183–194.

Nutini, H. *Todos los Santos in rural Tlaxcala*. Princeton, N.J.: Princeton University Press, 1988.

Rodríguez, R. *Hunger of Memory: The Education of Richard Rodríguez. An Autobiography*. Boston: David R. Godine, 1982.

Spindler, G., ed. *Anthropology and Education*. Stanford, Calif.: Stanford University Press, 1955.

Spindler, G., and L. Spindler. "Roger Harker and Schonhausen: From the Familiar to the Strange and Back Again." In G. Spindler (ed.), *Doing the Ethnography of Schooling*. New York: Holt, Rinehart and Winston, 1982, 20–47.

———. "Instrumental Competence, Self-Efficacy, Linguistic Minorities, and Cultural Therapy: A Preliminary Attempt at Integration." *Anthropology and Education Quarterly* 10, no. 1 (1989): 36–50.

Spindler, G., and L. Spindler, eds. *Pathways to Cultural Awareness: Cultural Therapy with Teachers and Students*. Newbury Park, Calif.: Corwin Press, 1994.

Suárez-Orozco, C., and M. Suárez-Orozco. *Transformations: Immigration, Family Life and Achievement Motivation among Latino Adolescents*. Stanford, Calif.: Stanford University Press, 1995a.

———. "Migration: Generational Discontinuities and the Making of Latino Identities." In L. Romanucci-Ross and G. DeVos (eds.), *Ethnic Identity: Creation, Conflict, and Accommodation*. 3d Ed. Walnut Creek, Calif.: Alta Mira Press, 1995b.

Suárez-Orozco, M. M. "California Dreaming: Proposition 187 and the Cultural Psychology of Racial and Ethnic Exclusion." *Anthropology and Education Quarterly* 27, no. 2 (1996): 151–167.

———. "State Terrors: Immigrants and Refugees in the Post-National Space." In H. T. Trueba and Y. Zou (eds.), *Ethnic Identity and Power: Cultural Contexts of Political Action in School and Society*. New York: State University of New York Press, in press.

Thompson, T. H., and A. A. West. *History of Santa Barbara County, California, with Illustrations and Biographical Sketches of Its Prominent Men and Pioneers*. Oakland, Calif.: Thompson and West Publishers, 1883 (reproduction of this volume in 1961 by Howell North Books, Berkeley, Calif.).

Trueba, H. T. *Raising Silent Voices: Educating Linguistic Minorities for the Twenty-First Century*. New York: Harper and Row, 1989.

———. "A Mexican Immigrant Community in Central California." Unpublished manuscript. Harvard University, 1997.

Trueba, H. T., C. Rodríguez, Y. Zou, and J. Cintrón. *Healing Multicultural America: Mexican Immigrants Rise to Power in Rural California*. London: Falmer Press, 1993.

Vigil, D. "Chicano Gangs: One Response to Mexican Urban Adaptation in the Los Angeles Area." *Urban Anthropology* 12, no. 1 (1983): 45–75.

———. "Group Processes and Street Identity: Adolescent Chicano Gang Members." *Journal for the Society for Psychological Anthropology, ETHOS* 16, no. 4 (1988): 421–444.

———. *Barrio Gangs*. Austin: University of Texas Press, 1989.

———. *Personas Mexicanas: Chicano High Schoolers in a Changing Los Angeles*.

Case Studies in Cultural Anthropology. Series editors George Spindler and Louise Spindler. Fort Worth, Philadelphia, San Diego: Harcourt Brace College Publishers, 1997.

Villenas, S. "The Colonizer/Colonized Chicana Ethnographer: Identity, Marginalization and Co-optation in the Field." *Harvard Educational Review* 66, no. 4 (1996): 711–731.

Zou, Y., and H.T. Trueba, eds. *Ethnic Identity and Power: Cultural Contexts of Political Action in School and Society.* New York: State University of New York Press, 1998.

2

Latino Diversity: Demographic, Socioeconomic, Occupational, and Educational Characteristics

The binational reality in the lives of millions of Latinos (called Hispanics by the Census Bureau) and the contributions they have made to our economy and quality of life, our culture, and democracy are discussed below. Latino people are racially, socially, and economically highly diversified; but they share culture, language, history, values, worldview, and ideals. Some of their ancestors lived in the Southwest before it belonged to the United States. Other ancestors have been coming for the last century and a half, seeking better employment and freedom. We are living through difficult times, characterized by fear of losing our jobs, increasing crime, and the erosion of family and community values. As Suárez-Orozco insightfully interprets it, our anxiety "generated by immigration today cannot be divorced from the world-wide reshaping of the socioeconomic and symbolic space." In a paradoxical turn of events, immigrants and refugees "have become an uncanny mirror of our own *dislocation*," [sic] and they "embody the very terrifying sense of home-less-ness which characterizes the age of rapid change and globalization" (Suárez-Orozco 1998:289, italics mine). In the face of drastic global sociopolitical and economic change, we turn to immigrants and blame them for all our sufferings, demonizing them as criminals who break our laws, abuse our services, and deprive us of employment. We ask ourselves: Who are these Latino immigrants? Why do they continue to come? How long will they stay? Can they adjust and become productive citizens? Is their culture compatible with ours? Do we need their labor? These workers have to be ghost workers, who must at the same time be there (to do the impossible jobs) but not "be there" (be voiceless and transparent). "When it be-

31

came public knowledge that Pete Wilson and his wife had hired an 'illegal alien' as a maid, his response was that he did not 'remember her' and that he had 'never seen her.' . . . These responses make perfect symbolic sense" (Suárez-Orozco 1998:301, 24). As stated earlier, the violence of county police officers in California, the border patrol, vigilantes, and bandits against undocumented immigrants reflects an epidemic of hatred by a number of organizations. Paranoiac and hateful law enforcement officers portray undocumented workers as terrorizing gangs of aliens who invade our country and break our laws. Nothing is further from the truth. In fact, Mexican workers seek only a chance to work and survive; they are the true victims, as Suárez-Orozco has amply documented (1998).

In some respects, my own biography exemplifies some of the content of the book. It is a book about *Latinos Unidos*, Latino people in the United States coming together in spite of the enormous historical, cultural, social, economic, religious, and racial differences. But we are together not only for political and cultural reasons of the past; that is, on the grounds of whatever our ancestors had in common in the old or in the new world. What binds us together is our experiences in the United States and our common response to the problems of "making sense" of our lives in American society. That means that we find similar interpretations, similar conflicts, and similar problem-solving efforts that force us to rediscover common and profound elements in our cognitive and emotional repertoire. In a very real sense, we create a new history and re-create our own ethnicity together in America through the assumption of new identities. The politics of self-identity and the psychological strategies needed to survive in the new country operate within the parameters and constraints of race, social class, religion, prearrival experiences, literacy level, degree of bilingualism, and the unique agencies of family, community, friendships, and mentorships. Although many efforts in the social sciences have been directed at the construction of broad, and at times rigid, explanatory models for differential achievement, self-identification, and upward mobility, more recently there is a trend to explore behavioral explanations with an eye to the specific impact of agencies and interventions that change the expected outcomes of failure or success. Another trend that is being modified is the rather righteous and narcissistic examination, via sophisticated discourse, of the oppressed or presumed "oppressed peoples" of the world, with little firsthand contact with them. Armchair social science research is always safer, less painful, more detached, and elegant. It pays off in terms of prestige, promotions, and incentives that feed the vanity of scholars, although in the end, little action results to benefit the oppressed. Whether the stimulating discourse produced by these scholars has any relationship to the reality of the daily lives of the oppressed peoples is another matter; one that, unfortunately, is often viewed as irrelevant by some postmodern researchers. Discourse on critical pedagogy, critical ethnography, and "critical" whatever (analysis, thinking, approach, and so on) has become a means to avoid the tough dilemmas involved in the actual face-to-face study of oppression; a study that can be not only methodologically difficult and time consuming, but epistemologically complex, psychologically risky and taxing, genuinely humbling, and often overwhelming. In the end, there is no substitute for field-based research in order to understand human behavior, especially the behavior of peoples from other languages and cultures.

Socioeconomic and Demographic Characteristics

In the study of U.S. Latinos, we cannot trivialize the ethnic, social, racial, and economic differences of Latino subgroups. Caribbean, Puerto Rican, and Cuban Latinos have experiences that may polarize them racially and economically. Their upward mobility varies a great deal, and their literacy levels, bilingualism, and educational needs differ. Latinos from Mexico tend to be represented more by the rural and Indian subgroups than by the European and mestizo subgroups. They come from diverse ethnolinguistic communities whose Indian roots, home languages, and cultures may be very distant from those of Mexicans from middle and upper classes living in large cities. Their religious practices, community social organization, and home and village lifestyles may be shockingly different, and their reactions to urban violence and poverty also differ a great deal. We know that the early experiences in urban centers tend to marginalize Mexican youth in the United States and destroy their family unity, often resulting in gang activity (see C. Suárez-Orozco and M. Suárez-Orozco 1995a and 1995b; Vigil 1983, 1988, 1989; Moore, Vigil, and Garcia 1983). In communicating with marginalized youth, it is extremely important to understand the social and political contexts in which Latinos function and try to survive.

Of the population sixty-five years of age and older, Whites are 85 percent, Blacks are 8 percent, Hispanics are 4 percent, and Asian and Pacific Islanders are 2 percent. Blacks, Hispanics, Asian and Pacific Islanders, and American Indians account for 34 percent of the U.S. population under eighteen years of age (*Population Today: News, Numbers and Analysis,* 24, no. 8, August 1996: 6). Equally shocking are the poverty rates for children. Of the more than sixteen million poor children, one-third (5.6 million) live in "working-poor" families (at least one parent working fifty or more weeks a year and making less than $11,821, the poverty standard for 1994). The number of working-poor families increased 30 percent from 1989 to 1994; most children in these working-poor families are born to women over age twenty-five, and half of these children live in two-parent households with one parent working all year. These children (27 percent of them have no health insurance) are often not immunized, don't do well in school, and are more likely to be poor as adults (*Population Today: News, Numbers and Analysis*, 24, no. 8, August 1996: 4). Overall, the state-by-state picture of U.S. children is depressing. From 1985 to 1993, the number of low-birth-weight babies increased 6 percent; the rate of violent deaths of youth aged fifteen to nineteen (suicide, homicide, accidents) increased 10 percent; violent crime arrests of youths aged ten to seventeen rose 66 percent; single-parent families with children increased 18 percent. There are, however, some positive signs. From 1985 to 1993 the infant mortality rate decreased 21 percent, the rate of deaths of children ages one to fourteen decreased 12 percent; the number of high school dropouts ages sixteen to nineteen decreased 18 percent; the number of idle teens ages sixteen to nineteen decreased 9 percent; and the rate of child poverty remained the same (*Population Today: News, Numbers and Analysis*, 24, no. 8, August 1996: 5).

In 1989, the Latino population was fourteen and a half million, or 6.4 percent of the total U.S. population (at that time of 228 million). By 1990, the Latino population had increased 5.6 million to a total of 20.1 million (that is, 8 percent of the whole U.S. population, then 248 million). The Latino population grew at a rate four times faster than the rest of the country (Valencia 1991, 15). This growth was felt primarily in California, Texas, New York, and Florida—the states that account for 75 percent of the total Latino population. California alone has 34 percent of all Latinos (6.8 million, mostly of Mexican ancestry); Texas has 21 percent of Latinos (4.3 million, also mostly of Mexican ancestry); New York has 10 percent (2 million, mostly Puerto Rican), and Florida has 8 percent (1.6 million, mostly Cuban). About 1.7 million Latinos live in Arizona, Colorado, and New Mexico (mostly of Mexican origin). In New Jersey there are some 640,000 Latinos, mostly Puerto Ricans. The remaining Latino population is scattered throughout the other states. It is expected that sometime in the middle of the next century, the Latino population will be nearly fifty-five million and become larger than the Black population (Valencia 1991, 15). Naturally, the population in some states will change more rapidly (Valencia 1991, 3–16; C. Suárez-Orozco and M. Suárez-Orozco 1995a, 48–81). According to Hayes-Bautista, Schink, and Chapa:

A state-by-state breakdown of the 1980 data gives a clue to possible future trends. At that time California had 4.5 million Latinos (or 30.8 percent of the total), Texas 2.9 million (19.8 percent), New York 1.7 million (11.4 percent), Florida 0.8 million (5.8 percent), and Illinois 0.6 million (4.1 percent). . . . Mexicans are by far the largest Latino subgroup in the United States, numbering 8.7 million in 1980, or 60 percent of all Latinos. Since it is widely agreed that undocumented people were severely undercounted in the census, this figure may be well off the mark. . . . Some 83 percent resided in California, Arizona, New Mexico, Texas and Colorado in 1980. The only other state with a significant Mexican population is Illinois. (Hayes-Bautista, Schink, and Chapa 1988, 129–130)

In 1980, Puerto Ricans made up the second largest Latino subgroup, about two million, concentrated in New York and New Jersey (61 percent) and Illinois (20 percent). The Cuban subgroup counted 803,226 in 1980, concentrated for the most part in Florida (59 percent). The three subgroups, Mexicans, Puerto Ricans, and Cubans, account for 11.6 million of the 14.7 million counted in the 1980 census (Hayes-Bautista, Schink, and Chapa 1988, 131). To understand the long-term population trends and the Latino impact, we must examine what we know about Latino immigrants from the last three decades. According to Rumbaut (1995, 16–69), in 1990 there were 19.7 million immigrants (defined as persons born outside U.S. territory) in the United States (or 6.8 percent of the U.S. population), of which 8,416,924 were Latinos (including Caribbean), from Cuba, Colombia, Jamaica, Nicaragua, Haiti, Dominican Republic, Guatemala, El Salvador, and Mexico; of them 4,298,014 were from Mexico. Of all Latino immigrants, 78 percent came between 1970 and 1989 (6.5 million, one-third of all immigrants), and 50 percent came in the 1980s; only 27 percent of the Latinos have become U.S. citizens, which is understandable given the recency of their arrival, type of work, rural background, and limited assistance. Sixty percent of Mexican immigrants live in California. The vast differences among these recent diverse Latino and Caribbean immigrant populations are summarized in Tables 2.1 and 2.2. The Cuban, Colombian, Jamaican, and Nicaraguan immigrants have educations comparable to those of mainstream Americans, and they have the highest numbers of workers in upper white collar jobs, with the highest percentage of homeowners. A person's educational level seems to predict economic level and employment. The highest rates of poverty are found among the populations with the least education—Mexicans, Salvadorans, Guatemalans, Dominican Republicans, and Haitians. The only exceptions are the Nicaraguans who, although they have a higher educational level, show a poverty level comparable to the less-educated populations. There is no a correlation between higher levels of educa-

Table 2.1

1990 Latino and Caribbean Immigrant Population by Country of Origin, Ranked by Percentage of College Graduates and by Labor Force Distribution

Country	Population	College Graduate	Labor Force	Self-Employment	Upper White Collar	Lower Blue Collar	Poverty Rate	Public Assistance	Own Home
Cuba	736,971	15.1	64.1	7.3	23	18	14.7	16.2	56
Colombia	286,124	15.5	73.7	6.6	17	22	15.3	7.5	38
Jamaica	334,140	14.9	77.4	4.0	22	11	12.1	7.8	44
Nicaragua	168,659	14.6	73.1	4.7	11	24	24.4	8.4	26
Haiti	225,393	11.8	77.7	3.5	14	21	21.7	9.3	37
Dominican Republic	347,858	7.5	63.8	5.1	11	31	30.0	27.8	16
Guatemala	225,739	5.8	75.7	5.2	7	28	25.8	8.3	20
El Salvador	485,433	4.6	76.3	4.7	6	27	24.9	7.1	19
Mexico	4,298,014	3.5	69.7	4.5	6	32	29.7	11.3	36

SOURCE: Adapted from Rumbaut 1995, 23–26. (Based on the U.S. Bureau of Census, *The Foreign Born Population in the United States*, CP-3-1, July 1992, tables 3–5; *Persons of Hispanic Origin in the United States*, CP-3-3, August 1993, tables 3–5; and data drawn from a 5 percent Public Use Microdata Sample, PUMS, of the 1990 U.S. Census.)

Table 2.2
1990 Latino and Caribbean Immigrant Population by Country of Origin
(Ranked by Percentage of College Graduates), Median Age, Fertility,
Percentage of Female Household Heads, of Families with Both
Parents, and of English Proficiency

Country	Median Age	Fertility*	Female Head of Household	Both Parents	English Only	Some/ No English
Cuba	49	1.8	16.5	72	5	40
Colombia	35	1.8	21.5	65	5	34
Jamaica	36	2.2	34.6	53	94	0
Nicaragua	30	2.5	21.0	66	4	34
Haiti	35	2.4	27.6	56	6	23
Dominican Republic	34	2.5	41.3	47	4	45
Guatemala	30	2.6	19.5	66	3	45
El Salvador	29	2.7	21.4	61	3	49
Mexico	30	3.3	14.1	73	4	41

SOURCE: Adapted from Rumbaut 1995, 23–26. (Based on the U.S. Bureau of Census, *The Foreign Born Population in the United States,* CP-3-1, July 1992, tables 3–5; *Persons of Hispanic Origin in the United States,* CP-3-3, August 1993, tables 3–5; and data drawn from a 5 percent Public Use Microdata Sample, PUMS, of the 1990 U.S. Census.)
*Number of births per woman 35–44 years of age.

tion (percentage of college degrees) and the use of public assistance. The Cubans have the highest educational level and the second highest use of public assistance.

There are other important differences among these recent immigrants. As can be seen in Table 2.2, although the most educated populations tend to be older, have lower fertility rates, and larger percentages of families with both parents, there is no clear correlation between the dominant language (Spanish) in the homes and their income, fertility, and college degrees. The largest, youngest, and least-educated populations seem to have the highest levels of fertility. This fact has significant implications for the future generations of Latinos, and it helps us understand the clusters of enduring poverty among them, especially among the farmworkers. It also suggests a lack of education and employment opportunities for women.

Latinos have benefited the least from the economic recovery of the 1980s and 1990s. High rates of poverty have continued in the Latino community. In 1979, 21.8 percent of Latinos were poor; in 1988, the rate was 26.8 percent. In 1979, 28 percent of Latino children lived in poverty; in 1988, 37.9 percent lived in poverty. In 1979, 13.1 percent of Latino families were living in poverty; in 1988, the number reached

16.1 percent. In 1978, 12.5 percent of Latino families with householders who were high school graduates lived in poverty. In 1988, this figure rose to 16 percent. While Latinas saw a small increase in their annual earnings from 1979 to 1988 (from $13,795 to $14,845), male Latinos saw a decrease (from $20,626 to $17,851) (Valencia 1991, 19–20). In 1993, out of the sixteen million children living in poverty (one-fourth of all children under six years of age), 3.9 million (40.9 percent) were Latinos (Rodgers 1996, 11–12). Between 1981 and 1993, the number of poor Latino families with children under eighteen years of age headed by the mother only almost doubled, from 374,000 to 706,000, about 60 percent of all Latino families (Rodgers 1996, 40).

The cited data is only part of the story for the country as a whole. Looking at the distribution of poverty among the various ethnic groups and at the age differences between the White and the ethnic or racial groups gives us a more accurate picture of the challenges ahead. One of the recent reports (Bureau of the Census, *Current Population Reports,* June 1996), examines longitudinal data poverty—the number of people who were poor in a given month during 1992–1993, the chronically poor, median durations of poverty spells, and so on. About 21.6 percent of people who were poor in 1992 were not poor in 1993; children and the elderly, however, were less likely to leave poverty; 4.8 percent, or 11.9 million people, were poor all twenty-four months of 1992–1993; one-half of all poverty spells lasted 4.9 months or longer, but Blacks had longer spells (6.2 months) than Whites. About 52.7 million people (or 20.8 percent) were poor two months or more in 1993; about the same number, 52.9 million, were poor in 1992. The median duration of poverty, 1992 to early 1994, for selected groups shows that those sixty-five years and older had a 7.2-month, and female householder families, a 7.1-month median duration; Blacks had a 6.2-month and Hispanics, a 5.2-month duration. Poverty trends show that 8.6 percent of Hispanics entered poverty in 1993, in contrast with 2.6 percent Whites, and 6.7 percent Blacks (*Current Population Reports,* June 1996, 2–5).

Migration and Economic Crises

Although population migrations are caused by many and complex factors, economists feel that one of the greatest incentives to go north is the economic opportunity vis-à-vis the poverty experienced by an ever-increasing unemployed group of able persons. Dussel Peters (1997) feels that the main motivation for Mexican immigration to the United States is economic. The chronic lack of stable and well remunerated jobs in Mexico has created a systematic and permanent flow of immigrants seeking employment in the United States. Part of the problem in Mexico seems to be related to the restrictive monetary and credit policies, the import liberalization trends that culminated with the 1994 peso devaluation, and Mexico's ever-increasing foreign debt, which all together created a surplus of labor, in spite of the successful economic improvement in the automobile, petrochemical, and electronic industries. In the end, Mexico has not been able to shake off its dependency on imports, and especially among the private manufacturing industries, the crises peaked in 1994. The rate of increase among the "economically active population" far exceeded the pace of economic growth and the demand for domestic labor (Dussel Peters 1997, 4–10). One of the most promising, growing industries in Mexico is the *maquiladora* with an increase from 5 percent to 40 percent of the manufacturing employment between 1980 and 1996 (or from 125,000 to 800,000 workers in those years, respectively). *Maquiladora* is a plant in which pieces produced in the United States are assembled by Mexican workers. But even that represents a very small part of the total economy and will not continue to grow at a fast pace because the market is becoming saturated (Dussel Peters 1997, 14–15).

The steady stream of immigrants from Mexico, Caribbean countries, and South America has become the single largest continental proportion (nearly 38 percent) of legal immigrants and more than 80 percent of undocumented immigrants (Gonzalez Baker, Bean, Escobar Latapí, and Weintraub 1997, 2). In addition to Mexico's role in modern migration movements into the United States, its economic and political importance was demonstrated by our government's pursuit of the North American Free Trade Agreement (NAFTA) and its diligent response to Mexico's 1994 economic crisis. Gonzalez Baker et al. believe that, regardless of what measures and immigration policies are adopted in the United States, the flow of immigrants will continue at a rapid pace and the mainstreaming of Mexican and other Latino populations will follow nonconventional and less-conspicuous routes. For example, people who extend their permanence period beyond that permitted by their visa, plus the annual net increase in undocumented immigrants from Mexico (about 92.4 percent of all undocumented persons in 1992; Gonzalez Baker et al. 1997, 4), along with the dramatic increases in nonimmigrant admissions in recent years, reflect a more intense globalization of our economies in the American hemisphere. In 1980 people of Mexican origin constituted 15 percent of foreign-born persons, in 1990, 20.7 percent, in 1994–1995, 28.4 percent (Gonzalez Baker et al. 1997, 6). The rapid increase of the Mexican population in the United States between 1960 and 1996 is as follows:

- 1960, 1.7 million (1 percent of the total U.S. population)
- 1970, 4.5 million (2.2 percent)
- 1980, 8.7 million (3.9 percent)
- 1990, 13.3 million (5.4 percent)
- 1995, 17 million (6.6 percent)
- 1996, 18 million (6.7 percent)

(Gonzalez Baker et al. 1997)

It is also significant that the 6.8 million people born in Mexico and living in the United States represent 38.2 percent of the total Mexican-origin population, and 25.8 percent of all the foreign-born persons in this country. Congruent with the previous indices of growth, the number of naturalized citizens of Mexican origin in 1980 was about half a million; and between 1980 and 1996, about 1.8 million. It seems that two additional factors have motivated Latinos to become naturalized since September of 1996: (1) the impending cuts in social benefits for all immigrants, and (2) in the case of Mexicans, the real or symbolic promise of dual citizenship, or at least the recognition by the Mexican government of their Mexican citizenship rights in principle, without any specific implications at the moment. In conclusion, Gonzalez Baker and her colleagues point to the increasing transnationalism and its implications for immigration policy, which means that the bridging of the borders may become a tangible reality or the tracking of Mexican immigrants (via IDs or other means) will assist authorities to curtail the flow of immigrants. It is not clear how all the above currents may converge into a rapid "browning" of North America.

The fear that recent immigrants from Mexico, who are now at the bottom of the economic ladder, may remain unassimilated in enduring pockets of poverty seems to be challenged by some scholars who feel that Latino progress is disguised by the large and ever-increasing numbers of newcomers. "So numerous are the poor arrivals that Hispanic poverty seems to grow even though many of the earlier arrivals are upwardly mobile. In fact, a recent report has proclaimed that the movement into the middle class is so strong that a majority of the middle class in the Los Angeles area will soon be comprised of Latinos" (Myers 1997, 3). This opinion is not shared by other scholars who feel that this "myth" of Hispanic progress does not stand up to rigorous economic analysis, or who portray the current Latino migrations as "importing Third World poverty." George Borjas (1985, 1995) has defended a model of consistent deterioration in the human quality of recent immigrants, attributing to them a low ability to acquire human capital and lower earnings in comparison with previous immigrants (who came from Europe) and with native-born Americans:

The "declining quality" thesis has been criticized on several grounds. The economic concept of quality has an unfortunate implication when expressed in common English. Some have feared the racist implication that the quality of immigrants is declining because the composition of the immigrant flow has shifted from European to Asian and Latin American origins. However, Borjas intended declining quality to signify the declining returns to human capital. Unfortunately, those declining returns are compounded by *relative* declines in the amounts of human capital as well. Recent immigrants actually have higher education and other human capital than their predecessors; their human capital is declining only in the relative sense that it is rising more slowly than that of native-born whites. (Myers 1997, 4)

Two factors seem to determine the apparent slow pace in the rise of human capital among Latino immigrants; one is that the rate of the flow of newcomers is faster than the rate of increase in their incomes, and another is the educational point of departure; that is, many newcomers arrive with relatively little formal education. As Myers points out, "prior to both occupation and earning achievement lies educational attainment, the key component of human capital used to signify skill level. Most studies of economic adaptation take education simply as a determinant; however, educational attainment is a fundamental aspect of economic adaptation in its own right. Within the lifetime of adult workers, this variable is relatively fixed, but in the context of intergenerational change educational development is a critical dimension of economic adaptation" (Myers 1997, 6–7). One of Myers's most significant observations is that of intergenerational educational growth. Often the main motivation for Latinos to come and stay in this country is to provide their children with a better education. The fact that immigrant parents cannot afford to pay for the education of their children becomes a family project; through an informal process of designation and anticipated success, one of the children is collectively supported to reach a higher educational level. The reality of the exploitation of new immigrants has been clearly stated by Portes. "The puzzle is whether today's children of immigrants will follow their European predecessors and move steadily into the middle-class mainstream or whether, on the contrary, their ascent will be blocked and they will join children of earlier black and Puerto Rican migrants as part of an expanded multiethnic underclass. As the deteriorating conditions of life in American cities suggest, the question is of more than passing significance for the future of American society" (Portes 1996, 3). Portes goes on to spell out the long-term role of immigration in the structure of the American economy in the sagas of immigrants who struggle to find political freedom and economic security. Then he adds:

The saga reflects accurately many individual experiences, but it is only part of the story. While individual motivations are undoubtedly important, a political economy analysis shows that what drives the process is not the dreams and needs of immigrants but the interests and plans of their prospective employers. Although geopolitical and other considerations have played roles in granting to certain foreign groups access to American territory, the fundamental reason for sustained immigration, at least since the post–Civil War period, has been the labor needs of the economy. . . . Employer associations played a decisive role in recruiting European and Asian labor during the nineteenth century. They organized dependable labor flows from Asia, southeastern Europe, and Mexico at the turn of the century and then succeeded in keeping the immigration door open against nativistic opposition until World War I. (Portes 1996, 3–4)

Portes's earlier discussion (1995) of what he calls the 1.5 generation (the emergent second generation) responds to a specially structured cohort for analysis. Myers tries a different strategy, the idea of age-at-arrival effects, measurable in the census through the intersection of year of arrival and current age of the immigrant. To accomplish this, Myers places birth cohorts inside arrival cohorts, and he finds no basis for the 1.5 generation but a "gradient of adaptation that extends from the oldest adult immigrants to the youngest child immigrants" (1997, 9). Myers selects for his study (the Southern California Immigration Project) a region encompassing the southern seven counties between Ventura and San Diego all the way to the border with Mexico. This area had 17.1 million people in 1990, 25.1 percent foreign-born, and a total population of Mexican origin of 4.2 million (46.6 percent of whom were foreign-born; Myers 1997, 11).

According to Myers, there are three broad temporal dimensions that help measure adaptation of immigrants: lifetime, intergenerational, and successive arrival cohort dimensions. Lifetime follows a path suggested by age and length of residence in the United States. But because individuals move with passing time cohorts are formed not only in length of residence but also in age. It is important to create "double cohorts" putting together birth cohorts with arrival cohorts. Myers explains:

Given that the younger generation of native-borns is falling behind the career progress of their more fortunate parents, failure to adjust for birth cohort leads to upwardly biased age effects. . . . Compounding this problem the Borjas method uses the upwardly biased native-born lifetime career as a reference for judging the relative adaptation of immigrants. The implication is that immigrants should advance at the same rate as the false standard linking younger and older men in the cross-section. By this method, both new immigrants and young native-borns might be judged to have declining quality. (1997, 8)

Intergenerational progress research assumes that immigrants pave the way for their children's adaptation and upward economic mobility. If there is a lack of upward economic mobility from one generation to the next, people assume that there is a resistance to assimilation or an incapacity to assimilate. Portes (1995) focused on the so-called 1.5 generation, or the young immigrant children emerging into the second generation that gives special importance to the age-at-arrival effects. Although there is no clear-cut age with which to identify the 1.5 generation, one could probably endorse Myers's suggested age of ten as the cut-off point. Overall, however, change over time is better examined across successive cohorts of newcomers as a measure of collective adaptation of immigrant groups to a new society. The statement about declining quality of immigrants (made by Borjas and others) is based precisely on this type of analysis of change between arrival cohorts (Myers 1997, 10).

From the southern California sample of seven counties, males of Mexican origin were studied. The database used was the Public Use Microdata Samples (PUMS), which compiles census data for states, counties, and cities of over one hundred thousand people in a given geographic location. The data collected by Myers from 1980 and 1990 permitted him to examine temporal effects and differences between various cohorts. He looked at earnings, occupation, and educational attainment. The emphasis on educational attainment was based on the assumption that education predicts occupational rank and earnings. He divided his sample into non–high school completion, high school completion and/or some college, and college graduates. The results were most interesting. Between 1980 and 1990, "the percentage of all Mexican-origin men with less than a high school degree fell 2.9 percentage points between 1980 and 1990, even though non-completion fell 15.7 percentage points for the native-born" (Myers 1997, 15). Data on those Mexican male immigrants who arrived in the ten years previous to the census date, that is, showing changes between 1980 and 1990 of successive cohorts of newcomers, indicates that "the percentage of lower-educated Mexicans declined by 9.8 percentage points between 1980 and 1990, mean occupation rose slightly, and mean weekly earnings fell by $36. In contrast, when the 1970s arrivals are traced forward from 1980 and 1990, we find that educational attainment improved relatively little over time, mean occupation rose by 2.0 status points, and weekly earning rose by nearly $53" (Myers 1997, 15).

This technique has permitted demographers and economists to examine temporal dimensions in immigrant adaptation that were previously camouflaged by the rapid flow of new arrivals. Indeed immigrants have two cohorts, one is a birth cohort and another an immigration cohort. And both age grouping and the length of immigration experience affect mobility and show differential impact (Myers 1997, 17). Thus, Myers has managed to assess the relative progress of immigrants. Indeed, occupational attainment follows educational level, although the main benefits accrue to younger cohorts and earlier immigrants. Myers concludes with an unequivocal statement establishing the relationship of education to economic progress:

> Educational attainment is the foundation of economic adaptation, and this reveals most clearly the importance of intergenerational progress. Within their lifetimes, adult immigrants or native-born Mexican-Americans experience relatively little educational change. The major adjustment occurs between cohorts, with successively younger immigrants being progressively more likely to complete high school. In fact, the youngest immigrants approach the educational level of the native-borns. This human capital investment lays the basis for the subsequent progress in the labor market. (Myers 1997, 33)

Myers's study shows that young immigrant children match or exceed the academic achievement of native-borns (they have a higher rate of high school completion; Myers 1997, 34) and that the intergenerational educational progress does not necessarily or directly translate into occupational mobility and higher earnings. This "economic ceiling" is the result of economic restructuring and has changed the pattern of returns on human capital investment. It is not clear what other factors determine the economic ceiling experienced by urban, educated, hard-working, recent-comer Latinos. Perhaps this ceiling is related to the prearrival experiences, educational level, family literacy tradition, and political sophistication of immigrants. In brief, rather than accepting an overly pessimistic view of the future of Latino immigrants, Myers opens the door to cautiously optimistic expectations of our returns on educational investments. These investments, however, are limited by the social and economic hardships of a population that is transitioning from rural to urban settings.

The Rural-Urban Continuum

Farmworkers constitute the most enduring underclass of the twentieth century in California, in spite of the fact that they are an extremely hard-working group. In some counties (such as McFarland, Madera, Santa Barbara, and San Luis Obispo) there are clusters of Mexican farmworkers in poverty working for very low wages and in subhuman conditions (working long hours, without appropriate clothing or protection, and living in deplorable housing). The population in these counties increased rapidly in response to a demand for manual labor for cultivation of specialized crops. We shall see later how California's failure to mechanize agriculture resulted in the *mexicanization* of commercial agriculture (Palerm 1994), which conflicts not only with immigration policy (extensions, changes in the immigration law, amnesty efforts to legalize cheap labor) but with public opinion about immigrants, their human rights, and the justification for their presence in this country. Aggressive recruitment efforts in Mexico on the part of employers were inconsistent with federal efforts to curtail the flow of immigrants from rural backgrounds. The excessive inflow of rural immigrants to the West Coast resulted in the creation of new ghettoes and pockets of poverty. Immigrant families and village networks are instrumental in managing the choice of jobs with persons from particular Mexican communities:

> The economies and labor markets of rural communities are increasingly layered or segmented in a manner that pushes many of the costs of seasonal farm work onto the most flexible or absorptive people present, recently-arrived immigrants. . . . Today's rural poverty is being created via the immigration of persons with low earnings and little education into an expanding fruit and vegetable agriculture that increasingly exports the commodities produced by immigrant farm workers. . . . Rural poverty affects California cities as local residents, particularly the children of immigrants, seek a livelihood outside agriculture. The transfer of rural poverty to urban poverty highlights the importance of education and training to improve the prospects for California's rural-to-urban migrants in the urban economy. (Martin and Taylor 1996, 2)

Added to these problems is the fact that the income growth benefits of unskilled labor are not evenly distributed. They often go to persons living outside the local communities. A cautionary note is relevant here. Although the permanence of poverty enclaves is undeniable, we do not have adequate methodological resources and funds to research upward mobility of individual immigrants or groups who transition from rural to urban settings; furthermore, the measurement of "urban poverty" (the length and intensity of poverty spells) and the characteristics of persons escaping urban poverty every year, may prevent investigators from producing a balanced picture of the impact of seasonal rural immigrants. Second, even when the main beneficiaries of seasonal farm labor are not part of the local community, the agricultural economy of this country as a whole continues to reap enormous benefits. Granted, often the communities that must bear the cost of serving the needs of low-skilled season farmworkers with minimum earnings and unstable jobs do not have sufficient resources. Martin and Taylor feel that in some rural towns, agricultural labor is divided into a three-tiered labor force; the smallest portion of workers, 14 percent, work year round; 20 percent are long-season local workers, and 66 percent are peak-season migrants (1996, 6).

To illustrate the impact of new immigrants in rural towns, Martin and Taylor describe the situation in Madera and Fresno. In Madera, a city with one hundred thousand residents (one-third are Hispanics), the cultivation of raisin grapes and other fruit is the responsibility of mestizo workers from Michoacán and other central and western Mexican states who gradually replaced white workers. More recently, however, Mixtec Indians from Oaxaca have become the new force replacing mestizos. In both instances, the reason for the change in the workforce was wages. Farmersville and McFarland (each with seven thousand residents) are also examples of towns that experienced replacement of older immigrants by an oversupply of new immigrants. Fresno is an excellent example of an expanding city with second-generation immigrants who do not wish to do farm labor. In 1993, Fresno County had a population of some eight hundred thousand people and powerful annual agricultural commodity sales of $3 billion (16.6 percent of California's total $18 billion agricultural commodity sales). Half of its total population lives in the city of Fresno, and two hundred thousand people live in fourteen incorporated, often segregated, cities—such as Mendota, Huron, and Parlier—and the remainder are scattered around. Unemployment in the county in 1992–1993 was 14 percent. In 1993, public assistance was received by 30 percent of the population, 10 percent for non-Hispanic Whites, 40 percent for Hispanics, and 60 percent for Blacks (Martin and Taylor 1996, 8). In the 1980s and 1990s low wages for farmworkers were compensated for by in-kind benefits. Now these benefits are shrinking and wages are not rising; as a consequence, seasonal farm jobs are less attractive to workers with other options.

Schooling, educational level, and literacy are considered by many scholars as pivotal for increasing social and economic mobility in immigrants and other populations. As we consider the future of Latinos, children's academic achievement in school, and a serious investment in their overall development, we come face-to-face with the neglect and instructional problems of schools having concentrations of Latinos.

The Struggle of Latino Children in Schools

The demographic predictions of the 1970s were too conservative. The increased immigration of Latino and Asian populations has rapidly shifted both the total number of children in schools and their racial and ethnic balance vis-à-vis the White non-Latino population. California will face radical changes before any other state. In 1970 there were only 30 percent ethnic and racial minority students in K–12 public schools. After 140 years of predominantly White enrollment, in 1990, 50 percent of the California public school students belonged to ethnic and racial subgroups. There is no longer a numerical majority of Whites. By the year 2030, White students will constitute about 30 percent of the total enrollment and Latino students will represent the largest group (44 percent of the total enrollment; Valencia 1991, 17). Other school demographic projections suggest that the White school-age population will decrease for the country at large and the Latino school-age population will continue to increase. Latino children (five to seventeen years of age) numbered six million in 1982 (9 percent of the national youth population); by 2020 they will number nineteen million (25 percent of the country's youth population). That is, the Latino school-age population will more than triple in eight years (Valencia 1991, 18–19).

In the late 1960s, there were more than three times as many Blacks as Latinos in the school population, and there was one Latino for every seventeen White students; twenty years later Latino enrollment is two-thirds that of the Black student population, and there is one Latino student for every seven Whites. The White student population decreased 17 percent, whereas the Latino student population increased 103 percent in that period (Orfield, cited by Valencia 1991, 18–20). This trend had been accentuated for complex historical reasons in the 1990s (Orfield and Eaton 1996). Paradoxically, the economic and technological future of this country will depend precisely on the educational success of Latinos, Blacks, and Asians, because by the mid–twenty-first century they will constitute half of the total United States population. Latino children will be the majority in many of our schools. The United States has not prepared for this challenging change. Educators need to be trained to communicate with Latinos effectively and to understand the critical role of Latinos in our future. Latinos will continue to view the family and community as the center of religious, economic, and social life. Latinos clearly occupy the most strategic position among immigrants as we approach the twenty-first century; the success of Latinos can easily become the success of America's democracy, as well as influence its economic, technological, and military survival. The world is increasingly complex and less controllable by the U.S. government and its political institutions. During the twenty-first century, American democratic institutions will struggle for survival in the face of the rising power of other nations.

Latino populations will continue to grow and will remain highly diversified. The education of Latinos will be the most critical challenge to be faced by the next century's educators. The survival of American democracy may well depend on the vision and wisdom of intellectual leaders and teachers who understand Latino communities and families, their values and needs, their exclusion and pain. Latino immigration is likely to continue to be strong given (1) the economic and political instability of Mexico, Central America, and South America, (2) the increasing need for hand labor in the United States for specialized crop agriculture and for laborers in other economic endeavors requiring the performance of undesirable and strenuous work, and (3) the Latino tendency to want to reunite families (Hayes-Bautista, Schink, and Chapa 1988, 132–134). According to W. Cornelius, Latino population growth will continue if economic development in this country demands low-skill, low-wage jobs, and if the political and economic crises in Mexico and Central America remain acute (Cornelius 1995, 2).

Preparing Teachers for Latino Students

The historical academic underachievement of Latino students is attributed to the lack of cognitively, culturally, and linguistically appropriate teaching methods, and the remedy is often presented in terms of methodological and mechanistic tools dislodged from the sociocultural and historical circumstances of children's family and community. There is a lack of understanding of the fundamental differences between Latino and other children. This "technical" approach to underachievement assumes that nothing is wrong with schools and teachers, and the problem rests with students themselves as being not "regular" or "normal," but having "special" needs. Technical refers here to the positivistic tradition in education that views teaching as a precise scientific undertaking and that sees teachers as technicians who practice preselected skills and strategies. Technical solutions (see American Association of School Administrators 1987; Carter and Chatfield 1986; Knapp and Shields 1990; Means and Knapp 1991) assume that schools and teaching are politically neutral and that consequently, change is required in children and families, not in schools and teachers. These basic assumptions absolve teachers from having to critically analyze exemplary and effective teaching approaches, and encourage them to grab "technical" solutions. One of the fundamental tenets of critical pedagogy as established by Freire (1967, 1973, 1985, 1993, 1995; Freire and Macedo 1987, 1996) and recently reaffirmed and reinterpreted by Gadotti is the political character of education:

> The pedagogy of dialogue is a historical pedagogy. As with any other pedagogy, it is always in evolution. . . . In this historical context of the failure of education and of new hopes, the concept of a pedagogy of dialogue acquires new systematization with the work of Paulo Freire (1921), a major figure in this movement. As a successor of Anisio Teixeira and the "new schoolists," Freire provides the best example of a renewed understanding of the first works—*Education as a Practice of Freedom* (1967) and *Pedagogy of the Oppressed* (1973)—Freire has given a dialogue a clear political character. In his work, the dialogue of the oppressed, oriented by a critical conscience of reality, tries to surpass the conflict between the oppressed and their oppressors. He conceives dialogue as an educator who takes the side of the oppressed. This position is the opposite of the educator who proclaims neutrality or doesn't take sides. (Gadotti 1996, 2)

In fact, there has been an increase in research studies that identify educational programs found to be successful in working with Latino student populations limited in their English proficiency (American Association of School Administrators 1987; Carter and Chatfield 1986; Lucas, Henze, and Donato 1990; Tikunoff 1985). In addition, there has been specific interest in identifying teaching strategies that more effectively teach culturally and linguistically "different" students, those who have limited English proficiency, and other "disadvantaged" and "at-risk" students (Knapp and Shields 1990; Means and Knapp 1991; Tinajero and Ada 1993). Although it is important to identify promising instructional programs and strategies, it is erroneous to assume that blind replication or teacher mastery of particular methods will guarantee successful student learning. Often, prospective teachers imbue the "new" methods and curricula with almost magical properties that render them, in and of themselves, capable of improving students' academic standing.

One great challenge in teacher education is to persuade new teachers that a myopic focus on methodology obfuscates the central question, which is: Why don't linguistically and culturally "subordinated" students (children from economically oppressed families), in general, succeed academically? Some scholars feel that it is perhaps because schools reproduce the existing asymmetrical power relations among cultural groups (Anyon 1988; Gibson and Ogbu 1991; Giroux 1992; Freire 1985). If this statement is correct, then how do we take teachers beyond the "methods fetish" (Bartolomé 1994) and away from ahistorical and apolitical assumptions to reality, to critical assessment of learning environments in their political contexts, and how do we inculcate in teachers a sophisticated understanding of such environments? I contend that teachers need to possess the necessary subject matter, knowledge, and methodological skills to teach, but they also need political clarity to critically analyze and translate exemplary pedagogical approaches into appropriate cultural and linguistic codes. We have to recognize that historically teachers have been "trained" in lock-step and mechanistic approaches. Despite this reality, efforts are being made to bring about changes in teacher preparation. The nature and extent of these changes are matters of speculation and experimentation, but the need for a fundamentally different ideological basis is firm. Gary Orfield and associates have vividly depicted the demographic projections of Latino and Black student populations from 1968 to 1994 in predominantly minority and 90–100 percent minority schools (see Table 2.3).

As these populations grow in our public schools, teachers continue to search for "technical" solutions. Paulo Freire (1973, 1993, 1995, passim) argues that technical expertise and mastery of content area and methodology are insufficient to ensure reflective and effective instruction and that without political clarity teachers cannot create, adapt, or reform teaching strategies intended to actively engage children in the learning process, while at the same time respecting and challenging them. This is particularly difficult with students from diverse cultural groups and low socioeconomic levels. If teachers recognize that getting a job, finding a home, and surviving are not politically neutral activities, then they will understand that teaching is not a politically neutral

Table 2.3
Percent of U.S. Black and Latino Students in Predominantly Minority and 90–100 Percent Minority Schools, 1968–1994

Year	Predominantly Minority		90–100% Minority	
	Blacks	Latinos	Blacks	Latinos
1968–1969	76.6	54.8	64.3	23.1
1972–1973	63.6	56.6	38.7	23.3
1980–1981	62.9	68.1	33.2	28.8
1986–1987	63.3	71.5	32.5	32.2
1991–1992	66.0	73.4	33.9	34.0
1994–1995	67.1	74.0	33.6	34.8

SOURCE: G. Orfield, M. Bachmeier, D. James, and T. Eitler. "Deepening Segregation in American Public Schools," *Equity and Excellence in Education* 30, no. 2 (September 1997).

undertaking either. Indeed educational institutions mirror the greater society—our culture, values, and norms. Thus, the asymmetrical power relationships among the various social and cultural strata of the larger society are reproduced within the school and classroom unless all participants make concerted efforts to prevent reproduction of power. Teachers can either maintain the status quo, or they can lead the transformation efforts by facing the sociocultural reality of the classroom and school and by creating a genuinely democratic environment where teachers' hegemonic discourse is replaced by active participation of all students in their own learning efforts. Teachers can support positive social change in the classroom in a variety of ways. Because of the increasing isolation of Latino children and the rapid growth of the Latino school population in the United States, it is important to explore ways of improving instruction in schools having heavy concentrations of Latinos. Latino enrollments from 1970 to 1994 have increased substantially (see Figure 2.1).

The rapid growth of Latino student populations has primarily affected California, Texas, New York, New Mexico, Florida, Arizona, Illinois, and New Jersey. The comparison of enrollment numbers in 1970 and 1994 shows a dramatic picture (see Table 2.4).

One possible intervention can be the creation of heterogeneous learning groups for the purpose of modifying low-status roles of individuals and groups. These groupings, however, will have to have pedagogical strategies that are socioculturally congruent and go beyond technical arrangements, that is, strategies that focus on maximizing the meaningful participation of culturally different children (see, for example, the work of Gutierrez 1994 and Gutierrez, Larson, and Kreuter 1995). Cohen (1986) shows that teachers can create learning conditions where students perceived as having low status (for example, limited English speakers in a classroom where English is the dominant language; students with academic difficulties, or those perceived by their peers as less competent) can indeed demonstrate their knowledge and expertise. In this way the students can see themselves, and be seen by others, as capable and competent. These "democratic" contexts are created by teachers who want to engage *all* students in peer learning activities without isolating or ranking them. Teachers' political awareness and clarity obviously are not enough to remedy structural inequities in society, but they can inspire students to strive for the democratic ideals that can foster equity, self-confidence, and motivation in academic achievement. Neither the teacher's role nor the role of educational institutions is ever neutral (Freire 1985, 1993, 1995; Freire and Macedo 1987, 1996). Teachers at times may uncritically follow school practices that perhaps unintentionally promote tracking

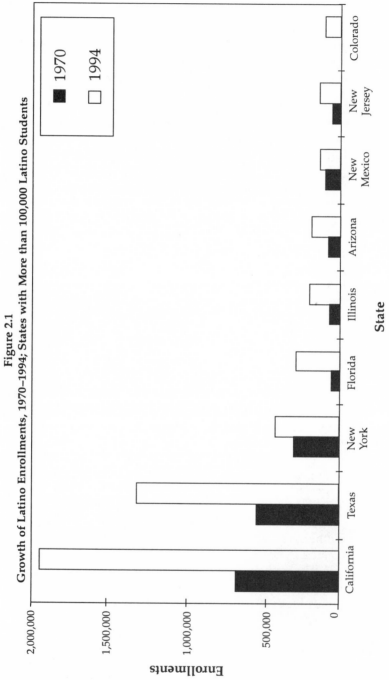

Figure 2.1
Growth of Latino Enrollments, 1970–1994; States with More than 100,000 Latino Students

SOURCE: G. Orfield, M. Bachmeier, D. James, and T. Eitle. "Deepening Segregation in American Public Schools," *Equity and Excellence in Education*, 30, no. 2 (September 1997).

Table 2.4
Growth of Latino Enrollments 1970–1994

	1970	1994	Change 1970–1994	
	Enrollment	Enrollment	Number	Percent
California	706,900	1,953,343	1,246,443	176.3
Texas	565,900	1,304,269	738,369	130.5
New York	316,600	440,043	123,443	39.0
Florida	65,700	301,206	235,506	358.5
Illinois	78,100	218,568	140,468	179.9
Arizona	85,500	203,097	117,597	137.5
New Mexico	109,300	148,772	39,472	36.1
New Jersey	59,100	148,345	89,245	151.0

SOURCE: G. Orfield, M. Bachmeier, D. James, and T. Eitle. "Deepening Segregation in American Public Schools," *Equity and Excellence in Education* 30, no. 2 (September 1997).

and segregation within school and classroom contexts, and they thus perpetuate the status quo. Low socioeconomic status and the racial or ethnic background of students of color are often perceptually framed in school as characteristics of "deficit" or "caste" individuals and therefore of low academic achievement (Anyon 1988; Bloom 1991; Cummins 1989; Ogbu 1974, 1978, 1981, 1982, 1983, 1987, 1991, 1992). The impact of the social structural arrangements is pervasive, for it covers the entire family's status, residential location, literacy environments, safety from violence, positive reinforcement from church, banks, and other institutions, and linguistic and cultural socialization to participate in the social activities of mainstream persons.

The present emphasis on (almost obsession with) methods must be broadened to examine issues of race, ethnicity, income, deficit mentality, and ideologies contrary to our democracy, especially that of *White supremacy* (McLaren 1997; Cummins 1989; Giroux and McLaren 1986; Flores, Cousin, and Diaz 1991). Taking a sociohistorical view of present-day conditions can help teachers understand the historical specificity of marginalized students and how the eradication of home languages and cultures can be interpreted as dehumanizing.

A Deficit View of Latino Students

The design, selection, and use of particular teaching methods, approaches, and strategies arise from teachers' perceptions of the academic ability and worth of students. The most pedagogically advanced strategies will be ineffective in the hands of educators who implicitly or explicitly subscribe to a *deficit* mentality, or a belief system that renders ethnic, racial, and linguistic minority students at best culturally disadvantaged, in need of fixing, or, at worst, culturally or genetically inferior, and consequently beyond hope of "fixing." The various models proposed to explain the academic failure of Latinos (described as *historical, pervasive,* and *disproportionate*) are deficit-based and deeply imprinted in our individual and collective psyches (Flores 1982, 1993; Menchaca and Valencia 1990; Valencia 1991, 1997). The deficit model has the longest history of any model discussed in the education literature. Valencia traces its evolution over three centuries. "Also known in the literature as the 'social pathology' model or the 'cultural deprivation' model, the deficit approach explains disproportionate academic problems among low status students as largely being due to pathologies or deficits in their sociocultural background (e.g., cognitive and linguistic deficiencies, low self-esteem, poor motivation). . . . To improve the reducibility of such students, programs such as compensatory education and parent-child intervention have been proposed" (1986, 3). Barbara Flores (1982, 1993) documents the effect this deficit model has had on schools' past and current perceptions of Latino students. Her historical overview chronicles descriptions used to refer to Latino students over the last century. The terms range from *mentally retarded, linguistically handicapped, culturally and linguistically deprived,* and *semilingual* to the current euphemism for Latino and other subordinated students: the *at-risk* student.

Similarly, recent research continues to lay bare our deficit orientation and its links to discriminatory school practices aimed at students from groups perceived as low status (Anyon 1988; Bloom 1991; Diaz, Moll, and Mehan 1986; Oaks 1986). Findings range from teacher preference for Anglo students, to bilingual teachers' preference for lighter-skinned Latino students (Bloom 1991), to teachers' negative perceptions of working-class parents as compared with middle-class parents (Lareau 1990), and, finally, to unequal teaching and testing practices in schools serving working-class and ethnic minority students (Anyon 1988; Diaz, Moll, and Mehan 1986; Oaks 1986). Especially indicative of our inability to consciously acknowledge the deficit orientation is the fact that the teachers in these studies (teachers from all ethnic groups) were themselves unaware of the active role they played in the differential and unequal treatment of their students.

The Isolation of Latino Students

The increasing segregation of Latino students is dramatically shown region by region for 1994–1995 (see Figure 2.2).

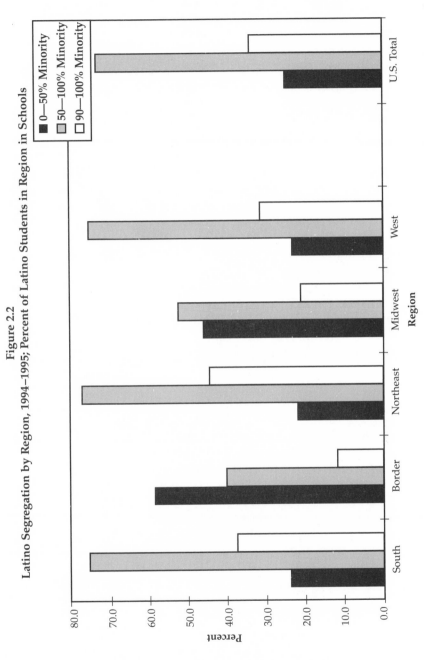

Figure 2.2
Latino Segregation by Region, 1994–1995; Percent of Latino Students in Region in Schools

SOURCE: G. Orfield, M. Bachmeier, D. James, and T. Eitle. "Deepening Segregation in American Public Schools," *Equity and Excellence in Education*, 30, no. 2 (September 1997).

Latino student segregation has worsened in the last few years. The deficit view of subordinated students has been critiqued by numerous researchers as ethnocentric and invalid (Boykin 1983; Diaz et al. 1986; Flores 1982; Flores et al. 1991; Sue and Padilla 1986; Trueba 1989; Walker 1987). Other research offers alternative models that shift the explanation of school failure away from the characteristics of the individual child, their families, and their cultures, and toward the schooling process (Au and Mason 1981; Heath 1983; Mehan 1992; Philips 1972). Unfortunately, however, many of these alternative models have unwittingly given rise to a kinder and more liberal, yet a concealed and pernicious, version of the deficit model that views subordinated students as being in need of either "fixing" or of "specialized" modes of instruction, a type of instructional "coddling" that mainstream students do not require in order to achieve in school. The deficit ideology with respect to Latinos has resulted in further isolation of these students from 1989 on (see Tables 2.5 and 2.6 for segregation rankings of Latino students in key states 1989–1990, and 1994–1995).

Despite the use of these less overtly ethnocentric models, the deficit orientation toward difference, especially as it relates to Latinos and other low socioeconomic and ethnic minority groups, is deeply ingrained in the ethos of our most prominent institutions and their visible educational programs.

Table 2.5
State Rankings in Segregation of Latino Students by Three Measures, 1989–1990 School Year

% in Majority White Schools		% in 90–100% Minority Schools		% Whites in School of Typical Latino	
New York	16.6	New York	54.1	New York	21.5
Texas	21.2	New Jersey	41.4	Texas	26.5
California	22.2	Texas	41.0	California	28.8
New Mexico	23.2	Connecticut	36.8	New Jersey	28.9
New Jersey	24.9	Illinois	35.5	Illinois	31.7
Illinois	25.9	California	33.4	New Mexico	33.3
Florida	32.2	Florida	30.4	Florida	33.8
Connecticut	33.8	Pennsylvania	26.4	Connecticut	33.9
Pennsylvania	40.1	Indiana	21.2	Pennsylvania	41.6
Massachusetts	41.0	New Mexico	17.9	Arizona	42.4

SOURCE: G. Orfield, M. Bachmeier, D. James, and T. Eitle. "Deepening Segregation in American Public Schools," *Equity and Excellence in Education* 30, no. 2 (September 1997).

Table 2.6
State Rankings in Segregation of Latino Students by Three Measures,
1994–1995 School Year

% in Majority White Schools		*% in 90–100% Minority Schools*		*% Whites in School of Typical Latino*	
New York	13.8	New York	57.3	New York	19.2
California	17.3	New Jersey	43.4	California	24.8
Texas	19.6	Texas	43.0	Texas	25.0
New Mexico	21.6	California	38.7	New Jersey	29.3
Rhode Island	24.8	Illinois	34.9	Illinois	30.9
Illinois	26.5	Connecticut	32.4	New Mexico	31.0
New Jersey	27.3	Florida	27.6	Florida	34.5
Connecticut	31.9	Pennsylvania	25.8	Connecticut	35.0
Florida	33.2	New Mexico	20.0	Rhode Island	38.0
Arizona	34.0	Arizona	18.9	Arizona	38.2

SOURCE: G. Orfield, M. Bachmeier, D. James, and T. Eitle. "Deepening Segregation in American Public Schools," *Equity and Excellence in Education* 30, no. 2 (September 1997).

Students' Cultural and Cognitive Capital

Well-known approaches such as cooperative learning, language experience, process writing, reciprocal teaching, and whole-language activities have the potential to be used to create humanizing learning environments where low-status Latino students cease to be treated as objects and yet receive academically rigorous instruction (Cohen 1986; Edelsky, Altwerger, and Flores 1991; Palinscar and Brown 1984; Pérez and Torres-Guzmán 1992; Zamel 1982). Unfortunately, however, even these approaches when implemented uncritically can produce negative results (Delpit 1986, 1988, 1995). Teachers' critical applications of these approaches can contribute to discarding deficit views of students from subordinated groups and produce many forms of academically rigorous, student-centered teaching strategies. What these approaches have in common is that they capitalize on students' existing knowledge (including linguistic and cultural) and experiences, and they are enriching and challenging cognitively. In mainstream society, the practice of learning from and valuing student language and life experiences occurs in classrooms where students speak a language and possess cultural capital closely matching those of the society at large (Anyon 1988; Lareau 1990; Winfield 1986). This is precisely what needs to happen for culturally different children. It is important for educators to recognize that no language or set of life experiences is inherently superior, yet our social values reflect our preferences for certain language and life experiences over others. We should not discount Latino experiences and cultural capital as strengths. Learning only occurs when prior knowledge is accessed and linked to new information. Beau Jones, Annemarie Palinscar, Donna Ogle, and Eileen Carr (1987) explain that learning *is* the act of linking new information to prior knowledge. According to their framework, prior knowledge is stored in memory in the form of knowledge frameworks. New information is understood and stored by calling up the appropriate knowledge framework and then integrating the new information. Acknowledging and using existing student language and knowledge makes good pedagogical sense, and it also constitutes a humanizing experience for those students who feel *de*humanized and disempowered in the schools. Many of the strategies identified as effective in the literature have the potential to offset reductive education in which "the educator as *the one who knows* transfers existing knowledge to the learner as *the one who does not know*" (Freire 1985, 114, emphasis added). The mere implementation of a particular methodological strategy identified as effective does not guarantee success, as the debate in process writing attests (Delpit 1986, 1988; Reyes 1991, 1992).

The incorporation of students' language, cultural, and experiential knowledge is not a laissez-faire policy, and it does not negate teachers' responsibility for providing students with particular academic content knowledge and learning skills. The teacher is the authority, but he or she does not have to be an authoritarian. Teacher and students jointly construct knowledge, building on what students bring to class. Teaching is not "fixing" students but discovering with students new ideas, new values, and new worlds of hope. Teachers must convey in their daily work the moral conviction that they are committed to humanize the educational experience of students by eliminating hostility and replacing messages of distrust or disdain with respect and love for all. This approach is precisely what Freire has taught us in his *Pedagogy of Hope* (1995).

References

American Association of School Administrators. *Raising Achievement among Minority Students*. Arlington, Va.: AASA, 1987.

Anyon, J. "Social Class and the Hidden Curriculum of Work." In J. R. Gress (ed.), *Curriculum: An Introduction to the Field*. Berkeley, Calif.: McCutchan, 1988, 366–389.

Au, K. H. and J. J. Mason. "Social Organization Factors in Learning to Read:

The Balance of Rights Hypothesis. *Reading Research Quarterly* 11 (1981): 91–115.

Bartolomé, L. I. "Beyond the Methods Fetish: Toward a Humanizing Pedagogy." *Harvard Educational Review* 64, no. 2 (Summer 1994).

Bloom, G. M. "The Effects of Speech Style and Skin Color on Bilingual Teaching Candidates' and Bilingual Teachers' Attitudes Toward Mexican American Pupils. "Unpublished doctoral dissertation, Stanford University, 1991.

Borjas, G. J. "Assimilation, Changes in Cohort Quality, and the Earnings of Immigrants." *Journal of Labor Economics* 3 (1985): 463–489.

———. "Assimilation and Changes in Cohort Quality Revisited: What Happened to Immigrant Earnings in the 1980s?" *Journal of Labor Economics* 13, no. 2 (1995): 201–245.

Boykin, A. W. "The Academic Performance of Afro-American Children." In J. T. Spence (ed.), *Achievement and Achievement Motives: Psychological and Sociological Approaches.* San Francisco: W. H. Freeman, 1983, 322–369.

Bureau of the Census. *Projections of the Hispanic Population 1983 to 2080.* (Current Population Reports, Series P-25, No. 995) Washington, D.C., U.S. Government Printing Office, 1986.

———. *Current Population Reports,* published by the U.S. Department of Commerce, Economics and Statistics Administration, June 1996.

Carter, T. P., and M. L. Chatfield. "Effective Bilingual Schools: Implications for Policy and Practice." *American Journal of Education* 95 (1986): 200–232.

Chronicle of Higher Education, Almanac Issue, *Chronicle of Higher Education* 43, no. 1, September 2, 1996.

Cohen, E. G. *Designing Groupwork: Strategies for the Heterogeneous Classroom.* New York: Teachers College Press, 1986.

Cornelius, W. "Educating California's Immigrant Children: Introduction and Overview." In R. G. Rumbaut and W. A. Cornelius (eds.), *California's Immigrant Children: Theory, Research, and Implications for Educational Policy.* University of California, San Diego. San Diego: Center for U.S.-Mexican Studies, 1995, 1–16.

Cummins, J. *Empowering Minority Students.* Sacramento: California Association of Bilingual Education, 1989.

Delpit, L. "Skills and Other Dilemmas of a Progressive Black Educator." *Harvard Educational Review* 56 (1986): 379–385.

———. "The Silenced Dialogue: Power and Pedagogy in Educating Other People's Children." *Harvard Educational Review* 58 (1988): 280–298.

———. *Other People's Children: Cultural Conflict in the Classroom.* New York: The New Press, 1995.

Diaz, S., L. C. Moll, and H. Mehan. "Sociocultural Resources in Instruction: A Context-Specific Approach." In *Beyond Language: Social and Cultural Factors in Schooling Language Minority Students.* Los Angeles: California State University. Evaluation, Dissemination and Assessment Center, 1986, 187–230.

Dussel Peters, E. "Recent Structural Changes in Mexico's Economy: A Preliminary Analysis of Some Sources of Mexican Migration to the U.S." Paper presented at the Conference on Immigration and Sociocultural Remaking of the

North American Space, David Rockefeller Center for Latin American Studies, Harvard University, April 11–12, 1997.

Edelsky, C., B. Altwerger, and B. Flores. *Whole Language: What's the Difference?* Portsmouth, N.H.: Heinemann, 1991.

Erickson, F., and G. Mohatt. "Cultural Organization of Participation Structures in Two Classrooms of Indian Students." In G. Spindler (ed.), *Doing the Ethnography of Schooling: Educational Anthropology in Action.* New York: Holt, Rinehart and Winston, 1982, 133–174.

Flores, B. M. "Language Interference or Influence: Toward a Theory for Hispanic Bilingualism." Unpublished doctoral dissertation, University of Arizona at Tucson, 1982.

———. "Interrogating the Genesis of the Deficit View of Latino Children in the Educational Literature During the 20th Century." Paper presented at the American Educational Research Association Conference, Atlanta, Georgia, 1993.

Flores, B., P. T. Cousin, and E. Diaz. Critiquing and Transforming the Deficit Myths about Learning, Language and Culture. *Language Arts* 68, no. 5 (1991): 369–379.

Freire, P. *Education As a Practice of Freedom.* Rio de Janeiro: Paz e Terra, 1967.

———. *Pedagogy of the Oppressed.* New York: Seabury, 1973.

———. *The Politics of Education: Culture, Power and Liberation.* South Hadley, Mass.: Bergin and Garvey, 1985.

———. *A Pedagogy of the City.* New York: Continuum Press, 1993.

———. *Pedagogy of Hope: Reliving Pedagogy of the Oppressed.* New York: Continuum Press, 1995.

Freire, P., and D. Macedo. *Literacy: Reading the Word and the World.* South Hadley, Mass.: Bergin & Garvey, 1987.

———. "A Dialogue: Culture, Language, and Race." In P. Leistyna, A. Woodrum, and S. Sherblom (eds.), *Breaking Free: The Transformative Power of Critical Pedagogy. Harvard Education Review,* Reprint Series No. 27, 1996, 199–228.

Gadotti, M. *Pedagogy of Praxis: A Dialectical Philosophy of Education.* Translated by John Milton. New York: State University of New York Press, 1996.

Gibson, M. A., and J. U. Ogbu. *Minority Status and Schooling: A Comparative Study of Immigrant and Involuntary Minorities.* New York: Garland, 1991.

Giroux, H. *Border Crossing: Cultural Workers and the Politics of Education.* New York: Routledge, 1992.

Giroux, H., and P. McLaren. Teacher Education and the Politics of Engagement: The Case for Democratic Schooling. *Harvard Educational Review* 56 (1986): 213–238.

Gonzalez Baker, S., F. D. Bean, A. Escobar Latapí, and S. Weintraub. "U.S. Immigration Policies and Trends: The Growing Importance of Migration from Mexico." Paper presented at the Conference on Immigration and Sociocultural Remaking of the North American Space, David Rockefeller Center for Latin American Studies, Harvard University, April 11–12, 1997.

Gutierrez, K. "How Talk, Context, and Script Shape Contexts for Learning: A Cross-Case Comparison of Journal Sharing." *Linguistics and Education* 5 (1994): 335–365.

Gutierrez, K., J. Larson, and B. Kreuter. "Cultural Tensions in the Scripted Classroom: The Value of the Subjugated Perspective." *Urban Education* 29, no. 4 (1995): 410–442.

Hayes-Bautista, D. E., W. O. Schink, and J. Chapa. *The Burden of Support: Young Latinos in an Aging Society.* Stanford, Calif.: Stanford University Press, 1988.

Heath, S. B. *Ways with Words.* New York: Cambridge University Press, 1983.

Jones, B. F., A. S. Palinscar, D. S. Ogle, and E. G. Carr. *Strategic Teaching and Learning: Cognitive Instruction in the Content Areas.* Alexandria, Va.: Association for Supervision and Curriculum Development (with the Central Regional Educational Laboratory), 1987.

Knapp, M. S., and P. M. Shields. *Better Schooling for the Children of Poverty: Alternatives to Conventional Wisdom: vol. 2. Commissioned Papers and Literature Review.* Washington, D.C.: U.S. Department of Education, 1990.

Lareau, A. *Home Advantage: Social Class and Parental Intervention in Elementary Education.* New York: Falmer Press, 1990.

Lucas, T., R. Henze, and R. Donato. "Promoting the Success of Latino Language-Minority Students: An Exploratory Study of Six High Schools. *Harvard Educational Review* 60 1990: 315–340.

Martin, P., and E. Taylor. "Immigration and the Changing Face of Rural California: Summary Report of the Conference Held at Asilomar, June 12–14, 1995." Unpublished manuscript.

McLaren, P. "Unthinking Whiteness, Rethinking Democracy: Or Farewell to the Blonde Beast; Towards a Revolutionary Multiculturalism." *Educational Foundations*, in press.

McLaren, P. *Revolutionary Multiculturalism: Pedagogies of Dissent for the New Millenium.* Boulder, Colo.: Westview Press, 1997.

McLeod, B. ed. *Cultural Diversity and Second Language Learning.* Albany: SUNY Press, in press.

Means, B., and M. S. Knapp. *Teaching Advanced Skills to Educationally Disadvantaged Students.* Washington, D.C.: U.S. Department of Education, 1991.

Mehan, H. "Understanding Inequality in Schools: The Contribution of Interpretive Studies." *Sociology of Education* 65, no. 1 (1992): 1–20.

Menchaca, M., and R. Valencia. "Anglo-Saxon Ideologies in the 1920s–1930s: Their Impact on the Segregation of Mexican Students in California." *Anthropology and Education Quarterly* 21, no. 3 (1990): 222–249.

Miranda, L., and J. T. Quiroz. *The Decade of the Hispanic: A Sobering Economic Retrospective.* Washington, D.C., National Council of La Raza, 1989.

Moll, L. C. "Writing As Communication: Creating Learning Environments for Students." *Theory into Practice* 25, no. 2 (1986): 102–110.

———. "Some Key Issues in Teaching Latino Students." *Language Arts* 65 (1988): 465–472.

Moore, J., D. Vigil, and R. Garcia. "Residence and Territoriality in Chicano Gangs." *Social Problems* 31, no. 2 (1983): 183–194.

Myers, D. "Dimension of Economic Adaptation by Mexican-Origin Men." Paper presented at the Conference on Immigration and Sociocultural Remaking of the North American Space, David Rockefeller Center for Latin American Studies, Harvard University, April 11–12, 1997.

Oaks, J. "Tracking, Inequality, and the Rhetoric of School Reform: Why Schools Don't Change." *Journal of Education* 168 (1986): 61–80.

Ogbu, J. *The Next Generation: An Ethnography of Education in an Urban Neighborhood.* New York: Academic Press, 1974.

————. *Minority Education and Caste: The American System in Cross-Cultural Perspective.* New York: Academic Press, 1978.

————. "Origins of Human Competence: A Cultural-Ecological Perspective." *Child Development* 52 (1981): 413–429.

————. "Cultural Discontinuities and Schooling." *Anthropology and Education Quarterly* 13, no. 4 (1982): 290–307.

————. "Minority Status and Schooling in Plural Societies." *Comparative Education Review* 27, no. 2 (1983): 168–190.

————. "Variability in Minority School Performance: A Problem In Search of an Explanation." *Anthropology and Education Quarterly* 18, no. 4 (1987): 312–334.

————. "Immigrant and Involuntary Minorities in Comparative Perspective." In Gibson and Ogbu, (eds.), *Minority Status and Schooling: A Comparative Study of Immigrant and Involuntary Minorities.* New York: Garland Publishing, Inc., 1991, 3–33.

————. "Understanding Cultural Diversity." *Educational Researcher* 21, no. 8 (1992): 5–24.

Orfield, G., M. Bachmeier, D. James, and T. Eitle. "Deepening Segregation in American Public Schools." *Equity and Excellence in Education* 30, no. 2 (September 1997).

Orfield, G., and S. E. Eaton, eds. *Dismantling Desegregation: The Quiet Reversal of* Brown v. Board of Education. New York: The New Press, 1996.

Palerm, J. V. *Immigrant and Migrant Farm Workers in the Santa Maria Valley, California.* Center for Chicano Studies and Department of Anthropology. University of California, Santa Barbara. Sponsored by the Center for Survey Methods Research, Bureau of the Census, Washington, D.C., 1994.

Palinscar, A. S., and A. L. Brown. "Reciprocal Teaching of Comprehension Fostering and Comprehension-Monitoring Activities." *Cognition and Instruction* 1, no. 23 (1984): 117–175.

Pérez, B., and M. E. Torres-Guzmán. *Learning in Two Worlds: An Integrated Spanish/English Biliteracy Approach.* New York: Longman, 1992.

Philips, S. U. "Participant Structures and Communication Competence: Warm Springs Children in Community and Classroom." In C. B. Cazden, V. P. John, and D. Hymes (eds.), *Functions of Language in the Classroom.* New York: Teachers College Press, Columbia University, 1972, 370–394.

Population Today: News, Numbers and Analysis, vol. 24, no. 8, August 1996.

Portes, A. "Children of Immigrants: Segmented Assimilation and Its Determinants." In A. Portes (ed.), *The Economic Sociology of Immigration.* New York: Russell Sage Foundation, 1995, 248–280.

————. "Introduction: Immigration and Its Aftermath." In A. Portes (ed.), *The New Second Generation.* New York: Russell Sage Foundation, 1996, 1–7.

Reyes, M. "Comprehension of Content Area Passages: A Study of Spanish/

English Readers in the Third and Fourth Grade." In S. R. Goldman and H. T. Trueba (eds.), *Becoming Literate in English As a Second Language.* Norwood, N.J.: Ablex, 1987, 107–126.

———. "A Process Approach to Literacy during Dialogue Journals and Literature Logs with Second Language Learners." *Research in the Teaching of English* 25 (1991): 291–313.

———. "Challenging Venerable Assumptions: Literacy Instruction for Linguistically Different Students." *Harvard Educational Review* 62 (1992): 427–446.

Rodgers, H. Jr. *Poor Women, Poor Children: American Poverty in the 1990s.* 3d ed. New York: M. E. Sharpe, 1996.

Rumbaut, R. "The New Californians: Comparative Research Findings on the Educational Progress of Immigrant Children." In R. G. Rumbaut and W. A. Cornelius (eds.), *California's Immigrant Children: Theory, Research, and Implications for Educational Policy.* University of California, San Diego. San Diego: Center for U.S.-Mexican Studies, 1995, 17–69.

Suárez-Orozco, M. M. "State Terrors: Immigrants and Refugees in the Post-National Space." In Y. Zou and H. T. Trueba (eds.), *Ethnic Identity and Power: Cultural Contexts of Political Action in School and Society.* New York: SUNY Press, 1998: 283–319.

Suárez-Orozco, C., and M. Suárez-Orozco. *Transformations: Immigration, Family Life and Achievement Motivation among Latino Adolescents.* Stanford, Calif.: Stanford University Press, 1995a.

———. "Migration: Generational Discontinuities and the Making of Latino Identities." In L. Romanucci-Ross and G. DeVos (eds.), *Ethnic Identity: Creation, Conflict, and Accommodation.* 3d ed. Walnut Creek, Calif.: Alta Mira Press, 1995b, 321–347.

Sue, S., and A. Padilla. "Ethnic Minority Issues in the U.S.: Challenges for the Educational System." In *Beyond Language: Social and Cultural Factors in Schooling Language Minority Students.* Los Angeles: California State University, Evaluation, Dissemination and Assessment Center, 1986, 35–72.

Tikunoff, W. *Applying Significant Bilingual Instructional Features in the Classroom.* Rosslyn, Va.: National Clearinghouse for Bilingual Education, 1985.

Tinajero, J. V., and A. F. Ada. *The Power of Two Languages: Literacy and Biliteracy for Spanish-Speaking Students.* New York: Macmillan/McGraw-Hill, 1993.

Trueba, H. T. *Raising Silent Voices: Educating Linguistic Minorities for the Twenty-First Century.* New York: Harper and Row, 1989.

Valencia, R., ed. *The Evolution of Deficit Thinking: Educational Thought and Practice.* The Stanford Series on Education and Public Policy. London and Washington, D.C.: Falmer Press, 1997.

Valencia, R. R. "The Plight of Chicano Students: An Overview of Schooling Conditions and Outcomes." In R. R. Valencia (ed.), *Chicano School Failure: An Analysis through Many Windows.* London: Falmer Press, 1991, 3–26.

Vigil, D. "Chicano Gangs: One Response to Mexican Urban Adaptation in the Los Angeles Area." *Urban Anthropology* 12, no. 1 (1983): 45–75.

———. "Group Processes and Street Identity: Adolescent Chicano Gang Members." *Journal for the Society for Psychological Anthropology, ETHOS* 16, no. 4 (1988): 421–444.

———. *Barrio Gangs*. Austin: University of Texas Press, 1989.

Walker, C. L. "Hispanic Achievement: Old Views and New Perspectives." In H. T. Trueba (ed.), *Success or Failure: Learning and the Language Minority Student*. New York: Newbury House, 1987, 15–32.

Winfield, L. F. "Teachers' Beliefs Toward Academically at Risk Students in Inner Urban Schools." *Urban Review* 18 (1986): 253–267.

Zamel, V. "Writing: The Process of Discovering Meaning." *TESOL Quarterly* 16 (1982): 195–209.

3

Race and Ethnicity in Academia: Latinos in Higher Education

The *Chronicle of Higher Education* (Chronicle of Higher Education Almanac, September 2, 1996: 17–26) has published college enrollment and other statistics on the educational gains of Latinos. In 1984 there were 535,000 Latinos enrolled in college, and in 1994 there were 1,046,000 (the actual Latino population more than doubled during this period); in 1994, there were slightly more women than men in college, and more in two-year colleges than in four-year colleges; 968,000 were undergraduates, 64,000 were graduate students, and 13,000 were professionals. The overall educational attainment of Latinos, in 1990, was the lowest in the country, with 30.7 percent of the Latino population having eight or fewer years of education, in contrast with Whites (with only 8.9 percent), Asians (12.9 percent), Blacks (13.8 percent), and American Indians (14.0 percent). Of the 64,000 graduate students, only 903 obtained doctorates in the 1993–1994 school year. In 1995, Latinos (U.S. citizens and permanent residents) obtained 1.8 percent of the nation's doctorates in business and management, 2.2 percent of doctorates in the physical sciences, 2.3 percent in engineering, 3.0 percent in life sciences, 3.1 percent in professional fields, 3.7 percent in arts and humanities, 4.2 percent in the social sciences, and 4.3 percent in education. In 1992, of the 526,222 full-time faculty members with regular instructional duties, Latinos held 12,076 positions. Latino men had 1.7 percent, and Latino women 0.8 percent of the total number.

In the last few years the backlash against affirmative action and the myths abut minority hiring have had a negative impact on the diversification of higher education. A study conducted among 300 recipients of three prestigious doctoral fellowship programs from the Ford, Spencer, and Mellon foundations (Ph.D.'s since 1989 from elite institutions) debunked the myths about minority hirings. The idea that in spite of the serious efforts made, universities failed to identify qualified minorities because the pools are small and the competition intense was challenged by D. G. Smith (1996, B3–B4). About the myth that "because so few potential faculty members of color are in the graduate school pipeline, they are highly sought after" Smith states, "Only 11 percent of the scholars of color (and only 9 percent of the entire group) fell into this category. Even from the 11 percent of the minority-group Ph.D.'s who were sought after—that usually meant being called by no more than two institutions—often not the ones that were the candidates' top choices. Among the rest of the minority-group Ph.D.'s, 14 percent took the only faculty positions they were offered; 10 percent were underemployed, taking campus staff or administrative positions that did not utilize their doctoral work; and 20 percent took postdoctoral positions" (Smith 1996, B3). Latinos were particularly sensitive to the neglect and lack of support in obtaining new jobs. Even the minority scientists had a hard time finding jobs. The most shocking finding was that "[t]he study showed that white men with expertise in the latest scholarship in their disciplines concerning race, class, and gender had a significant advantage in the job market; indeed, many of them fell into our 'sought-after' category. A number of these men commented on the resistance they saw to diversifying the faculty. As one said, 'There is a lot of talk about diversifying, but when push comes to shove, there is still a lot of hiring of white males' " (Smith 1996, B4). In the end, the individual success of minority faculty had to do with the dedicated job of a champion who not only recommended the candidate, but coached him or her through the hiring process. As the pipeline of qualified minority college graduates becomes smaller owing to the lack of support, funding, and academic mentoring in the previous education years, it is imperative to examine our policies and commitment at the higher education level.

In an age of anonymity, homelessness, genocide, and mass hysteria with anti-immigrant sentiments, what difference does it make for an ethnic to have an awareness of his or her own personal self-identity? Who cares? Being "the other," "us," whoever we are, and looking different (whatever we look like) are enough clues to the world to classify us, taxonomize us, and handle us in a predictably rotten fashion. Perhaps color and race alone don't matter. But if other clues are present as well, such as signs of poverty, gestures, sounds, smells, and symbols of being foreign—such as a strange accent, or a dressing pattern typically not American, or a pattern in touching, walking, laughing, looking, or carrying oneself that is clearly not middle-class American—along with dark skin, then a powerful set of markers is present and even dangerous at certain times and in certain places. Yet, it is precisely here that the power of many Latinos lies, in their potential to represent multiple identities in extreme polar positions of American socioeconomic strata. A *vato loco* (crazy guy), if dressed in certain ways, can trigger an arrest as a potential gang member; but if dressed in a three-piece, $400 suit with expensive shoes and driving a Mercedes, is treated like an executive (at least in most places—shades of darkness count also for Latinos, not only for Black people).

What is fascinating in the social sciences is that we build up a rather sophisticated paraphernalia to create the impression of absolute objectivity in discussing ethnic, racial, and social identities, yet we know how to stereotype, characterize, and brand almost any group of people we do not like, or we fear, or we do not understand. The amazing ability of many Latinos to pass for white, to disappear in the crowds of mainstream people, is a function of our physical and psychological characteristics. Part of our survival kit is an extraordinary degree of stoic resiliency in the face of conflict, and the capacity to adapt, imitate behaviors, and survive. Although these qualities enhance the Latino image as congenial and dependable, they also signal to the suspicious mind, a danger of untrustworthiness, of duplicity, lack of sincerity, and lack of loyalty and patriotism. It is in this political context of race, ethnicity, and images that both public opinion and social science research function. For this reason, the biases existing in public opinion, newspapers, movies, radio, and TV are also present in social science research.

Race, Ethnicity, and Xenophobia

As Paulo Freire has eloquently stated, "*Nâo há mudança sem shonho como nâo há sonho sem esperança.*" "There is no change without a dream, as there is no dream without hope" (Freire 1993, 91). What keeps our hope alive in the struggle for equity is the understanding of the nature of oppression and our right to regain control of our lives. The concepts of race and ethnicity continue to be at the center of public discourse and passionate political debate in Europe and the Americas, including Latin American countries with populations of European descent. It is no secret that although the precise biological meaning of race becomes more elusive, the sociocultural meaning of race takes new dimensions and becomes central in our daily lives, especially in pluralistic societies that have become de jure racially and ethnically integrated, but de facto economically and socially segregated and stratified. In higher education, these concepts take on a special significance and carry over serious consequences to the next century for future generations. McLaren speaks about American predatory culture in modern sociopolitical and racial contexts. "With few, if any, ethically convincing prospects for transformation—or even survival—we have become cyber-nomads whose temporary homes become whatever electronic circuitry (if any) is available to us. In our hyper-fragmented and predatory postmodern culture, democracy is secured through the power to control consciousness and semioticize and discipline bodies by mapping and manipulating sounds, images and information and forcing identity to take refuge in the forms of subjectivity increasingly experienced as isolated and separate from larger social contexts" (McLaren 1995, 117).

Physical anthropologists and biologists have essentially discarded "race" as an operational concept because there is an infinite number of combinations and permutations of human characteristics beyond eye and skin color, bone structure, weight and stature, distribution of fat, and overall appearance. Medical technology and genetic studies go beyond the chemical and physiological structure of internal organs, blood types, and genes, to more fundamental possible combinations of similar and dissimilar traits. People are the products of their physical and human environments and of personal experiences that tend to leave a lasting mark on our genetic constitution over a period of several generations. And because there is evidence of genetic exchanges and "miscegenation" across human groups all over the world, the human species has produced the most diversified and bizarre combinations of both visible and invisible characteristics crossing ethnic and religious groups, nations, and continents. Ultimately, the interplay between ecological, biological, sociocultural, and genetic factors makes it impossible to conceptualize an accurate racial taxonomic system of human groups. In contrast, socially defined concepts of race become vital in human relations and determine norms of interaction, judgments about intelligence, expectations about performance, and daily interaction, thoughts, and behavior.

The social concept of race is also elusive in the abstract, but it is fleshed out in specific interactional (and often conflictive) contexts: Black versus White, brown versus White, Black versus yellow, and others. This elusiveness is compounded by the fact that our sociological concept of race often brings ethnicity into the picture, even to the point of using both terms interchangeably. The word *ethnicity* comes from *ethnos* (meaning *people* in Greek), and it has been the center of anthropological studies for over a century. Scholars dedicated millions of hours collecting descriptions of ethnic groups around the world (called *ethnographies*): their language, culture, environment, occupations, marriage patterns, family life, kinship system, property, law, and so on. The knowledge accumulated by these scholars under the leadership of

George Peter Murdock is organized in the *Human Relation Area Files,* which are frequently used for purposes of cross-cultural studies (called *ethnology*). As an integral part of ethnographic research, scholars use ethnolinguistics or sociolinguistics to make inferences about the way members of ethnic groups think from the way they talk. As immigrants from all over the world become part of modern industrial societies, they bring with them their languages, cultures, and lifestyles. Thus ethnicity, within the contexts of modern industrial societies, is compounded by contacts among the cultures of immigrants and mainstream peoples in the larger society.

The term *ethnic groups* in the Western world, especially in Europe and the United States, refers to socially and culturally stratified subgroups of Americans who are recognized as collectively retaining unique and different characteristics in comparison with mainstream folks (see Trueba, Jacobs, and Kirton 1990; Trueba, Rodríguez, Zou, and Cintrón 1993; Trueba, Cheng, and Ima 1993; Trueba and Zou, 1994). Their language, culture, religion, art, values, lifestyle, family organization, children's socialization, and worldview are viewed by the members of the group as uniquely linked to their home country and ancestors. At times physical appearance separates them from the rest of society and from other subgoups in the larger society. Consequently, ethnicity refers to that complex set of characteristics of groups who share historical or mythical common ancestors and maintain their own identity "in contrast or opposition" to mainstream society. Ethnicity is the other side of the assimilation coin. Common opinion has it that in order to become a "real" or "assimilated" American, one must forget his or her ethnic identity. In Europe, according to the media, birthplace and several generations of ancestors born in Europe, does not guarantee to persons of color (especially from non-Christian religions) the right to be considered a European citizen. By the same token, in the United States, a nonwhite person who is a second- or third-generation immigrant, even one with perfect command of the English language (without a trace of a foreign accent), is still asked what country he or she comes from. In contrast, Latin Americans of European descent are rapidly assimilated and pass for full-fledged Americans.

Racial or ethnic identification becomes pivotal in American society to determine a person's relative status and chances for success. Sheer statistical, demographic, and residential information serves to predict educational achievement, income, dropout and suspension rates, size of family, mortality trends, incarceration, tendencies to violence, use of welfare, and other presumed dysfunctional characteristics that configurate the American justice system, investment and banking policies and operation, and even the distribution of resources and liabilities (from the location of banks, grocery stores, movie theaters, to that of waste disposal, prisons, and nuclear sites). As Ladson-Billings and Tate have emphasized, social class and gender considerations alone "are not powerful enough to explain all the difference (or variance) in school experience and performance," and consequently we must conclude that "race continues to be a significant factor in determining inequity in the United States" (Ladson-Billings and Tate 1995, 48–49). Because of the fact that elementary and secondary school performance is affected by race and ethnicity, the size and quality of pools of racially and ethnically different candidates for higher education positions become limited. Additionally, the racial and ethnic prejudice in the society at large is reflected not only in the elementary and secondary public schools but also in higher education institutions, and extended to the most critical areas of hiring, promotion, and retention norms and procedures.

In a broader historical perspective, the pendulum-like cycles of tolerance or intolerance for racial and ethnic diversity in the United States are often associated with military, socioeconomic, cultural, and political crises. These crises bring an intensity to the stereotyping, scapegoating, and persecuting of immigrants, rationalized as a legitimate concern for national security or crime prevention or the protection of our economic interests or cultural purity. A critical analysis of the history of immigrants in Europe and the United States (see M. Suárez-Orozco 1991; and C. Suárez-Orozco and M. Suárez-Orozco 1995a and 1995b) should help us understand the reality of the hardships faced by all immigrants. Indeed we must go far beyond the romantic fantasies of America as the archetypal country of immigrants with an exemplary democracy, the land of opportunity for all and the land of freedom. Unfortunately, as in other countries America has also been the land of exploitation of the ignorant, the poor, and the needy; the land in which children of color are neglected, warehoused in awful places called "schools" that are placed under freeways or in unsafe ghettoes; the land where young immigrant women still work in the most abject, unsanitary, and oppressive conditions in sweatshops, packing companies, or in the agricultural fields exposed to toxic pesticides from dawn to sunset as pickers, without health insurance and for a fraction of the salary earned by Whites making less than the minimum salary (Trueba 1996). The reality is that without the cheap labor of these immigrants the wealth of the U.S. textile companies and agribusiness corporations would not exist. Many of these immigrants stay in this country for one reason only: to help their children get a good education and a better life.

Leo Chavez, in a case study in a cultural anthropology collection edited by George and Louise Spindler, entitled *Shadowed Lives: Undocumented Immigrants in American Society* (1992), cites a *New York Times* editorial of 1880. "There is a limit to our power of assimilation. . . . [W]e are not in need of any more aliens at present. Foreigners who come here and herd together like sheep remain foreigners all their lives. We know how stubbornly conservative of his dirt and his ignorance is the average immigrant who settles in New York, particularly if he is of a clannish race like the Italians. Born in squalor, raised in filth and misery and kept at work almost from infancy, these wretched beings change their abode, but not their habits" (Chavez 1992, 14).

The use of the words *race* and *clannish race* is indicative of the historical confusion between race and ethnicity. There is nothing new in the recent efforts to "close our borders" and do away with illegal immigration. The impact of xenophobia within the university walls is subtle and does not have the dramatic effect of the high-tech flamboyant cavalry of new immigration officers riding along the wall dividing Tijuana and San Diego. Nonetheless, when search and personnel committees meet to discuss candidates, the nativistic tendencies of White Americans of European ancestry come across loud and clear. Yet, many immigrants excel in school and eventually join universities; but they also continue to face difficult years, as other immigrants suffered from the turn of the century until the mid-1920s, when they were accused of moral turpitude and socially ostracized only because they used their home language to communicate with one another and with some students.

Although immigration trends have changed drastically since the 1920s with the dramatic increase in Hispanic and Asian populations, the working conditions and exploitation of many immigrants have not changed. Many immigrants (for example, farmworkers in California) are willing to sacrifice their lives working in the fields at low wages and in unhealthy conditions because they hope to open up educational opportunities for their children. Education is the only hope they have to get their families out of poverty. In this context, racial and ethnic intolerance in higher education profoundly affects the access and quality of education for racial and ethnic minority students. In the final instance, an institution primarily created and maintained by White faculty will present perspectives and values that exclude, penalize, or ignore students of color. The consistent reluctance of higher education institutions to diversify its faculty is clearly impinging on the quality of education offered for all students. Even White students need to understand ethnically and racially diverse populations in this country. The isolation from exposure to minorities perpetuates prejudice and the inability to deal with populations of color.

Debate on Affirmative Action

Although the basic historical facts on the origin of affirmative action as a national policy are clear, it is less clear what the meaning of the concept and its public interpretation has been. Affirmative action grew out of the 1964 Civil Rights Act, as amended in 1972. Title VII of the 1964 Civil Rights Act prohibits discrimination based on race, religion, gender, color, and national origin. Affirmative action was introduced by President Lyndon Johnson through Executive Order 11246 in 1965. The executive order allowed volunteer programs to remedy problems of exclusion or discrimination on the basis of race, ethnicity, and gender, and to take historical records into account in trying to overcome past discrimination in employment, education and contracting. Affirmative action implies a determined effort to ensure that those ethnic groups that are significantly underrepresented in colleges or the workplace are more equitably represented. The definition of affirmative action has been expanded to include persons with disabilities and other groups that have historically been underrepresented in certain fields. Properly applied, affirmative action is most definitely not a handout. Instead, it is an opportunity that meets the students or employees halfway. They must respond with their own hard work and enthusiasm to succeed.

It is precisely in the interpretation of affirmative action that the debate lies. If conceived as a quota system, one can argue that it is inherently unfair to any other student deprived of preferential treatment, of the advantages and additional consideration given to persons on the grounds of their race, ethnicity, gender, or other characteristics not related to qualifications. If conceived as an additional mechanism to identify qualified students and to assess the special nature of their qualifications in the larger context of long-term benefits for all students, for the appropriate representation of all ethnic, racial, linguistic, and socioeconomic groups of society, then affirmative action must presuppose the existence of a level of academic excellence (a standard required from all students). The additional consideration given to the richer experience and other qualifications brought by socioculturally diverse students can be constructed as enriching the experience of all students and providing a fair opportunity to students from underrepresented groups.

The fundamental assumption in this concept is that society does not create fair and equal conditions for academic success; indeed, the literature indicates that society perpetuates the social order precisely through schooling by continuing to give an advantage to those students whose culture, language, social class, economic class, and ethnicity are closer to the mainstream, middle-class university personnel. To the degree that affirmative action is not punitive of previous unjust practices by making today's mainstream students suffer for the sins of their parents, it can be constructed as fair and within the limits of justifiable policies at the university. Indeed, many universities have for years added preferential criteria for admission beyond tests and scores (as of themselves not completely reliable). Affirmative action can only be understood in the context of societal changes that place a great deal of value on recognizing as part of the civil rights of all Americans the opportunity to achieve an education of comparable quality regardless of race, gender, language, religion, ethnicity, and social class.

In the opinion of highly credible social scientists (including Suárez-Orozco and Suárez-Orozco 1995a, 1996, 1998; and Cornelius 1995; Rumbaut and Cornelius 1995; Chavez 1992), the issue of affirmative action does not occur in a vacuum, rather it is part of a national current stimulated by political agendas during a general malaise, a crisis of national identity, desire for ethnic and cultural purity, and struggle over control. Affirmative action, in this context, is seen as one additional mechanism initiated by "those others," who do not belong in this country, to take over the nation. The "paranoic conspirational theories," the conspicuous crimes against immigrants of color, the intolerance of law enforcement officers, and all the data presented by Suárez-Orozco help us to understand the subtle and not so subtle strategies of conservatives determined to "regain" control of "their" country by limiting the access of persons of color to positions of power. In this context, Proposition 209 is read differently by different persons/people and interpreted in entirely different ways. The text alone, as cited here, presents a language that seems acceptable at face value: "The state shall not discriminate against, or grant preferential treatment to, any individual on the basis of race, sex, color, ethnicity, or national origin in the operation of public employment, public education, or public contracting." The end of affirmative action by Proposition 209 was interpreted as a serious and profound threat to the future of the students of color, including Black, Latino, and Filipino student associations (supported by gay, lesbian, and bisexual student groups). Minority student reaction to the end of affirmative action was in the form of (1) demonstrations to protest the decrease in the number of Black and Latino students admitted to public colleges, (2) support for ethnic studies, clubs, organizations, and opposition to an overall exclusive presence of non-Anglo students in public colleges, and ultimately (3) protest against any attack on people of color, women, low-income, and other marginalized groups (J. Shackelford and P. Shackelford, in press).

The blocking of Proposition 209 by Federal Judge Thelton E. Henderson on the grounds of a strong probability that it is unconstitutional angered a number of politicians. In his ruling, the judge suggested that courts "must look beyond the plain language" of the amendment and determine whether the burden imposed by it "necessarily falls on minorities and women." Judge Henderson said he was issuing the restraining order because Governor Wilson and Attorney General Lundgren appeared to be acting "with considerable dispatch" to carry out the measure, which could cause "irreparable harm" to the rights of the state's minority citizens. Mr. Wilson and Mr. Lundgren had asked state agencies to provide a list of all affirmative action programs that could conflict with the proposition (Smith 1996). The American Civil Liberties Union lawyer Edward Chen felt that Proposition 209 would turn the glass ceiling for women and minorities into an iron cage (Smith 1996). Public reflection was also heightened by the expediency of other states to replicate California's iniative. Racial tension also resurfaced in corporate America. We know that in the first week of April 1997, the final outcome was that the U.S. Federal Court of Appeals Ninth Circuit upheld the California measure barring racial preferences in a unanimous ruling that Proposition 209 does not violate the U.S. Constitution's equal-protection clause and other federal laws.

As Bob Herbert stated in his *New York Times* article on the Texaco scandal, in the context of the remarks revealed by executive Richard A. Lundwall's tapes, "Who needs affirmative action when discrimination is a thing of the past? . . . Racial discrimination is as common as commercials on television" (Herbert *New York Times*, November 11, 1996, A15). In those tapes, Blacks had been called porch monkeys, orangutans, uppity so-and-sos, black jelly beans and niggers; the executives found funny the fact that "all the black jelly beans seem to be glued to the bottom of the bag," referring to the lack of upward mobility of Black employees.

Obviously racial and ethnic prejudice are not exclusive to business and industry; in fact, they begin in the school setting with the way children are socialized into academic achievement, and they continue through the entire educational process, especially at the university level. Much of the work in critical theory is devoted to this issue (Freire 1973, 1993, 1995; Apple 1989, 1993, 1996; Aronowitz and Giroux 1991; Gadotti 1996; Giroux and McLaren 1994; Leistyna, Woodrum, and Sherblom 1996). Perhaps less optimistic than others, Michael Olivas, judging from current public sentiment on academia, feels that we cannot assume that in the near future there will be serious change toward a fair representation of Latino and African American faculty in higher education; not even a continuation of the efforts that followed the rhetoric of diversification in the last two decades (Olivas 1994, 117–138).

My Personal Experience

Most strategies adopted in the name of affirmative action, equity, curriculum reform, competitiveness in the college market for the minority student, or adopted simply for the sake of political expediency (to retain state or federal dollars) have failed to produce sustained gains in the numbers of tenured Latino or African American faculty. The outcomes have been disappointing. In some institutions the "revolving-door" syndrome prevails, with minority faculty being hired and leaving soon after. In other institutions honest recruitment efforts are neutralized by aggressive opposition of White faculty and other traditional gatekeeping mechanisms. In the end, minority candidates often do not meet the expected performance criteria required to be tenured and are "legitimately" rejected; not counseled, mentored, assisted, supported, and taught to become productive intellectuals like White faculty. Instead ethnically different faculty are placed in a rather hostile environment and then simply dismissed.

I have had firsthand experiences in gatekeeping and rejection. My first shock in this country was in seeking a job in a somewhat recognized White institution. With a very good record in graduate work and very strong letters of recommendation, and even with support from the faculty, my first interview resulted in a rejection by the dean of the college; he said publicly that he did not like my "Mexican" accent. My main professor, George Peter Murdock (an internationally renowned anthropologist), called that dean to give him a piece of his mind and helped me get an interview and a job at another institution the next day. I felt vindicated but insecure.

While advancing my career in academia as an administrator, I witnessed at close range the political contortions displayed by White faculty to rationalize their biases and the invocation of the sacred academic values, educational philosophy (read "cultural values"), academic freedom (read "White faculty control of academic processes"), and "harmony" (read "fear of brown, Black, and other ethnics"). Personnel and search committees ready to veto a candidate of color may open the discussion with a calculated speech (often with an inflated and artificial air of solemnity) on the justification of preserving departmental quality and traditions. The commentary can be typified by the following:

We are committed to academic excellence and equity at any cost. And we are equally committed to oppose activism because it will destroy our solidarity and jeopardize the quality of our work. In principle, we open our door to all minority candidates, and we will treat them well, the same way we treat other candidates. However, we oppose any political action (read "affirmative action") to favor one candidate over others. We cannot give any advantage to any racial or ethnic group because that would violate senate policy and compromise our academic freedom. The candidate with the best academic record, the one who meets our departmental needs and best fits our institution (read "our White faculty"), will be given the position.

As a point of departure, those hiring for this position will exclude any conscious and systematic effort at attracting racially and ethnically different faculty. The criteria used to judge the qualities and suitability of a candidate are interpreted and applied by committees without ethnic representation because "homogeneous committees understand the needs and sentiments of departmental faculty" as a dean once explained to me. But even those departments that recognize the need for hiring faculty of color and that do not object philosophically to searches for "qualified" candidates from specific ethnic and racial groups (especially searches for "targets of excellence" intended to bring persons with the highest academic records) often raise serious questions about the appropriateness of minority searches. Such committees often ask, Are these searches compatible with our academic freedom? Are they an effective means of attracting African American, Latinos, and other minorities? Why don't we let the good candidates surface during the search? What are the payoff, the expected benefits, and the ultimate goal of minority searches? But even we who assume that these searches make sense question if they can become effective without creating conflict and divisiveness in the university (summary from recollection and field notes).

What many faculty who see themselves as fair, democratic, and conscientious citizens of academia would like to know is whether (1) the political contexts and circumstances under which these searches take place do in fact render them unsuccessful, and whether (2) the short- and long-term strategies for recruiting minority faculty have adopted a new philosophy of education and have undergone other important changes. These questions are legitimate and deserve answers. I hope to offer at least some partial answers to these questions, using my own experience.

I have worked in higher education since 1969. My first teaching and administrative job was as an assistant professor and the interim chair of the Anthropology/Sociology Department at Western Illinois University in a small town called Macomb. I then taught briefly at California State University at Sacramento and worked for a number of years at the University of Illinois at Champaign-Urbana. Subsequently I became departmental chair at San Diego University for a short time and in 1982 went to the University of California at Santa Barbara, where I stayed eight years. From there I went to the University of California at Davis, to the University of Wisconsin at Madison, and only recently to the University of Houston. I also had the opportunity to work as a visiting professor at the University of Alaska at Fairbanks, the University of Leuven in Belgium, Stanford, Michigan State, at the University of California, Santa Barbara, and most recently (during FY 1996–1997) at Harvard. I have also had short-term visits at many other institutions in Sweden, Spain, Brazil, and particularly in Mexico, where I was born and spent thirty years of my life; I know the *universidades autónomas* system, the *technológicos* and had extended contacts with other universities and research centers in Tijuana, Ciudad Juárez, Monterrey, Mexicali, Querétaro, Puebla, and Mexico City. This broad experience across institutions in different countries has helped me to notice the unique and persistent patterns of interethnic interaction in universities in the United States. Drawing on my twenty-seven years of academic experience I shall describe the main challenges and dilemmas that faculty members and administrators face in their attempts to create a pluralistic and culturally diverse environment in higher education. Also I would like to suggest additional strategies for pursuing the goal of diversification. These strategies will be directed to increase the size of the pool and to establish fair and effective university policies and procedures to recruit, hire, and retain the best-qualified candidates from underrepresented ethnic and racial groups. I will select specific examples from institutions I know best: the University of California at Davis (where I was associate dean of letters and science and the director of the Division of Education), the University of Wisconsin at Madison (where I was the dean of the School of Education and I worked closely with Donna Shalala, who was chancellor at that time), and the University of Houston where I worked as the senior vice president for academic affairs and provost. I will describe concrete examples to illustrate specific points without revealing names of persons or institutions in order to protect their anonymity.

Recent controversies on the meaning of affirmative action, its philosophy, policies, and practices in the California higher education systems have made evident that there is not only a wide range of interpretations and positions on affirmative action but also that there is profound discontent with the performance of higher education institutions. Indeed, these debates have reopened the question: How realistic and appropriate is the California Master Plan? At the very least there is a need to redefine the goals of higher education in the context of savage budget cuts, decreasing public support, and lack of state resources. According to the media, the public is limiting public resources going to universities because of the presumed overpoliticization of the university's intellectual life and its focus on racial and ethnic conflicts. The assumption is that discourse on race and ethnicity becomes a "disruptive factor" in academia and compromises the quality of higher education institutions. These concerns are not new; they have been expressed in various academic communities over the past three decades in different forms and forums. There is a righteous tone among some academicians who claim to protect the purity of academia.

The academicians taking a purist approach emphasize the sanctity of academic institutions with all their traditions, practices, and the significance of scholarly endeavors (research and instruction), which must be protected from the destructive politics of minority activists. Minority hiring and promotions are seen as the cause (some say the effect) of political activism in the university, which ultimately could destroy the excellence of an institution. For university administrators to tolerate political activism is nothing else than to preside over the demise of research institutions, to witness in silence their deterioration, in the end, to compromise the foundations of American democracy. In the minds of some faculty, diversification is perceived as the number one enemy of social harmony, scientific and technical development, and democracy.

This puritanical approach to the maintenance of the racial and ethnic status quo in academia carries a number of contradictions and dilemmas even for righteous academicians. It is so much easier said than done. A liberal discourse sounds great, but in real academic life many liberals pay only lip service to their own principles. Learning and teaching are political, literacy education is cultural action for liberation. This position was defended by Freire (1973, 1993) and many of his followers, especially critical theorists and sociologists of education such as Apple (1978, 1982, 1985, 1989, 1990, 1992, and 1993), Aronowitz and Giroux (1985, 1991), Giroux (1983, 1992), Giroux and McLaren (1986, 1994), McLaren and Leonard (1993), and McLaren (1995). Yet, in the United States political action in the form of genuine defense for the rights of minority faculty is viewed as dysfunctional, irreverent, not acceptable, and ultimately deplorable by most academicians (including some who write as liberals). Their concern is that our universities may turn into political arenas (as happened in Mexico and Latin America) where political turmoil often causes disorder and prevents instruction and research. Never mind that in American institutions there are few instances of publicly questioning White hegemonic control of the hiring, promoting, and tenuring processes. Political action, however, on the part of White faculty to resist changes in these processes is seen as perfectly all right, indeed, admirable and required.

Why is it so disturbing for White faculty to hire and retain African

American or Latino faculty? The discomfort that the mere thought of diversification brings to some faculty is a basic fear of the unknown; it is the kind of profound discomfort that comes with uncertainty about the outcomes of diversification for the White lifestyle and control of educational institutions. Fear of change is not necessarily racism. Organized resistance to change can be motivated by racism or simply by the fear of discomfort. Ultimately, permitting change toward diversification in higher education can mean losing the power to control the institutional resources, status, and benefits that come with a faculty position. Losing power is also losing comfort. In order to secure some measure of comfort, White faculty develop unusual abilities to rationalize their politics of tacit reluctance to attract or retain faculty of color. They may argue that:

- "The candidate does not have the qualifications required for the job."
- "The candidate could not adjust to the modus operandi and traditions of the institution."
- "The position is not good for the candidate; he or she won't be happy in the company of Whites."
- "The students will not like and will not learn from people of color; worse still, students may destroy the candidate."

Specific Cases of Exclusion

In spite of the opposition, some candidates of color do manage to gain support and make their way to a short list and a final interview. When the process of selection is focused on a candidate of color whose qualifications are comparable to those of White candidates, there is a red light calling for "spontaneous" caucusing of the faculty in communication with the search committee; a period of deep anxiety and intense political action. New inquiries are made into the candidate's qualifications and background. White faculty communicate with each other and debate. Political pressure requires that White faculty appear to be liberal, fair, open-minded, and concerned citizens, willing to "give a chance" to candidates of color. But what if the candidate of color turns out to be antiwhite and difficult, yet academically sound? The reaction of some faculty is then fear, confusion, and anger. The closer the possibility of hiring a person of color gets, the more vicious the arguments against the candidate become. I have several examples.

A Chicana in a Research Institution

A Chicana (a female Mexican American), who, coming from a low-income family (farmworkers from Mexico) and having arrived in the United States at ten years of age with very irregular schooling, was mentored by her teachers and urged to leave home and go to college. She then went to Stanford and obtained her doctorate. After two years of part-time employment and a postdoctoral fellowship, she made her way to a final interview for a tenure-track position in a research institution. Her qualifications and performance were acceptable and, in comparison with other candidates, superior. The search committee was divided along ethnic lines. The faculty discussed the candidate in the halls, cafeteria, and offices. A departmental meeting was called to assess faculty reaction after her formal lecture and visit. Immediately at the beginning of the meeting, the negative comments started to come: "She could not teach here"; "She is a self-deprecating Chicana who does not know how to finish a sentence"; "Her research is marginal"; "We don't want any trouble with ethnic groups"; and so on. As a Chicana who had moved up from poverty to earning a doctorate from Stanford University, the tacit hostility during the interview did not bother her. From the time she was working toward finishing high school in order to go to college, through her admission interview at Stanford, but especially after her major adviser abandoned her at the point of dissertation, she was resolved to succeed at any cost. The chair of her dissertation committee, a famous woman researcher, had no tolerance with drafts that contained any typographical errors. After noticing a few typos in the first eight pages, she picked up the dissertation draft and threw it into the wastepaper basket, making a disgusted face. Normally, when students bring their first drafts, the committee chair goes over the entire manuscript primarily for content and organization in order to check the main ideas, the conceptual framework, and the findings and conclusions. After the major organizational issues are cleared up, the chair recommends a careful checking of the entire text for syntax, punctuation, correct spelling, format, and other details. The gesture of throwing away somebody's dissertation is inappropriate and insulting. If the chair was angry and wanted to make the point that she demanded a perfect draft, she could have returned the draft saying, "When you correct this draft, I will be happy to read it." As the Chicana's peers often stated, she was a trooper and had *muchos huevos*) ("lots of guts"), as Mexicans say. She completed the dissertation and received her doctorate, and she was proud. It would have seemed that opportunities for teaching and research positions would open up everywhere, but it was very difficult for her to even get an interview. When this interview came at a major research university, it was a major event and somewhat traumatic. At the departmental meeting the secretaries counted the votes cast by the faculty and passed the results to me. I realized then that several full professors who had not even attended the lecture had commented negatively about the presentation. It was obvious that several negative votes from full professors had been cast without even meeting this Chicana. In addition, there were two or three anonymous letters sent to the search committee that I had the opportunity to read. The tone of the letters was violent and the attacks vicious; her appearance, work, speech, everything was targeted. I began to recognize the handwriting in one of the letters and decided to confront the professor in question. He was embarrassed and felt justified to try his best to prevent this Chicana from coming to the university. He confessed he had never spoken to her directly, instead he had relied on the testimony of his colleagues. The search committee negotiated an extra position from the vice chancellor and hired this woman. She has done extremely well and now has the respect of her colleagues.

A Dean's Search

During one search for dean of a college, the pool of candidates was very large and competitive. The college was extremely political and factionalized. The search committee proposed a short list containing the names of an African American candidate, a White woman, and two White men. After a series of controversial faculty meetings, and for a number of complex procedural and political reasons (White male faculty caucused and questioned the African American candidate's credentials), the original support given to the African American as one of the finalists decreased. There was an offer made to a White male, who turned it down, the search was closed, and an inside member of the faculty was appointed as dean. During the conflict of the various factions, there were many attacks from one group of faculty against the others, and there were letters with vicious remarks directed against particular members of ethnic groups (against one Hispanic and against two Jewish faculty). The passion and almost hatred among professors were a shock to me.

A Hispanic Singled Out

In a small college that had fiscal and personnel problems, an inside White member of the faculty was appointed as dean. This new dean had earlier expressed his misgivings about the quality of a Hispanic woman who entered the college as "a target of opportunity hire." Gradually, for a number of personal reasons, the dean decided to remove this woman and a Hispanic male from their tenure-track positions. During the third probationary year, assistant professors can be let go if there is evidence of underperformance or for other strong reasons. From the first year on it was clear that the dean wanted to remove these two faculty members from the college. In order to obtain support from the administration to remove them he declared "financial exigency" on the grounds that the previous year's cuts had left the college without funds to keep all assistant professors. Financial exigency was not an appropriate action for the dean to take because the budget cut had been small and, under normal circumstances, the central administration would negotiate ways of absorbing the budget cut. The dean requested approval to transfer the two Hispanic faculty to temporary positions immediately in order to terminate them the following year. The Hispanic male was already nationally recognized as an extremely talented individual, well published, and indeed committed to scholarship. The faculty resisted the move against him. For the Hispanic woman there was less support among the faculty. Convinced that the dean was unfair and biased, she threatened to sue. She contacted the Office of Civil Rights, and the ensuing pressure finally persuaded the dean to give up the idea of an early transfer from a tenure-track to a temporary position. This woman was devastated and demoralized to the point that she could not function effectively for several months. She agreed to stop her civil rights inquiry when her status as a tenure-track faculty member was clarified.

Not Retaining and Hiring Outstanding Latino Faculty

The dean of a very large college, generally liked by Latinos, learned that several departments had identified (through regular searches) two Latino women of high caliber. The internal struggles in those departments made it "politically risky" to support the best candidates (the Latino women) found by the search committee. The dean decided not to hire anybody and thus avoided displeasing one of the groups—the White senior faculty. The same dean knew about an award-winning Latino associate professor who was the author of an outstanding book in his field. This professor was underpaid and had received a number of invitations to visit other campuses that wanted to pursue his appointment. There were several mechanisms available to the dean to retain this faculty member (a salary increase, a chair position, support in terms of new resources, public recognition ceremonies, and so on, or a combination of the above). The dean did not communicate with the chair of the department, and the Latino began to look for a different position. Fortunately, a group of Latino faculty provided him with advice and support and persuaded him to stay. This faculty member is demoralized and, if his wife can find a job elsewhere, he is willing to move. Why would a dean who has the funds and the opportunity to hire or keep outstanding Latino candidates give in to the pressure of senior faculty? Obviously because the dean does not have the stature and courage to do what is right and defend the quality of a department.

The Power of the Chair and of the Faculty in Rejecting Latinos

There was a case that involved a Latino male with an international reputation as a scholar and researcher, extremely productive—a person who wrote in five different languages and maintained a publication record that was extraordinary, was considered one of the best in his field, and was at the time teaching in a very prestigious institution. An invitation to bring the top five finalists reached my desk, and I realized that the Latino professor was not among them. I requested from the department chair and the chair of the search committee the folders of all the finalists for the position and asked them to compare all the finalists with the Latino professor. I ended a long session with the committee chair and was persuaded that the committee could not find any valid reason to exclude the Latino professor; he just intimidated the White faculty. The main reason given for selecting the White candidates (some of whom could not be compared with the Latino in terms of their academic level, experience, and achievements—in fact, they were extremely junior and had weak recommendations) was that they suited departmental needs and had obtained greater faculty support. Current faculty (some with publication records inferior to that of the Latino candidate) attacked him viciously. This was a department with a history of rejecting Latinos. At different times two outstanding Latino candidates with doctorates from Stanford and strong letters of recommendation were invited to apply for positions and interviewed. These candidates should have been the highest ranking candidates. Their visits were mishandled, the faculty was divided in their support, and some professors expressed concerns about the possible overlapping of their specializations in comparison with the existing faculty. Neither candidate was hired, and both ended up in first-rate institutions (one at Harvard and the other at UCLA). In the same college, a junior Chicano faculty, with a doctorate from Stanford and a highly promising publication record, was hired as assistant professor. He was made the chair of Chicano Studies and in addition received a heavy teaching load. His teaching evaluations were the highest ever in the department. However, his writing slowed down and he became demoralized. He felt that nobody, especially no senior faculty, ever made an effort to make him feel welcomed or help him in any way. He resigned and took a position in a very competitive institution, where he obtained tenure and renewed his publishing career. An almost identical case occurred in the same department, except in this case the Chicano faculty had spent six years hoping to be tenured, and in the end other faculty began to spread rumors that he was not going to receive tenure. He left and was hired with tenure at a highly prestigious university. His publications are received well, and he is the editor of an important journal in his field.

I could cite many more examples. These examples, however, are sufficient to make my point. In subtle ways at some times, and in explicit and vicious ways at other times, underrepresented minority persons are mistreated and rejected in higher education without reason and against all principles of equity and fairness. These examples are anonymous because my purpose is not to point fingers at anybody or at any institution. I have the feeling that in most of the cases I described, White faculty members felt justified to act the way they did, had no guilty feelings, or even any sense of responsibility to assist, mentor, and help young minority faculty trying to succeed in the competitive White academic institutions. But I know that even the most outstanding White faculty often lack sensitivity to these issues.

In the final analysis, the "balancing act" for some White faculty consists of keeping academia "pure" by rejecting underrepresented minorities but doing it without guilt or penalties (without lawsuits, loss of status and credibility, loss of federal funding and public support). Perhaps this is done in a more subtle manner in institutions of high caliber that enjoy the status of being "research institutions" with the highest academic standards and are associated with liberal and progressive thought. Being liberal and progressive does not mean that faculty of color are recruited for tenured positions or that the core of decisionmakers has become less White. In fact, some of these liberal institutions attract some minority faculty but keep very few; they have very strict retention criteria that either discourage faculty of color from applying or that bring candidates of color for a short time, only to screen them out periodically.

The treatment just described, along with other reasons, explains why so few Hispanics are in tenured faculty ranks. First of all, the pipeline of well-trained, highly qualified racial and ethnic minority faculty is quite reduced. Second, who among them would want to pursue a career in those "liberal progressive" institutions that offer only a revolving door option to most minority faculty? The pool of minority faculty is relatively small because (1) few minorities have the minimum qualifications to enter doctoral programs, (2) the mentoring of doctoral students is deficient, and (3) these students' academic socialization is deficient, and they tend to become ignored or marginalized. In my experiences in a number of institutions, and according to the testimony of many colleagues with whom I discussed this matter, White students are more frequently cultivated, guided, and supported because they know how to obtain support and exhibit the appropriate behaviors at every inch of the journey. So much so that often my Latino colleagues exchange bizarre stories about their days in the doctoral program; tough days of anxiety, humiliation, and abandonment by an insensitive faculty member who could not see the talent behind the color. For example, successful faculty, now teaching in various institutions, who came originally from Stanford in the 1980s bring back stories similar to the ones just discussed; how in the end, they had to beg a kind older faculty member to help them complete their dissertation because they did not feel they had enough support from their main faculty. At Harvard there are Latino doctoral students who left the University of California for those very reasons, and they remember instances in which their main faculty adviser not only failed to guide them, but when they were attacked by other faculty, their main adviser did not even attempt to offer some support.

We are always amazed that in spite of many obstacles, the students manage to finish and graduate. Faculty have little faith in our intellectual capacity and motivation; as a consequence, they do not give us their time, do not share their ideas with us, do not ask us to participate in their projects, and even, in disdain and anger, throw in the wastepaper basket the first draft of a dissertation. In other instances, they resign from our doctoral committees at the last minute, or stay but show total disregard for our ideas and field of interest. In order to finish the doctorate, many Latino men and women have to beg for help and attempt to negotiate for support of their ideas, which are often ridiculed by faculty. Having struggled to get the doctorate, a minority candidate for a position is not surprised by the abuse of White faculty but is deeply offended and demoralized. I know many current faculty whose stories have been confirmed by other students of color. They see the hiring and promotion processes as a logical sequence to their treatment as minority doctoral students. Their wounds stay open a long time, and their scars never disappear.

Is it difficult to gatekeep and reject ethnic and racial minorities? It is not, and it happens often. Can it be justified or rationalized? Yes. In the ultimate instance, resistance to incorporate underrepresented minorities into the rank and file of the faculty in higher education is justified by one or several of the following arguments:

- Quality control considerations ("there are no qualified candidates and we need to preserve the quality of our department in order to generate knowledge and compete well").
- The need to preserve academic freedom from the imposition of affirmative action hirings ("our field has other needs, and we must be free to pursue the right candidates to meet such needs").
- The need to prevent ethnic conflict ("hiring minorities will bring political activism and disorder; we must protect the harmony of our academic climate").

Quality control, academic freedom, and harmony would seem to be important attributes of research institutions, and therefore, deserving of our commitment. If we analyze quality-control considerations, we realize that the criteria for discerning quality are not applied with equity.

The initial assumption by faculty members is that candidates of color are of lower quality than White candidates; the resulting exclusion of people of color can lead to inbreeding, intellectual rigidity, and conceptual poverty. We deprive ourselves of views, opinions, talents, and options advocated by people with different cultural experiences. The enrichment and challenging intellectual exchanges taking place with diversified faculty cannot exist where uniformity and conformity are preferred over a rich variety of views and experiences. Universities are the intellectual arena par excellence for conceptual growth, creative thinking, and the acquisition of specialized discourse and linguistic repertoires. Universities are, furthermore, the place for intensive reflection on acquired knowledge and the joint construction of new knowledge. In this arena, the significance and timeliness of contributions by thinkers with other cultural (ethnic, linguistic, and social) experiences are critical to the education of all. People of color are most urgently needed in higher education institutions because they help prepare all students to face the real world, which is culturally diverse; indeed, faculty of color can be the most instrumental education in White institutions. The analytical skills, the discourse patterns, and the rich experience of faculty of color will transcend the taboos and cultural codes of White faculty in undiversified institutions. Without faculty of color, the academic experience of students can only be impoverished.

In the social and medical sciences, in education, art, music, law, business administration, technology, and other fields the contributions of researchers and professors of color are essential to the full understanding of the field as it changes vis-à-vis population changes in America, Europe, and other countries. The relevancy of cultural differences for those fields is at the essence of their growth and success. In the other fields, such as engineering, the natural sciences, mathematics, and so on, a better understanding of cultural differences and sensitivity to such differences can represent success or failure in attracting international markets, outstanding talent, financial support, and, ultimately, a broad network of scholars and researchers involved in the field for the benefit of all. Academia is, of itself, universal; restrictions based on race or ethnicity can only decrease the potential of any institution to compete well nationally and internationally. Racial and ethnic biases are most destructive to the institution and its students in all fields.

Conflict Resolution

In the United States, democracy is supposed to serve as a model to other nations. In order for our universities to live up to the democratic principles of equity (equal opportunity, fair treatment of all, equal access to knowledge, faculty, and resources) they must start by attracting individuals who, having the disciplinary—theoretical and methodological—qualifications, are also capable of understanding the racial and ethnic characteristics of students, community, and other populations affected by the university. In order to teach effectively one needs to communicate effectively. Individuals who are competent in dealing with diverse ethnic and racial groups can best serve their pedagogical needs.

First of all, we have to face the fact that in the minds of some academicians committed to high-quality instruction and research, affirmative action policies and practices, indeed any extradepartmental hiring initiatives, are viewed as intrinsically incompatible with academic freedom and doomed to fail. The fundamental assumption is that hiring is the quintessence of academic freedom and that imposing color as a required characteristic of a potential faculty may exclude the most talented and suitable individuals. The experiments in faculty diversification on a quick-time basis created the revolving door phenomenon. Rather than forcing departments to hire or promote persons of color, I think that chairpersons, deans, and vice presidents for academic affairs must create positive incentives for diversification in the long term. Two important working assumptions of administrators are:

- Retain as the primary criterion for hiring, the highest academic qualifications of the candidate, and his or her potential to bring about significant contributions to the field and the academic unit.
- Conduct searches with equity for all candidates regardless of color, race, ethnicity, gender, or disability.

Positive incentives to attract White faculty into volunteering for the diversification effort will help avoid the appearance of "forcing" faculty or "violating" their academic freedom, or in any way infringing on their rights. At times and in some political contexts, positive incentives offered by administrators to departments, in the form of additional financial resources to hire minorities—with maximum flexibility to select their specialization, gender, ethnicity, and race—can be viewed as an infringement of academic freedom or as bribes to impose a direction considered detrimental to the overall quality of academia. It is a very delicate matter faced by administrators who find themselves in the cross fire of opposite and conflicting factions. An administrator can persuade and encourage but cannot impose personnel decisions on departmental chairs, search committees, or faculty. Consequently, the only avenue open to an administrator is often indirect action somewhat detached from personnel decisions. This action can take the following forms:

- Financial resources and the flexibility to use them; visibility, moral support, and recognition;
- Help to the department (or other units) to expand searches, negotiate joint positions, and obtain additional resources to attract a candidate; and
- Negative sanctions imposed on units or factions that consistently and systematically organize to defeat qualified persons from ethnically or racially underrepresented groups. These sanctions can take the form of budgetary reduction or fiscal restrictions, denial of moral support, recognition, information, and so on.

The best higher education institutions often consider themselves the most liberal (or least biased against underrepresented groups). Yet, they may also be the ones with the least representation of diverse ethnic and racial groups in tenured positions, that is, with the fewest African American and Latino tenured faculty. In these institutions you have fewer conspicuous efforts to block the entrance of qualified candidates. The reluctance to tenure African American and Latino faculty may be based on a deep commitment by all faculty to keep "their" standards of academic excellence and their conviction that most members of minority groups do not possess the necessary qualifications. As a result, and given the composition of most hiring committees, that is, mainstream persons with their particular social networks, it is often very difficult to attract sufficient numbers of African American or Latino candidates with records comparable to those of mainstream candidates. This fact makes the job of hiring committees rather difficult even when these committees show some willingness to consider a wide range of candidates.

The exclusion of underrepresented groups may be more the result of myopia and insensitivity than of organized racism. If we accept the above assumptions and in good faith accept also the willingness of some institutions to oppose engineered racism or exclusion, that is, a clear rejection of overt political action to ignore, neglect, reject, and fail potential faculty from underrepresented ethnic or racial groups, then we must create the mechanism to enlarge the pool of candidates and socialize them to succeed. Having accepted these assumptions, academicians (admnistrators and faculty) must therefore explore creative mechanisms to resolve the fundamental challenge of expanding the pool of candidates from underrepresented groups.

Concluding Thoughts

Expanding the pool is only a necessary condition, not a sufficient one, for successful hiring, promotion, and retention of persons from underrepresented racial and ethnic groups. Additional strategies must address the serious problem of mentoring, guiding, developing, and nurturing minority faculty so they become genuine, active, and vital participants in academia. In order to accomplish these two goals, I would like to propose the establishment of what I will call university centers of excellence in prestigious universities. Through a combination of partnerships with and grants from federal, state, and private organizations, as well as with the wise investment of private donations and revenues from services and publications from the centers, selected universities could sponsor further training and specialization of doctoral candidates (at the dissertion level) and of recent graduates as postdoctoral fellows in disciplinary fields of the greatest need and also in fields lacking faculty from underrepresented groups. The organization and functions of the centers could be as follows:

1. Under the leadership of key university administrators, a group of mentors, ideally senior and highly recognized scholars, would be

able to give a portion of their time to conduct joint research and teaching activities with specific center members.

2. Mentoring of center members would be extended to their participation in seminars, conferences, and research projects across institutions.

3. A central part of the experience of center members would consist of an intense socialization in conducting research and writing, in acquiring additional methodological and analytical skills, in developing networks with peers and senior scholars, and in exploring interdisciplinary approaches to the study of socioeconomic, educational, and political problems of minority achievement.

4. The centers would provide members with continuous guidance, administrative internships, and rich academic experiences and multiple contacts in order to identify adequate tenure-track positions in universities where their professional growth is considered a top priority.

5. Centers would hold annual conferences and bring back alumni who would help place and nurture center members.

Ultimately, the end result of the centers would be to create adequate networks and support systems to assist potential faculty from underrepresented groups in finding adequate positions and to ensure their intellectual and professional maximum development.

In conclusion, the time has come for investing intellectual and material resources seriously, consistently, and substantially to create a strong pool of underrepresented minority faculty who can take university positions in administration, research, and instruction and who can demonstrate a level of performance above that of mainstream faculty. This is doable if we carefully plan the processes of academic socialization in order to select, support, and mentor new faculty members. The social and intellectual significance of a movement toward minority excellence is bound to have an impact at all levels of education; one that will give this country the momentum it needs to continue to live up to its ideal as a democratic society.

References

Apple, M. *The New Sociology of Education: Analzing Cultural and Economic Reproduction,* 1978.

———. *Cultural and Economic Reproduction in Education.* New York: Macmillan. 1982.

————. *Education and Power.* Boston: Ark Paperbacks, 1985. First published in 1982.

————. *Teachers and Texts: A Political Economy of Class and Gender Relations in Education.* New York: Routledge, 1989. First published in 1986.

————. *Ideology and Curriculum.* London: Routledge and Kegan Paul, 1990. First published in 1979.

————. "Do the Standards Go Far Enough? Power, Policy, and Practices in Mathematics Education." *Journal for Research in Mathematics Education* 23, no. 5 (1992): 412–431.

————. *Official Knowledge: Democratic Education in a Conservative Age.* New York: Routledge, 1993.

————. "Power, Meaning and Identity: Critical Sociology of Education in the United States." *British Journal of Sociology of Education* 17, no. 2 (1996): 125–144.

Aronowitz, S., and H. Giroux. *Education Under Siege.* South Hadley, Mass.: Bergin and Garvey, 1985.

————. *Postmodern Education: Politics, Culture and Social Criticism.* Minneapolis: University of Minnesota Press, 1991.

Au, K. H., and J. M. Mason. "Cultural Congruence in Classroom Participation Structures: Achieving a Balance of Rights." *Discourse Processes* 6 (1983): 145–168.

Chavez, L. R. *Shadowed Lives: Undocumented Immigrants in American Society: Case Studies in Cultural Anthropology.* G. Spindler and L. Spindler, eds. New York: Harcourt, Brace, Jovanovich College Publishers, 1992.

Chronicle of Higher Education, Almanac Issue, 43, no. 1 (September 2, 1996), 17–26.

Cornelius, W. "Educating California's Immigrant Children: Introduction and Overview." In R. G. Rumbaut and W. A. Cornelius (eds.), *California's Immigrant Children: Theory, Research, and Implications for Educational Policy.* University of California, San Diego. San Diego, Calif.: Center for U.S.-Mexican Studies, 1995, 1–16.

Freire, P. *Pedagogy of the Oppressed.* New York: Seabury, 1973.

————. *Pedagogia da Esperança: Um Reencontro Com a Pedagogia do Oprimido.* São Paulo, Brazil: Editora Paz e Terra, S. A., 1993.

————. *Pedagogy of Hope. Reliving Pedagogy of the Oppressed.* New York: Continuum Press, 1995.

Gadotti, M. *Pedagogy of Praxis: A Dialectical Philosophy of Education.* Translated by John Milton. New York: State University of New York Press, 1996.

Giroux, H. "Theories of Reproduction and Resistance in the New Sociology of Education: A Critical Analysis." *Harvard Educational Review* 53, no. 3 (1983): 257–293.

————. "Introduction." In P. Freire, *The Politics of Education: Culture, Power and Liberation.* South Hadley, Mass.: Bergin and Garvey, 1985, xi–xxv.

————. *Border Crossing: Cultural Workers and the Politics of Education.* New York: Routledge, 1992.

Giroux, H., and P. McLaren. "Teacher Education and the Politics of Engagement: The Case for Democratic Schooling." *Harvard Educational Review* 26, no. 3 (1986): 213–238.

Giroux, H., and P. McLaren. *Between Borders: Pedagogy and the Politics of Cultural Studies.* New York and London: Routledge, 1994.

Herbert, Bob. "Is Affirmative Action Needed?" *New York Times,* November 11, 1996, A15.

Ladson-Billings, G., and W. Tate IV. "Toward a Critical Race Theory of Education." *Teachers College Record* 97, no. 1 (1995): 47–68.

Leistyna, Pepi, Arlie Woodrum, and Stephen A. Sherblom, eds. *Breaking Free: The Transformative Power of Critical Pedagogy. Harvard Educational Review,* Reprint Series No. 27, 1996.

McLaren, P. *Critical Pedagogy and Predatory Culture: Oppositional Politics in a Postmodern Era.* London and New York: Routledge, 1995.

McLaren, P., and P. Leonard, eds. *Paulo Freire: A Critical Encounter.* London and New York: Routledge, 1993.

Olivas, M. "Latinos and the Law: An Essay on Crop Cultivation." *UCLA Law Review* 14 (1994): 117–138.

Rumbaut, R. "The New Californians: Comparative Research Findings on the Educational Progress of Immigrant Children." In R. G. Rumbaut and W. A. Cornelius (eds.), *California's Immigrant Children: Theory, Research, and Implications for Educational Policy.* University of California, San Diego. San Diego, Calif.: Center for U.S.-Mexican Studies, 1995, 17–69.

Rumbaut, R. G., and W. A. Cornelius, eds. *California's Immigrant Children: Theory, Research, and Implication for Educational Policy.* University of California, San Diego. San Diego, Calif.: Center for U.S.-Mexican Studies, 1995, 17–69.

Shackelford, J., and P. Shackelford. "Affirmative Action in Engineering Education: A Case Study." In Y. Zou and H. Trueba (eds.), *Ethnic Identity and Power: Cultural Contexts of Political Action in School and Society.* New York: State University of New York Press, 1998.

Shackelford, P., and J. Shackelford. "Affirmative Action Defended: Case Studies in Engineering Education." *Multicultural Education* 3, no. 1 (1995): 25–26.

Smith, D. G. "Faculty Diversity When Jobs Are Scarce: Debunking the Myths." *The Chronicle of Higher Education,* September 6, 1996, B3–B4.

Suárez-Orozco, M. M., ed. *Migration, Minority Status, and Education: European Dilemmas and Responses in the 1990s. Anthropology and Education Quarterly* 22, no. 2 (1991) (entire theme issue).

Suárez-Orozco, C., and M. M. Suárez-Orozco. *Transformations: Immigration, Family Life and Achievement Motivation among Latino Adolescents.* Stanford, Calif.: Stanford University Press, 1995a.

———. "Migration: Generational Discontinuities and the Making of Latino Identities." In L. Romanucci-Ross and G. DeVos (eds.), *Ethnic Identity: Creation, Conflict, and Accommodation.* 3d ed. Walnut Creek, Calif.: Alta Mira Press, 1995b, 321–347.

Suárez-Orozco, M. M. "California Dreaming: Proposition 187 and the Cultural Psychology of Racial and Ethnic Exclusion." *Anthropology and Education Quarterly* 27, no. 2 (1996): 151–167.

————. "State Terrors: Immigrants and Refugees in the Post-National Space." In Y. Zou and E. Trueba (eds.), *Ethnic Identity and Power: Cultural Contexts of Political Actions in School and Society*. New York: State University of New York Press, 1998, 283–319.

Trueba, H. T. "The Study of a Rural Mexican Town." Unpublished manuscript. University of California Linguistic Minority Research Institute. University of California, Santa Barbara, 1996.

Trueba, H., L. Cheng, and K. Ima. *Myth or Reality: Adaptive Strategies of Asian Americans in California*. London: Falmer Press, 1993.

Trueba, H. T., L. Jacobs, and E. Kirton. *Cultural Conflict and Adaptation: The Case of the Hmong Children in American Society*. London: Falmer Press, 1990.

Trueba, H. T., C. Rodríguez, Y. Zou, and J. Cintrón. *Healing Multicultural America: Mexican Immigrants Rise to Power in Rural California*. London: Falmer Press, 1993.

Trueba, H., and Y. Zou. *Power in Education: The Case of Miao University Students and Its Significance for American Culture*. London: Falmer Press, 1994.

Mexican Immigrant Families in California

—Porque somos los mojados siempre nos busca la ley
Porque estamos ilegales y no hablamos el inglés
El gringo terco a sacarnos y nosotros a volver.
—Si unos sacan por Laredo, por Mexicali entran bien
Si otros sacan por Tijuana, por Nogales entran seis
Ahi no'más saque cuenta cuántos entramos al mes.

—Because we're *wetbacks* the law is always after us,
Because we're illegal and don't speak English.
The gringo is determined to get us out, and we are determined to come back.
If some are kicked out through Laredo, they make it through Mexicali all right.
—If others are kicked out through Tijuana, six more come in through Nogales.
Just figure out how many enter each month.

—Luis Armenta, *Vivan los Mojados*

Very few examples of Mexican resiliency are more eloquent than the case of Mexican migrant women in central California. Their resiliency is based on their profound commitment to maintain a "community" in which their children can prosper and make their ancestors proud but also retain their language and culture. These women's endurance is shown not only in their daily agricultural labor but also in their capacity to organize, negotiate, and fight for their children's education. They seem to understand how American society functions and how to motivate children to achieve academically. Their daily work in the fields and packing houses, under precarious conditions, has affected their health significantly (they suffer from arthritis, bronchitis, allergies, malnutrition, and high blood pressure). Yet, neither these problems, nor the frequent verbal abuse of racist bosses, nor the lack of employment security have broken their spirit. They feel very proud of the fact that they are tough people who can survive in the worst of circumstances. These physically and spiritually strong women own and manage their own voices. Who am I to "give" them a forum? I did not have to give them anything, they took the opportunity and redirected my inquiry to make their voices heard. Yet, I am not sure I listened carefully enough. They will tell me when they read my account of their narratives.

Sociopolitical Context of Mexican Farm Labor

Mexican immigrant women are self-sufficient and empowered to run their own lives. My role as an ethnographer was to recognize the magnitude of their contributions to American democracy and to their children's education. I will comment in more detail about my methodological dilemmas in the next chapter. But it was obvious to me that the social and political currents surrounding the educational expectations of immigrant children, their parents, and their teachers were always higher than those of mainstream society. This phenomenon is alluded to by contemporary scholars. For example, Mike Rose says that the public opinion condemning schools runs counter to his personal experience and studies over several years, and the reality he observed embodies "the hope for a free and educated society." Furthermore, he adds:

> We seem to be rapidly losing that hope. Our national discussion about public schools is despairing and dismissive, and it is shutting down our civic imagination. I visited schools for three and a half years, and what struck me early on—and began to define my journey—was how rarely the kind of intellectual and social richness I was finding was reflected in the public sphere. We have instead a strange mix of apocalyptic vignettes—violent classrooms, incompetent teachers, students who think Latin is spoken in Latin America—and devastating statistics: declines in SAT scores and embarrassing cross-national comparisons. We hear— daily, it seems—that our students don't measure up, either to their predecessors in the United States or to their peers in other countries, and that, as a result, our position in the global economy is in danger. We are told, by politicians, by pundits, that our cultural values, indeed our very way of life is threatened. We are offered, by both entertainment and the news media, depictions of schools as mediocre places, where students are vacuous and teachers are not so bright; or as violent and chaotic places, places where order has fled and civility has been lost. It's hard to imagine anything good in all this. (Rose 1995, 1)

The reason it is easy to despair and give up our commitment to education is that we do not believe in the potential, resiliency, and talents of the new generation of Latino immigrants. And the reason we lack confidence in them is the overwhelming literature depicting them as failures. However, as I mentioned earlier, the recent work of scholars (Myers 1998 and González Baker, Bean, Escobar Latapí, and Weintraub 1998) helps us understand the dynamics of success and failure, the long-term, intergenerational economic and educational progress of Latinos, and their inexhaustible energy and determination to keep trying. As the song that begins the chapter says, "el gringo terco a sacarnos y nosotros a volver." As the Suárez-Orozcos point out:

> The obvious difficulties that most migrants face include language inadequacies, a general unfamiliarity with the customs and expectations of the new country, limited economic opportunities, poor housing conditions, discrimination, and what psychologists term the "stresses of acculturation." . . . Despite these obstacles, many migrants often consider their lot as having improved from what it was in their country of origin. Because of a perception of relative improvement, many migrants may fail to internalize the negative attitudes of the host country toward them, maintaining their country of origin as a point of reference. (C. Suárez-Orozco and M. Suárez-Orozco 1995b, 325)

Indeed, migrants hold their belief of improvement by visiting their villages of origin and displaying some wealth conspicuously (showing new trucks, good clothes, and spending money). The Suárez-Orozcos suggest that immigrants do not see their new life in terms of the ideals of the majority society but in terms of the "old culture," thus holding to a "dual frame of reference" (Suárez-Orozco and Suárez-Orozco 1995b, 325).

A number of scholars feel that the education of Latinos is worse now than in the previous decade (Portes 1996; Suárez-Orozco and Suárez-Orozco 1995a, 1995b; Durán 1983; Valencia 1991). Yet, recent studies of academic success of Latino students in high school and their continued efforts to succeed in their adult lives invite reflection on the supportive role of the family and home environment (Díaz Salcedo 1996). The narratives of academic achievement, in the midst of the narratives of inequity for many Latino students, represent a surprising success where failure was expected. Immigrants' adaptive responses vary according to their prearrival experiences. But their social and political sophistication seems to enhance their survival opportunities in North American society. This factor affecting the nature of adaptive strategies chosen by Mexican immigrants is literacy (in a broad Freirian sense), that is, their understanding of the complex social, economic, and political systems in this country, and their ability to handle text related to those systems (contracts, government documents, bank documents, hospitals documents, immigration papers, and so on). The marginalization of many Mexican families started long before they arrived in this country. Their naive notions about the politics of employment, the organization of schools, and the demands of society reflect more a change from rural to urban settings, above and beyond the change from one country to another. Of course, the added dimension in this country is that in order to acquire the necessary sociopolitical knowledge of appropriate conduct in urban settings, immigrants must first acquire the communicative skills to do so in a second language. To compound the problem, immigrants often take jobs that are exhausting and that leave them little time to acquire communicative skills in English. The consequences for the children of immigrants is that soon they are forced to play adult roles in making momentous decisions for their parents because the children know some English and understand the social system a bit better.

A serious problem facing young immigrant families at their arrival is the neglect and malnutrition of their children. This not only occurs in the case of migrant workers but also among urban dwellers who are isolated and cannot afford to pay for the cost of child care. Again, to compound these problems, families who have any members without full documentation feel the most vulnerable and cannot seek help from social agencies even if they rightfully qualify to receive aid. In many instances workers do not have health insurance or welfare, and they do not have access to a physician prior to childbirth or even beyond a few weeks after childbirth. The dysfunctional housing conditions increase the chances of health problems and child neglect. In some cases, the safety of the children is jeopardized because they live in dilapidated housing infested with drug addicts and vandals. These conditions are also associated with the phenomena of early recruitment of Mexican children into gangs and rising school dropout rates.

If, given the precarious conditions in which families live, the school lacks the resources or interest in providing special attention to immigrant children, then the chances for academic failure increase dramatically. The experiences of discrimination and of verbal and physical abuse on the part of mainstream children, combined with the predominant opinion among teachers that Latino children are low achievers, certainly do not help either the children or their families. These experiences create for immigrant children a complex setting in which they must redefine themselves in the United States, and these experiences often motivate them to reject their own family, language, and culture. These symbolic "self-rejections" and the formation of a new identity do not necessarily result in a desire to embrace school and North American society. A number of scholars have recently dealt with these problems of adaptation in the context of the school environment (Wilson 1991; Gutierrez 1994; Patthey-Chavez 1993; Delgado-Gaitan 1994; Deyhle and Margonis 1995; Gutierrez, Larson, and Kreuter 1995; Bartolomé 1996; Bartolomé and Macedo 1997). Several scholars, using critical pedagogy, offer as a solution "transformative" strategies for teachers and students (based on Freire 1973, 1995, scholars such as Giroux and McLaren 1994; Freire and Macedo 1987; and McLaren 1995, among others).

    There is an intimate relationship between the successful adaptation of Mexican immigrant families to our society and the academic success of their children. For example, a recent study in central California (Trueba 1997) shows that the most serious problems faced by the children of immigrants on the West Coast are the alienating experience of schooling, the rapid marginalization of these children, and their confusion regarding personal identity, cultural values, social acceptance, the ability to achieve, and overall self-worth. Consequently, if children manage to retain a strong self-identity and remain as part of the sociocultural community, they can achieve well in school. Carola and Marcelo Suárez-Orozco have also shown in their recent studies (1995a and 1995b) that immigrant children's learning ability and social skills deteriorate the longer they are exposed to American society's alienating environment, which undermines their overall school achievement and adaptation to this society. The traumatic experience of being uprooted and the confusion about family values and personal survival, coupled with the need for peer support, are bound to lead many young people to become affiliated with gangs (Vigil 1983, 1988, 1989, and 1997) and to disregard the codes of behavior prescribed by mainstream society.

Frequently, a family takes special precautions to salvage the moral character and overall well-being of a youth by taking him or her back to Mexico for a period of time, to complete his or her education, work under supervision, and marry a local person. There are cases when the entire family returns to Mexico in order to reeducate teenagers in family values. This is often associated with a serious reassessment of the family's finances and the risks involved in continuing to work in the United States. The number of repatriated ex-farmworkers in Colima, Michoacán, and Jalisco is increasing rapidly. However, in contrast with the alienation of Mexican immigrant children in major metropolises (such as Los Angeles, Chicago, New York, Houston, and so on), those children who live in settings where they can manage to retain their home language and culture, their familiar cultural institutions and networks, seem to survive the trauma of American schooling and to achieve well; this, of course, is the result of a carefully executed plan of education engineered primarily by the mothers who monitor schooling, and who defend their language and culture by creating vast networks on both sides of the border to support their children's strong Mexican identity and their ability to live in a binational and bicultural world.

In some rural communities of the West Coast, for example, there is a correlation between immigrant population increases and the ratios of children in schools. The number of children per immigrant family is higher than among other families. Also the economic and health needs of Mexican immigrant families are greater than those of families born and raised in the United States. This phenomenon can be understood in the context of unstable employment for immigrant families and the recruitment of new immigrants for cheap labor among the most needed economically in Mexico. Immigrant families and village networks are instrumental in managing the choice of jobs for persons from particular Mexican communities.

> The economies and labor markets of rural communities are increasingly layered or segmented in a manner that pushes many of the costs of seasonal farm work onto the most flexible or absorptive people present, recently-arrived immigrants. . . . Today's rural poverty is being created via the immigration of persons with low earnings and little education into an expanding fruit and vegetable agriculture that increasingly exports the commodities produced by immigrant farm workers. . . . Rural poverty affects California cities as local residents, particularly the children of immigrants, seek a livelihood outside agriculture. The transfer of rural poverty to urban poverty highlights the importance of education and training to improve the prospects for California's rural-to-urban migrants in the urban economy. (Martin and Taylor, 2)

The sense that there is no end in sight to the waves of immigrants is pervasive, and this has created serious reflection on the contradiction between immigration and integration policies, especially considering that children of seasonal farmworkers raised in the United States do not choose seasonal farmwork. A fundamental question is whether we are allowing unregulated immigration to create rural poverty, and if so, what is likely to happen to the children of migrant laborers? If the only option left for growers is to import new farm labor from Mexico, then new immigration will bring new poverty and more segregation. If the United States wants to curtail immigration from Mexico, we must invest in rural Mexico to develop sources of employment there so that rural Mexican seasonal farmworkers can repatriate. Otherwise, "the continued arrival of unskilled immigrants transforms the economy into something resembling the migrants' place of origin or the 'import-third-world-immigrants-and-get-third-world-conditions syndrome.' . . .

On the one hand, their labor is critical to an expanding labor-intensive agricultural sector. On the other hand, immigration into rural communities is associated with rising poverty, public assistance, and underemployment rates" (Martin and Taylor 1996, 4).

In Chapters 2 and 3 we discussed the isolation, economic hardships, and the psychological cost of coming to the United States and trying to survive, adjust, and achieve. As Suárez-Orozco insightfully has pointed out, the United States is currently going through difficult times when fear of losing one's job, the increase in crime, and the erosion of family values signal social chaos. Anxieties have focused on immigrants and refugees who are blamed for our problems and our lack of belonging in this society (Suárez-Orozco 1998, 9–24). Some of this anxiety is related to the vast changes in immigration patterns. To understand long-term population trends and the impact of Latino immigrants, we must examine what we know about Latino immigrants from the last three decades (see Chapter 2).

Mexican Immigrants in Migrant Town

At dawn, at times with temperatures in the mid-forties, old cars from "Migrant Town" (a fictitious name for a rural town in central California) rush to the surrounding fields. Farmworkers arrive carrying bags containing food and drinks for their morning break and lunch. They wear jackets or sweaters, and many cover their faces and head with a piece of cloth. During a few minutes of stretching exercises they receive last-minute instructions, they prepare the bands and packing boxes on the tractor, and the labor begins; the pickers on the ground and the packers on top of the tractors; the pickers pull out their little knives and start cutting broccoli (or lettuce, cauliflower, celery, and so on). Loud ranchero music from portable radios and cheerful conversation energize the group.

Mexican immigrants from the central Mexican states (particularly from Jalisco, Michoacán, Colima, and Guanajuato) during the last fifty years have made their way to Migrant Town in the central California valley of Santa Barbara County, 175 miles north of Los Angeles. They began to come after World War II and have worked since in the fields as pickers, tractor drivers, and packers. For a number of historical and economic reasons they have developed a binational, bicultural existence commuting between central Mexico and central California. As a very important survival strategy, they have developed extensive networks with Mexican families on both sides of the border, and they have provided their children with skills to function effectively in two very different cultures and languages. Consequently, they have maintained their home language and culture and their traditional family values through the annual civil and religious celebrations (baptisms, confirmations, weddings, funerals, Patron Saints, fiestas, and so on), which reinforce the hierarchical structure of the family. How and why would these immigrant families commit to educational excellence? Because they believe that the economic survival of the entire family will ultimately depend on the education of the children. A good education in the United States (so they think) will open up new cultural and linguistic panoramas in the near future. Thus, for example, Mexican junior high school students talk about becoming engineers, doctors, computer technicians, journalists, and architects; their dream is to provide for their parents and make them feel proud. Their success in math, English, and science is carefully crafted by Chicano mentors (graduate students from the California Polytechnic University at San Luis Obispo) via intensive after-class working sessions for students who commute forty-three miles daily to attend high school.

The strong commitment of Mexican families to their children's education is only part of a more ambitious plan for the future. Immigrant mothers have no hesitation stating three major goals for their families: (1) to retain at any cost their Mexican identity and cultural traditions, (2) to obtain economic security for the entire family (nuclear and extended), and (3) to prepare their children for better employment (hopefully a professional career) in the pursuit of upward mobility.

Migrant Town is a small agricultural community of between 6,500 and 8,000 people (95 percent Mexican immigrants). It is situated in the northwestern corner of Santa Barbara County, seventy-five miles north of the city of Santa Barbara. It has 260 square miles of rich farmland that yields amazingly vast volumes of vegetables and other specialized crops such as lettuce, cauliflower, broccoli, celery, and strawberries. The streets of Migrant Town are named after the European pioneers who arrived there in the nineteenth century, such as John Dunbar, a sailor born in Scotland, who reached Migrant Town in 1871 after passing through Louisiana and Texas; Thomas Hart, from England, who arrived in Migrant Town in 1872; Battista Pezzoni, born in Switzerland and transplanted to Australia, who finally settled in Migrant Town in 1875 and later started a prosperous dairy business; and Antonio Tognazzini, who arrived in Migrant Town in 1876 (Mason 1883). In 1895, the railroad was finally open to trains from San Francisco, and the burgeoning town established its own newspaper. Soon thereafter, and for a number of economic, political, and sociohistorical reasons, Migrant Town lost importance and failed to compete with the fast-growing neighboring cities. Immigrants played an important role in Migrant

Town. Japanese farmworkers had started to come to Migrant Town at the end of the nineteenth century, and by 1940, they represented about 50 percent of the population. Japanese children (who had after-school classes) were the highest achievers at school. The confinement of Japanese families in relocation camps in the 1940s is a very sad chapter in the history of the United States and of Migrant Town. It is particularly difficult to get anyone to discuss this sordid piece of Migrant Town history. The Japanese, of course, lost everything and only a small group ever returned to Migrant Town. In the town cemetery, however, the conspicuous and massive stones marking the tombs of ancestors are visited and redecorated often by relatives coming from all over California.

The Chinese, who had arrived with the construction of the railroad at the turn of the century, had formed a small community and had secret gambling casinos, restaurants, and laundries, but they began to leave town by the early 1920s when some Filipino and Mexican populations began to arrive in response to demands for agricultural labor. The Mexican population that started to come to Migrant Town in 1920 did grow substantially until 1942 with the beginning of the Bracero Program (Palerm 1992, 1994; Palerm and Urquiola 1993; Garcia 1992). Mexican farmworkers and their families began to permanently reside in Migrant Town in the 1960s; and from that time on, the increase in population has been dramatic. Migrant Town's population grew from 3,225 in 1960, to 5,479 in 1990. In 1960, the Mexican-origin population constituted only 18 percent of the total population, but by 1990 they were 83 percent of the town's population. In 1996, the Mexican population was estimated to be about 95 percent of the total population (Garcia 1995, 43). The Bracero Program, started in 1941, was highly instrumental in bringing Mexican nationals in large numbers to work in the fields of central California. Although the program was officially terminated in 1964, Mexican labor continued to be in high demand. The termination of the program, however, changed the status of guest workers from "legal" to "illegal" or undocumented. By the mid-1960s, California had already substantially expanded its agricultural industry based on specialty crops in response to an ever-increasing national and international appetite. At first, growers ignored the undocumented status of farmworkers. Later on, as pressures from the federal government mounted, the powerful agricultural industry lobbied to obtain the Immigration Reform and Control Act of 1986, which was intended to legalize workers already in the United States. This measure did not stop additional immigration of undocumented workers recruited by growers, and it did not affect the continued lobbying of the multibillion-dollar agricultural industry bosses to obtain a Special Agricultural

Worker and Replenishment Agricultural Worker program extending legal protection to more recent workers. This program offered amnesty to many undocumented workers and enabled them to become legal residents. Originally the program was expected to legalize some 250,000 farmworkers; to the shock of the immigration authorities, 1.3 million workers requested amnesty and obtained it.

Yet many Mexican farmworkers did not request amnesty because they found the procedures cumbersome, or they were hoping to go back to their villages of origin shortly. For most of them, however, going back to their villages was a dream that never came true. Poverty in rural Mexico was, and still is, rampant. A desperate search for employment took thousands of Mexican rural persons to the fields of California during the 1980s. According to Palerm (1992, 1994) and to Palerm and Urquiola (1993), more than 1.1 million Mexican immigrants in California work the land in the most difficult conditions and are often abused, neglected, and exploited. According to Palerm:

- Health care services are urgently needed in enclave communities because of the crowded and substandard conditions of the workers' residences.
- Farm workers have no health insurance and the job is plagued with accidents and injuries. Most farm workers know of Medicare or Medicaid, but the problems to gain access to these benefits (because of the paperwork and the language and cultural differences) are insurmountable.
- Farmers often rely on home remedies and traditional rural healing practices. Health education continues to be the most urgent need. (Palerm 1992, 365–366)

Working conditions and health care improved a great deal with the intervention of Cesar Chavez and the United Farm Workers of America. In the homes of many farmworkers, next to the Virgen de Migrant Town and other saints, there is a picture of Cesar Chavez. Older farmworkers always describe their working life in two periods, before Cesar Chavez and after him. National awareness of the injustices and subhuman working conditions of agricultural laborers was the target of Cesar Chavez's sacrifices and political efforts; there were important changes in the life of Migrant Town workers.

Farmworkers constitute the most enduring underclass during the twentieth century in California, in spite of the fact that they are an extremely hardworking group and that they do achieve a measure of family and personal success. In some counties (such as McFarland, Madera, Santa Barbara, and San Luis Obispo) there are clusters of Mexican farmworkers in poverty working for very low wages and in subhuman conditions (without appropriate clothing or protection, in deplorable housing and working long hours, at the will of the foremen). These counties rapidly increased their population in response to the demand for hand labor in the cultivation of specialized crops. The much discussed automation of California's agriculture never became a reality. Specialized crops, which saved California's economy in the 1960s and 1970s, always required intensive hand labor. As Palerm points out, in the last three decades (1960–1990) we did not see the *mechanization,* but the *mexicanization* of commercial agriculture (Palerm 1992, 364).

Arguments from both quantitative economic data and from ethnographic studies are presented to counter the view that Mexico–United States migration discourages independent economic growth in Mexico. The inflow of "migradollars," estimated at some $2 billion a year, directly and indirectly stimulates higher levels of economic activity, investment, employment, and income growth (Durand, Parrado, and Massey 1996, 423). The use of savings and remittances from the United States for workshops to produce tennis shoes (as in San Francisco del Rincón, Guanajuato) or to invest in farming (as in Ario de Rayón, Michoacán) is a typical example of the direct impact of migradollars. Other examples are the monies invested in the production of handicrafts for export (as in Santiago Tangamandapio, Michoacán) and in the purchase of sewing machines to decorate knitted clothing (as in Nahuatzen, Michoacán). Investments in large cities, however, are used for educational purposes such as the foundation of English academies, as in the case of Guadalajara, León, and Morelia (Durand, Parrado, and Massey 1996, 426–427). But there are also many indirect ways in which such investment stimulates the Mexican economy through consumer spending and the increase of service industries. As Durand, Parrado, and Massey state, even the conspicuous consumption of beer and other products during the traditional fiestas are important means of sharing the benefits of farm labor, and these are "a widely-sanctioned mechanism for the redistribution of wealth and income. In the fiesta, those who have money are expected to spend for the benefit of those who do not. Returning United States migrants with substantial savings feel obligated to spend a share of their funds for the general welfare, covering the lion's share of the costs of the music, fireworks, dances, parades, and religious celebrations—all of which are presented publicly and enjoyed by all, rich or poor" (Durand, Parrado, and Massey 1996, 428). Therefore, the overall impact of the migradollars in the Mexican economy is substantial. Of the $2 billion annually received in Mexico, $718 million is sent by skilled urban workers, $666 million by unskilled urban workers, $554 million by landless rural workers, and $62 million by small farmers. Furthermore, the additional income for Mexicans is estimated at $5.8 billion a year (3 percent of the gross domestic product in 1989), which benefits primarily skilled urban workers and investors, with annual gains of $1.9 million each. Beyond this impact, those two billion migradollars could well generate $6.5 billion in manufacturing and services. Thus, in conclusion, unlike other investments, migradollars benefit the people that need money the most, and very little is diverted to those of higher incomes occupying positions of authority (Durand, Parrado, and Massey 1996, 426–441).

The enormous economic contribution of farmworkers to the Mexican economy is only a small fraction of the extraordinary contribution they have made to the California agribusiness economy. In 1992, in Santa Maria Valley in Santa Barbara County alone, the cultivation of broccoli, strawberries, lettuce, cauliflower, grapes, celery, asparagus, cabbage, peas, cilantro, and artichokes demanded near twenty million hours of labor (Palerm 1994, 11), which is equivalent to 9,500 full-time jobs. In reality, employers used 23,000 workers; 13,000 of them were based on the border or somewhere else in Mexico and came only during the peak of the season—from April to August. Other workers, including established residents, were employed erratically as needed. Therefore, for different reasons, the majority of workers (permanent and temporary, documented and undocumented) had to maintain a binational existence in order to survive economically. Hence children were able to retain their Mexican identity while they acquired the linguistic and cultural skills necessary to function in this country. During periods of unemployment in the United States, entire families returned to their villages of origin and strengthened their cultural ties with Mexico. Of course, this pattern changes as children get older and establish a network of friends in the United States.

In 1992, 55 percent of households had one wage earner, 35 percent had two, and 10 percent had three or more. Only 6 percent of the families used State Disability, 5 percent had Assistance to Families with Dependent Children, and 7 percent had Social Security Insurance for unemployment (Garcia 1992, 392). The most recent changes occurring among second-generation Mexican immigrants show some improvement in their economic condition. I conducted a small economic survey of twenty families in January 1996 and found that the median annual income per family was $17,450. Thirteen households had two adults working temporary jobs. The average number of persons per household was 5.6, and the median pay per hour was $6.90. These facts are in contrast with the previous extensive survey conducted by Garcia, as well as with the realities of more recent comers. In his 1992 survey,

Garcia found that the average number of members per household was 5.3 for the entire population of migrant and immigrant workers in Migrant Town (Garcia 1992, 55).

An important recent change in the agricultural labor structure of central California occurred with the development of the *contratista* (contractor) system. In the last decade, a few powerful corporations have bought from the landowners and growers the right to manage the cultivation and harvest of specialized crops. To minimize their costs, these corporations now control the hand labor. They have isolated the landowners who have been replaced by Mexican American *contratistas* whose job is to find the cheapest labor (often the most recent comers). There is neither stability nor security in agricultural employment; and as a result families have much less take-home pay than they had ten years ago. Workers feel less protected and see the system becoming more dehumanized and insensitive to workers' needs. There are no health benefits for temporary laborers, and if they are injured, they lose their jobs. There is very limited medical assistance offered to immigrants or legal residents, including those who work in packing companies. In some cases, the worker is asked to take responsibility for personal injuries as a condition for receiving employment; if an injury occurs, the worker may be fired and, after recovery, may be made to compete with other workers for employment opportunities regardless of experience or seniority. If the *contratista* needs five additional persons, he calls ten new workers and retains the five fastest and cheapest. In fact, this system creates a revolving door that tends to penalize older workers and those whose health has suffered—most of the time precisely because of their work in agriculture.

The obviously pernicious consequences of working in unhealthy and oppressive environments affect women in the most critical period of their lives—during childbearing age—and this, in turn, affects children and the entire family. Exposure to pesticides, malnutrition, strenuous physical activities, and high stress, coupled with lack of medical attention, results in serious chronic health problems for Mexican families. Farmworkers do not have medical insurance, and they can't afford to pay doctors' fees. They resort to home remedies and prayer. When they are laid off, they can use unemployment benefits, go on welfare, and receive medical assistance only if they are legal residents or U.S. citizens. All farmworkers have access to a small local clinic that helps with vaccinations, information, and referrals. This clinic, the Migrant Town Community Health Center, has received meager state support from the Health Department of the State of California. According to a recent report from this clinic, Migrant Town's population is 38.5 percent under nineteen years of age; only 7.6 percent was above sixty-five years of age. Life expectancy in Migrant Town is lower than in urban areas. Migrant Town's economic indices suggest extreme poverty and malnutrition: 5.13 percent of all live births are low weight, and 16.22 percent are births to women under nineteen years of age. Medical attention for pregnant women is scarce and late; in 37 percent of the pregnancies, women did not have access to a doctor until after the first trimester. Infant mortality is 6.76 deaths per one thousand live births (Health and Welfare Department of California 1994). Visiting families and walking around in Migrant Town, one gets the impression that workers are always exhausted and that physical survival demands a great deal of energy every day. In fact, paradoxically, the only time people rest is when they are out of work, when they are sick, or when they are preparing to travel to Mexico. The women's stamina and their greater share of the home obligations is perhaps related to their very significant role in the entire immigration experience and the quality of life among immigrant families.

The Role of Women in the Family

The most intensive part of my ethnographic fieldwork study started in July 1995 and continued until mid-June of the following year. I conducted individual and group interviews with working mothers (audiotaped or videotaped and transcribed or summarized at a later time); and I did systematic observations of farm activities such as planting, fertilizing, cutting, and packing of crops. The study also included classroom observations, participation in teacher-parent meetings, interviews with the superintendent, principals, and teachers, and with the mentors of the middle and high school students. I also conducted a detailed survey (via a questionnaire and personal interviews) of one hundred families. The questionnaire focused on the place of origin, length of residence in the United States, language use and proficiency in English and Spanish, income, employment, and the role of adults in the education of the children. This survey was of great help to guide me in the personal interviews with the working mothers. I also conducted group interviews with middle school and senior high school students, and with staff from the Family Services Center, an office that handles problem students and family emergencies. The commitment to a good education for their children led women to organize community action in the 1970s to remove the school administration; this action resulted in the dismissal of the superintendent and the two principals. The new administration (led by a Mexican American superintendent) adopted new policies in support of Mexican families, which sent a clear

message of respect for the home language and culture of the farmworkers.

In Migrant Town, women maintain cultural ties with their communities of origin in Mexico. They organize themselves economically and
politically in the United States. Women have developed an extensive
organization of relatives and friends all over California. Women have
also become key decisionmakers for major events such as family celebrations, trips, changes of residence, final settlement in a town, purchase of a home and loans negotiations, and most importantly, becoming citizens of the United States. With respect to their children, women
keep very close supervision of their children's school work, attend
school meetings, and hold teachers and administrators accountable for
the achievement of the children. In the end, it is the mothers who engineer the quality of education and their children's choice of careers.
Women become the intellectual leaders of the family; their determination and vision are crucial during times of crisis, and they stand in
sharp contrast with the confusion and indecision of men.

What prepares women to play such an important role in the traumatic journey from the home culture to that of the United States? Many
of them are left alone in Mexico for years, and they alone have to become fully responsible for their children; furthermore, women have
more years of schooling, reach a higher literacy level, and are more
competent than men in handling budgets, contracts, interaction with
mainstream agencies, and simply better understand the social and cultural life of the United States. In brief, women in Migrant Town are
the organizers and initiators of change. They are courageous in their
demands from authorities, and, as a collectivity, they command great
public respect.

The Case of Consuelo

Consuelo is the archetype of the many young women interviewed: although in poor health—with arthritis, ear infections, allergic reactions
to pesticides, at times physically weak, and unable to obtain medical
care—she is committed to continue the struggle for a better life. She is
decisive in her actions and passionate about her beliefs. She talks about
her parents (both worked in California as farmworkers) with great respect as role models in the fields, who taught her early in life the importance of working hard, never giving up, and never taking anything
from others. She demands the respect of the Americans with her digni-
fied behavior. She emphasizes to her four children ages six to sixteen
the need to be responsible and persistent. The oldest and two youngest

are boys, and all three are considered gifted in school; their scores in mathematics are among the highest in their classes. The twelve-year-old girl is mentally retarded and goes to special education classes. At times with a laugh and at times in tears, Consuelo described incidents of racial prejudice and hostility by U.S. schoolchildren. She is bitter about the insensitivity of some bosses at work; recent humiliations and insults suffered at work still bring to the surface deep feelings of anger and shame. Most of all, she is deeply sorry that as a young mother she missed important intimate moments with her young children, such as not being able to hug them when they were asking for affection because she was always too busy or too tired. In protest, for many years she refused to speak English. Only recently has she decided to use English and prepare for her citizenship examination in order to stay in this country. This is a major change in her life, but she thinks she will eventually have dual citizenship, Mexican and United States. What follows is a summary of Consuelo's narrative.

Early Socialization and Experiences of Exclusion

Consuelo's family started coming to the United States together as a family in 1961 (prior to that Consuelo's father had worked as a farmworker for several years). Her father was not comfortable sending his children to the local schools because he knew they would not be treated well. Later on, Consuelo was sent back to Mexico to get some schooling in Michoacán. However, although there was sufficient work in Articia (near Los Angeles, California), Consuelo worked at home. "I was eight, my brother, ten, and my older sister, twelve. Then the *patrón* (the boss) who needed hands hired them both for half salary. I was helping drive the tractor. When I was nine and ten, I became responsible for our house. I had to make corn tortillas in a machine, clean the house, prepare the meals for the family, and baby-sit younger children." People began to notice that Consuelo and her siblings did not attend school and put pressure on her father to send them to school. But her father instead sent them back to Mexico where Consuelo finished elementary school. Her older siblings only finished the third grade. The youngest brother (ten years younger than Consuelo) never did farmwork and remained in Michoacán most of his life, where he became an accountant. Consuelo learned discipline as a very young child:

> Chona [Consuelo's younger sister] was very restless and was bothering all the other children and would not let me do my work. I would then tie her with a rope, but she knew how to untie herself; then she would say

that she had the *diablo* (devil). One day my father showed up to pick up his lunch and I did not have it ready. I started to cry and explained that Chona did not let me work and said she had the *diablo*. My father says: "Oh, she does, eh! Come here Chona, I will take the *diablo* out of you." Then he hit her so hard with the rope that Chona was sick and had a high fever all day and night. She never bothered me any more and I was responsible for the home.

Chona que era muy inquieta. Yo le decia, "Chona, ponte en paz." Iba la Chona y hacía llorar a los niños. Decía que tenía el diablo adentro. Pues la amarraba para poder seguir trabajando, para hacer el lonche, y nada, ella se quitaba la reata. La amarré del palo y de la cintura y me fuí a hacer el lonche. Llegó mi papá y yo no tenía el lonche listo y me puse a llorar. Le dije a mi papá: "Chona no me deja trabajar, dice que tiene el diablo." "¿Ah, sí?" Dice mi papá. "Pues te voy a sacar el diablo; ven para acá." Mi papá le pegó bien feo, hasta se enfermó ella con fiebre. Cuando llegaron del trabajo en la noche, la encontraron can fiebre y dormida. Desde entonces ya no tuve problemas y yo me hice responsable de la casa.

Later on Consuelo explained that her father rarely spanked them (two or three times in the life of each child) and tried to persuade them to do the right thing in order to not break their father's heart.

Rural Mexican children had bitter experiences with their peers. Consuelo was supposed to attend the fourth grade in Articia, but the U.S. children made her life impossible, so she was sent back to Mexico. She just did not want to attend school:

The kids were so bad! They would wait till the school bus got near to throw water balloons and get me and my girlfriend all wet and without being able to go home and change. Other times they would kick us, pull our hair. I would tell them "get off," but they continued. Then I began to insult them, and they would call us names. One day they began to kick me, and I held this girl's foot and she fell down. They call me and scolded. During lunch they would grab us. The Americans did not like us.

¡Los niños eran muy malos! Se esperaban hasta que el bus viniera y luego nos echaban bombas de agua y nos mojaban a mí y a mi amiga; de modo que no teníamos tiempo de irnos a cambiar a la casa. Otras veces nos pegaban con el pié, nos jalaban los cabellos. Yo les decía "Estense quietas," seguían. Entonces yo empecé a decirles grocerías, y ellas también las decían. Luego me empezaron a patear, y yo le agarré el pié a una de ellas y se cayó. Nos mandaron llamar y nos regañaron. Y cuando estábamos en el lonche, nos agarraban. No nos querían los americanos.

As children, Consuelo and her siblings felt the oppression and abuse of the bosses, but they also learned from their parents to respond to abuse by defending one's own rights. Consuelo was only fourteen years old and was already picking strawberries at six in the morning. At the end of the strawberry season, the entire family drove to Fresno to pick blueberries. The boss promised each member of the family (man, wife, and three children) ten dollars per box (a fairly large box). At the end of the day each had made about thirty dollars. The boss said, "Go to this address to pick up your money." When they showed up at the address, the boss threw a ten-dollar bill at them and dismissed them. "My father was angry and said, 'You are cheating us.' The old man replied, 'If you don't shut up and leave, I will call the Migra.' Because we were legal, my father said, 'I should call the police on you because you are a thief.' "

Indeed the next day the father went to the place where Mexican workers are hired and explained to the others that the man was dishonest and would cheat them. Most of them stayed, however, because they needed work. Bad experiences with bosses are a central theme providing women with a deep motivation to fight for their children and encourage them to learn in school so they cannot be cheated. Consuelo was about fifteen years old when she had a most humiliating experience.

> I remember one time, we had this bad *patrón* who would not let us go to the bathroom [in the fields you had to take a long walk to get out of sight] all morning long, and I could no longer hold it. Well, I held and held and could no longer hold. So I urinated right there on my clothes and was so embarrassed that I began to cry. My mother, who was working nearby, came and covered me so the others would not notice, and I just cried and cried out of shame.
>
> Una vez, yo me acuerdo, el patrón era muy malo y no nos dejaba ir a orinar toda la mañana, y a mí ya me andaba. Pues, me aguanté y me aguanté, y ya no podía más. Me oriné en la ropa y me dió tanta pena que me puse a llorar. Mi mamá andaba por allí cerca trabajando y vino y me cubrió para que los demás no se dieran cuenta, y yo no más lloraba de la vergüenza.

After twenty-two years of work in the fields, Consuelo finally graduated to work in one of the packing companies, but working conditions were just as inhumane there as they were in the fields. She soon found out that there was pressure to work fast all the time, the hours were long and often unpredictable; she ended up working the night shift. Any worker who refused to come to a shift was fired. So after a long career of service in the worst of conditions, at the age of thirty-seven, with arthritis, loss of hearing because of ear infections, suffering many allergic reactions to the chemicals used in the fields and packing companies, with four children ranging in grades from first to senior high school (one of them mentally retarded), and without medical insurance, Consuelo reflected on her life and found that the only reason for all these sacrifices was the education of her children.

The Role of Women in the Family

Women are the stronghold, the foundations of the immigrant family. They make most of the hard decisions, manage the budget, go to school meetings, deal with the teacher and principal of the schools, discipline the children, check their homework, and help them plan for the future. Working in the fields or packing houses entails painful sacrifices. Consuelo confesses:

> To me all this has been very hard, especially when my children were younger. I had to prepare lunches and clothing for my oldest son and my daughter (who were eleven and seven years of age) the night before and wake them up early to go to school. Then I had to take my two youngest sons (who were two and four years of age) to my sister's house so she would take care of them here in Migrant Town. I came back home exhausted. I had to see them with pity, because I could not even hug them, I did not have time. "Mami, Mami," they said, crying. I would reply. "Let me make supper" or "Let me take a shower." Real hard! That is how I spend years in the field, until I moved to the packing company.
>
> Para mí ha sido muy duro, sobre todo cuando uno tiene sus niños chiquitos. Desde la noche preparaba su lonche, su ropita y tenía que levantarlos para llevarlos a la casa de mi hermana para que los cuide, aquí mismo en El Rocío. Regresaba a la casa muy cansada. Tenía que estar viendo a los niños así con lástima, porque no podía ni abrazarlos por que no tenía uno tiempo. "Mami, mami," me decían, llorando. Y yo les contestaba "déjame hacerles de comer," o "déjame darme una bañadita." Bien duro. Así me la pasé años trabajando en el campo, hasta que me cambié a la empacadora.

Working in the packing companies demands a great deal of physical strength, and the job is always done under continuous supervision. The bosses are mean and yell all the time. A bad boss demands faster work but calls you a thief if you pick up a small bag of tomatoes and vegetables from the floor that would otherwise be discarded that night. To keep your job you not only have to tolerate verbal abuse, but you must sign a paper accepting full responsibility for any accidents or injuries that might occur while working, as if they were your fault. As Consuelo explained, one of her *compañeras* (coworkers) was pushed and hit by a negligent forklift driver. The day after her injury, the company doctors told her she should go back to work. She could hardly move, one hour after she started crying, "I can't stand the pain." She went back to the doctor and was sent to therapy, but she had to pay for it. Several months afterward she is still hurting and cannot walk well. "They are so arbitrary and demand so much!"

Consuelo and her sisters have many stories about the packing companies. What is clear is that in some respects, working in the fields is healthier and less stressful. In the packing companies, they are always worried about accidents. "Women workers can get cuts, and the machinery is very dangerous. There are bands that can grab persons who have loose clothing, and sometimes can drag them near the cutting machines, and one must stop them and push [the button] to prevent accidents."

In the ultimate analysis, working at night while you have young children is extremely difficult. As Consuelo explains:

> At 3:00 A.M. I arrived from work and could not sleep. From 7:00 to 9:00 A.M. I would send the kids to school and tried to sleep a little. When I got back from the packing company I could not sleep because I was frozen, with my fingers frozen, bent over, cramped up, without being able to move them, because we work in rooms with very low temperatures. That is how I got very sick with bronchitis. I arrived home frozen, so in order to be able to sleep, I would get into the shower with very hot water and then I relaxed, but later my bones began to hurt.
>
> A las tres de la mañana llegaba y luego no podía dormir. De las 7 a las 9 A.M. mandaba a todos a la escuela y luego dormía un poquito. Cuando llegaba del empaque no dormía, porque llega uno congelado, con los dedos así doblados, agarrotados, sin poderlos mover, porque trabajábamos en temperaturas muy bajas. Yo allí me enfermé feo de los bronquios. Llegaba a la casa congelada y para poder dormir me metía a la regadera con agua bien caliente y con eso me relajaba, pero luego me empezaron a doler los huesos.

Consuelo feels that her arthritis, her hearing loss, and her allergic reactions after touching vegetables (even with gloves on), have worsened since she began to work in the packing companies.

Consuelo's Dilemmas

There is no other theme more frequently discussed by Mexican families or so often alluded to by popular songs on any of the five Spanish-speaking stations in the area that the one of loyalty to the *Raza* (your own people). Loyalty starts by recognizing *paisanos* (people from your country) wherever you go. To pretend not to recognize them, or to assume an air of superiority, is one of the worst offenses that can be committed against another Mexican. Disdain or arrogance is presumed when a Mexican pretends to speak only English and *presume* (brags) of his or her new identity as a Mexican American (*pocho* is a derogative word for persons refusing or unable to speak correct Spanish). The reason for this value on ethnic loyalty is that it protects the ethnic identity and close relationships of many Mexicans who, by and large, are unprotected and abused in rural California. The fact that women insist that their children speak Spanish to them and the rest of the family is based on the belief that once the language is lost, there is nothing one can do to maintain the family unit. Consuelo would never allow their children to respond to her or her husband in English. Their periodic visits to Michoacán to see the grandparents and cousins and the annual visits from their many Mexican relatives, are always used as an opportunity to enhance the children's Spanish-language skills and the cultural values of the entire family. The strong ethnic identity of Mexican immigrant men and women and their profound attachment to their native land gives them the motivation to make big sacrifices. Mexican immigrants know that in the end they will overcome the difficulties. In the final analysis, loyalty to the *Raza* is not in contradiction with the important goals of education for one's own children. As Consuelo noted, "I feel that my dad wanted to achieve something here in order to take us back there in Tangancícuaro [Michoacán] so we do not stay here where they mistreat us. But our children need to study here, because there are more opportunities here. I wish I could go to Tangancícuaro, but I must stay for the sake of my children."

Consuelo's oldest son is now sixteen years old and has already started senior high school outside Migrant Town. What concerns Consuelo is that Migrant Town children attending high school in the neighboring mainstream city are now in danger because of the gangs and the lack of support on the part of the school personnel. Everything is fine until they leave Migrant Town.

> While they are in elementary school all goes well; but as soon as they go to the secondary school [in the large mainstream city] they become at risk. I have been thinking that my children are going to go through what I went through [discrimination and abuse]. I believe that if my children are at risk and they want to leave school, I would let them do so. I worry about the gangs! My son tells me, "They want to beat me, they call me *Oaxaca* [derogatory term meaning Indian or primitive] and treat me as inferior." I tell him, "With this [pointing at her head] show them you are better than they." He replies, "That is why they hate me, because I get better grades than they do."
>
> Mientras que están en la primaria todo va bien; pero apenas se van a secundaria, entran en peligro. Yo he pensado que los niños van a pasar

por lo mismo que yo [discriminación y abuso]; yo creo que si los niños están en peligro en la escuela secundaria y si ellos quieren salir, yo los dejo que se salgan de la escuela. ¡Me preocupan las pandillas! Me dice mi hijo: "Me quieren pegar. Me llaman 'Oaxaca' y me tratan como que yo soy menos." Yo le digo, "con esto [pointing at her head] demuéstrales que eres más que ellos." Y el contesta: "por eso me tienen coraje, porque yo saco mejores calificaciones que ellos."

No doubt the challenge for the next generation of immigrant children will be defined with U.S. society's backlash of racial and ethnic prejudice and the efforts to prevent cultural diversity.

The Personal and Family Contextual Features of Resiliency

The following facts provide the reader with a broader context with which to understand Consuelo's resiliency:

- She enjoyed little respect in the United States but had a very high social status in Tangancícuaro.
- She was sent back to Michoacán by her parents to complete six years of schooling (more than any other member of the family).
- At the age of eight, she handled adult responsibilities such as taking care of young children and cooking for the family.
- She took over the home finances to remedy her husband's lack of responsibility.
- She planned and executed the purchase of land in Michoacán and the planting of avocado orchards (now a prosperous business).
- She goes personally to school to check on her children's performance, supervises them, and motivates them daily in the home. Her oldest son is a gifted artist who can draw portraits and create architectural designs. His best scores are in mathematics. He imitates his mother in motivating the two youngest boys.
- She never shows signs of lacking self-confidence.
- She organized study groups of women taking the U.S. citizenship examination.
- She explored the housing market in the Migrant Town area and negotiated a loan to buy a home.

Consuelo's role and that of other immigrant mothers in Migrant Town has been clearly defined in the maintenance of the home language; yet, there is a steady acculturation among the youngsters reflected in their fluent use of English and their preference for country or rock music, American clothing, and the American lifestyle. This, however, is not in conflict with their obvious commitment to the Mexican values of respect for elders, attendance at church functions, and the observance of curfew and other restrictions.

Migrant Town's Mexican working women represent the quintessence of Mexican culture as they set up the lifestyle and pace of change in their families, articulate a vision of the future, and inspire their children to study hard in order to pursue ambitious careers. The many activities of women in all aspects of the cultural life of Migrant Town demonstrate an underlying organization that translates into economic and cultural survival of groups of families in Migrant Town. It is rather paradoxical that the very essence of American democracy and the survival of the American dream will be in the hands of those children we so easily neglect and look down on. We hope that the unfortunate marginalization resulting from neglect and mistreatment will only be a temporary obstacle. Indeed, marginalization does not necessarily have to be a terminal problem. Critical pedagogy shows us that understanding one's own marginal status is the very beginning of empowerment and ethnic redefinition. In fact, we know that Mexican immigrant women are committed to the academic success and cultural survival of their children and that they have engineered ingenious ways of providing their children with motivation and higher aspirations for academic excellence. Their unique role has advanced the process of empowerment a great deal in central California.

Working women are proud "pickers" and feel empowered to engineer the survival of their families via the educational success of their children through bilingual skills and high academic achievement. They pursue the maintenance of a strong cultural identity, but they accommodate if necessary. Critical ethnography, based on the principles of critical pedagogy, can help us to understand the empowerment of these women. We cannot let the shocking reality of the challenges blind us or preempt careful analysis of American education, the quintessence of our democratic structures. As Rose states:

> If, for example, we try to organize schools and create curriculum based on an assumption of failure and decay, then we make school life a punitive experience. If we think about education largely in relation to our economic competitiveness, then we lose sight of the fact that school has to be about more than economy. If we determine success primarily in terms of test scores, then we ignore the social, moral and aesthetic dimension of teaching and learning—and, as well, we'll miss those considerable intellectual achievements which aren't easily quantifiable. If we judge one school according to the success of another, we could well diminish the

particular ways the first school serves its community. In fact, a despairing vision will keep us from fully understanding the *tragedies* in our schools, will reduce their complexity, their human intricacy. We will miss the courage that sometimes accompanies failure, the new directions that can emerge from burn-out, the desire that pulses in even the most depressed schools and communities. (Rose 1995, 2–3)

As we will discuss in the next chapter, because Mexican immigrant families have different prearrival experiences and varying degrees of literacy skills and socioeconomic and social status, their early experiences in the United States and their children's academic success also vary a great deal. The adaptive strategies adopted by new immigrants reflect their previous experiences, and this determines the pace of adaptation and its ultimate success. One of the least investigated strategies is the binational, bicultural approach to adaptation. Naturally, education is most important to Mexican families. In fact, some children are sent back to Mexico for their elementary education if their experience in American schools becomes unproductive or unbearable. Often, however, children from migrant families in the entire Southwest are known to experience absences from school in relation to their parents' unemployment cycles. There are important recent changes associated with the unemployment of immigrants; for example, the replacement of traditional farmworkers (those who started to come in the 1960s from central Mexico) by Mixtec or Mayan Indians aggressively recruited by *contratistas* (contractors) in Northern Mexico (seeking the cheapest hand labor for agricultural jobs in California). The least sophisticated new workers often tolerate the low pay and abuse because they need work. Although the rural Mexican population in the United States is only about 20 percent (although urban Mexican immigrants are the majority), many of the urban immigrants in the United States come from rural backgrounds and resort to networks and cultural traditions in the United States. The reality of their binational experience is most instrumental in their survival—judging from the testimonies of "repatriated" immigrants in Mexico.

Binational Lives

From the preliminary reports of repatriation studies, it seems that communication between family members on both sides of the border never stopped. The economic interdependency of members of the same family residing on either side of the border permitted them to engage in a resource exchange and the investment of modest capital to run small businesses. The use of both languages and cultures, as well as the use of capital and labor to support family ventures, continues to provide these families with new economic resources and higher social status. The conspicuous consumption that is discussed by Durand, Parrado, and Massey (1996) has important symbolic functions to mark success and build confidence in those who left Mexico. It is indeed an indirect repayment in respect that compensates the many degrading incidents suffered in the United States. In fact, families and their networks on both sides of the border create the most efficient informal social insurance that provides small cash and emotional support to any person in trouble, with the implied commitment that eventually all will have to reciprocate in kind when crisis or need arises. The penalty for not complying with this reciprocal obligation is to be abandoned by the family and network on both sides of the border. Children, as they grow up and become fully bilingual, are an integral part of the network, and they are often called on to play a role as interpreters and assistants. During important life events, all these relationships are played out and ritually sanctioned with religious ceremonies during baptisms, weddings, funerals, and so on. Also, during certain celebrations (patron saint festivities, Day of the Dead, and so on) relatives get together on either side of the border to renew their commitment to help. An intergenerational agreement is always renewed and, more recently, women play a major role in these events, because in many instances, they have become the financial experts for the family.

In order to understand better the nature of the binational experience and the lives of the increasing number of repatriated workers in Mexican towns, research centers in Mexico (for example at the University of Colima and at the Tamaulipas Research Center) are collecting substantial data. The following questions greatly intrigue researchers in Mexico:

1. What is the nature of the process of ethnic and social reidentification of the inner self and repatriated workers' consciousness about their increased social status relative to peers who did not work in the United States?
2. What is their socioeconomic level, especially if it is associated with earnings sent from the United States by themselves or their family?
3. What fundamental changes in values and lifestyle are evident, and what is the relationship of such changes to their experience in the United States?
4. What is the impact of their experience in the United States for their participation in the political system of the *municipio*?

Binational, bicultural existence is a fact that is increasing everyday both in central Mexico and in the southwestern United States. This phenomenon seems to be an adaptive strategy for surviving the economic and psychological hardships alluded to by Suárez-Orozco and Suárez-Orozco (1995a, 1995b), Hondagneu-Sotelo (1994), and Trueba, Rodríguez, Zou, and Cintrón (1993) associated with the experience of working and living in the United States, often in poverty and under oppression. The expected benefits of schooling in this country are often wiped out by the early dropout of Mexican youth and their exposure to gangs and drugs. However, Rose (1995) warns us about the neglected beneficial impact on the families of those individuals exposed to schools—even with a limited exposure—and about the extraordinary success of minority students in some schools. Martin and Taylor (1996, 6) suggest that in some rural towns agricultural labor is divided into a three-tiered labor force; the smallest portion of workers, 14 percent, work year-round; 20 percent are long-season local workers, and 66 percent are peak-season migrants. However, there is a great deal of networking across rural-urban continua within the families of immigrants. In Migrant Town, for example, most of the second-generation children who reached high school work in urban areas, in spite of the fact that they were born into migrant Mexican families. I suspect that there is an overall career ladder starting from the lowest paid jobs in the rural United States to better-paying skilled labor, to professional jobs and businesses. The mobility from rural to urban within the United States may be within one generation in most cases (Trueba 1997; and personal interviews in central California). The creative entrepreneurs that repatriate permanently in Mexico, or continue their binational existence, are intimately connected to the flow of "migradollars" sent to Mexico.

Economic entrepreneurship and a strong sense of belonging in a community are important factors for a successful adaptation of Mexican immigrants, but in the long range educational level is a necessary condition for social upward mobility and greater economic power. High academic achievement, however, is possible if we pay attention to what Sonia Díaz Salcedo (1996) discovered in her study. She states, "They spoke at length about the issues they faced with their parents or guardians, and the impact that their relationships at home have had on their success in school. The themes that surfaced were: resilience and survival, relating to family, the importance of connecting with the culture and ethnicity, developing a sense of responsibility and independence, communication, and spirituality or religious affiliation" (Díaz Salcedo 1996, 129). Díaz Salcedo describes how students spoke lovingly of their parents who gave them a "loving and caring home life that provided what they perceived as a supportive environment."

These students were appreciative and grateful for their parents. They stated that they valued the support, the love, and the nurturing that they received from their parents. Additionally, they claimed that they felt fortunate that their parents supported them and provided constant encouragement. In some specific cases, students spoke of the sacrifices made by their mothers in the way they provided a caring, nurturing home for them. This is consistent with the perception of hardships articulated by mothers during the years they had to work and take care of their children. In the Díaz Salcedo study, however, not all of the families of successful students were ideal and exemplary. Those students whose families were less than ideal, found other sources of support. Their resourcefulness led them to find the support of "surrogate" parents and to find within themselves and their school environment additional support through a strong spiritual life, a strong belief in God, and trust in various church groups. In all cases "the students also formed their ideas about resilience and survival in the context of their home lives. In turn, they had made the connection to parental support or lack of support in discussing their success at school. For all of them it appeared to be important for someone to say that 'they matter.' In many cases this 'someone' was the mother; in other cases it was someone at school or in their lives outside of school or home" (Díaz Salcedo 1996, 131).

In the end, students were aware that they had not chosen their family, but they had many choices open to them; they felt in control of their future. All felt a close emotional connection with their Latino culture, which was "implicit in certain dynamics, and tended to be more explicit in their home contexts" (Díaz Salcedo 1996, 132). These findings are congruent with the work of Carola and Marcelo Suárez-Orozco (1995a, 1995b) and with the work I did in central California regarding the unique role that a strong ethnic affiliation plays in the maintenance of the motivation to achieve in school.

References

Delgado-Gaitan, C. "Russian Refugee Families: Accommodating Aspirations through Education." *Anthropology and Education Quarterly* 25, no. 2 (1994): 137–155.

Deyhle, D., and F. Margonis. "Navajo Mothers and Daughters: Schools, Jobs, and the Family." *Anthropology and Education Quarterly* 16, no. 2 (1995): 135–167.

Díaz Salcedo, S. "Successful Latino Students at the High School Level: A Case Study of Ten Students." An analytical paper presented to the Faculty of the

Graduate School of Education of Harvard University, in partial fulfillment of the requirements for the degree of Doctor of Education, 1996.

Durán, R. *Hispanics' Education and Background: Predictors of College Achievement.* New York: College Entrance Board Publications, 1983.

Durand, J., E. Parrado, and D. S. Massey. "Migradollars and Development: A Reconsideration of the Mexican Case." *International Migration Review* 30, no. 2 (1996): 423–444.

Freire, P. *Pedagogy of the Oppressed.* New York: Seabury, 1973.

———. *Pedagogy of Hope. Reliving Pedagogy of the Oppressed.* New York: Continuum, 1995.

Freire, P., and D. Macedo. *Literacy: Reading the Word and Reading the World.* Critical Studies in Education Series. Boston: Bergin and Garvey Publishers, 1987.

Garcia, V. *Surviving Farm Work: Economic Strategies of Mexican and Mexican American Households in a Rural California Community.* Doctoral dissertation. Anthropology Department, University of California at Santa Barbara, 1992.

Giroux, N., and P. McLaren. *Between Borders: Pedagogy and the Politics of Cultural Studies.* New York and London: Routledge, 1994.

González Baker, S., F. D. Bean, A. Escobar Latapí, and S. Weintraub. "U.S. Immigration Policies and Trends: The Growing Importance of Migration from Mexico." In M. M. Suárez-Orozco (ed.), *Crossings: Mexican Immigration in Interdisciplinary Perspectives.* Cambridge, Mass.: Harvard University Press and David Rockefeller Center for Latin American Studies, 1998, 79–105.

Gutierrez, K. "How Talk, Context, and Script Shape Contexts for Learning: A Cross-Case Comparison of Journal Sharing." *Linguistics and Education* 5 (1994): 335–365.

Guiterrez, K., J. Larson, and B. Kreuter. "Cultural Tensions in the Scripted Classroom: The Value of the Subjugated Perspective." *Urban Education* 29, no. 4 (1995): 410–442.

Hondagneu-Sotelo, P. *Gendered Transitions: Mexican Experiences of Immigration.* Berkeley: University of California Press, 1994.

Leistyna, P., A. Woodrum, and S. Sherblom, eds. *Breaking Free: The Transformative Power of Ctirical Pedagogy. Harvard Educational Review Reprint Series No. 27,* 1996.

Martin, P., and E. Taylor. "Immigration and the Changing Face of Rural California: Summary Report of the Conference Held at Asilomar, June 12–14, 1995." Unpublished manuscript.

Mason, J. "History of Santa Barbara and Ventura Counties, California." In W. A. Tompkins (ed.), reproduction of Thompsons and West's *History of Santa Barbara and Ventura Counties, California, with Illustrations and Biographical Sketches of Its Prominent Men and Pioneers.* Thomas H. Thompson and Albert A. West (eds.). Berkeley, Calif.: Howell North Books, 1883.

Myers, D. "Dimensions of Economic Adaptation by Mexican-origin Men." In M. M. Suárez-Orozco (ed.), *Crossings: Mexican Immigration in Interdisciplinary Perspectives.* Cambridge, Mass.: Harvard University Press and David Rockefeller Center for Latin American Studies, 1998, 157–200.

Palerm, J. V. "Cross-Cultural Medicine a Decade later: A Season in the Life of a Migrant Farm Worker in California." *The Western Journal of Medicine* 157 (1992).

————. *Immigrant and Migrant Farm Workers in the Santa Maria Valley, California.* Center for Chicano Studies and Department of Anthropology. University of California, Santa Barbara. Sponsored by the Center for Survey Methods Research, Bureau of the Census, Washington, D.C., 1994.

Palerm, J. V., and J. I. Urquiola. "A Binational System of Agricultural Production: The Case of the Mexican Bajío and California." In D. G. Aldrich Jr. and L. Meyer (eds.), *Mexico and the United States: Neighbors in Crises.* U.C. Mexus Conference Proceedings. Los Angeles, Calif.: The Borgo Press, 1993, 311–367.

Patthey-Chavez, G. "High School as an Arena for Cultural Conflict and Acculturation for Latino Angelinos." *Anthropology and Education Quarterly* 24, no. 1 (1993): 33–60.

Portes, A., ed. *The New Second Generation.* New York: Russell Sage Foundation, 1996.

Rose, M. *The Promise of Public Education in America: Possible Lives.* New York and London: Penguin Books, 1995.

Suárez-Orozco, C., and M. Suárez-Orozco. *Transformations: Immigration, Family Life and Achievement Motivation among Latino Adolescents.* Stanford, Calif.: Stanford University Press, 1995a.

————. "Migration: Generational Discontinuities and the Making of Latino Identities." L. Romanucci-Ross and G. DeVos (eds.), *Ethnic Identity: Creation, Conflict, and Accommodation.* 3d ed. Walnut Creek, Calif.: Alta Mira Press, 1995b, 321–347.

Suárez-Orozco, M. M. "California Dreaming: Proposition 187 and the Cultural Psychology of Racial and Ethnic Exclusion." *Anthropology and Education Quarterly* 27, no. 2 (1996): 151–167.

————. "State Terrors: Immigrants and Refugees in the Post-National Space." In Y. Zou and H. T. Trueba (eds.), *Ethnic Identity and Power: Cultural Contexts and Political Action in School and Society.* New York: SUNY Press, 1998.

Trueba, H. T. "A Mexican Immigrant Community in Central California." Unpublished manuscript. Harvard University, 1997.

Trueba, H. T., C. Rodríguez, Y. Zou, and J. Cintrón. *Healing Multicultural America: Mexican Immigrants Rise to Power in Rural California.* London: Falmer Press, 1993.

Valencia, R., ed. *Chicano School Failure: An Analysis Through Many Windows.* London: Falmer Press, 1991.

Vigil, D. "Chicano Gangs: One Response to Mexican Urban Adaptation in the Los Angeles Area." *Urban Anthropology* 12, no. 1 (1983): 45–75.

————. "Group Processes and Street Identity: Adolescent Chicano Gang Members." *Journal for the Society for Psychological Anthropology, ETHOS* 16, no. 4 (1988): 421–444.

————. *Barrio Gangs.* Austin: University of Texas Press, 1989.

————. *Personas Mexicanas: Chicano High Schoolers in a Changing Los Angeles. Case Studies in Cultural Anthropology.* Series editors George Spindler and Louise Spindler. Forth Worth, Philadelphia, San Diego: Harcourt Brace College Publishers, 1997.

Wilson, P. "Trauma of Sioux Indian High School Students." *Anthropology and Education Quarterly* 22, no. 4 (1991): 367–383.

5

Critical Ethnography and a Vygotskian Pedagogy of Hope: The Case of Mexican Immigrant Children

We could argue that in a strictly historical sense, the first critical ethnography was constructed in 1542 by an oppressed Indian, Francisco Tenamaztle, who had led the revolt against the Spaniards in the states of Jalisco, Michoacán, and Colima in central Mexico. He was captured and exiled to Spain, where, assisted by Fray Cristóbal de las Casas, he defended the human rights of all the Indians by stating,

> Los indios tienen por ley natural, divina y humana, [el derecho] de los hacer pedazos [a los blancos barbudos], si fuerzas y armas tuvieren, y echarlos de sus tierras.
>
> The Indians have, by natural and divine law, [the right] to cut in pieces [the white bearded], if they [the Indians] had the strength and weapons, and to throw them [the bearded whites] away from their land. (Cited in León-Portilla 1995, 30)

In a more technical sense, critical ethnography has deep theoretical roots in psychological anthropology and was later refined in sociology and philosophy by the seminal work of Paulo Freire. The ideal of early anthropologists to improve the schooling and overall human development of all children was revealed in a conference held at Stanford University on June 9–14, 1954, organized by George Spindler. Renown scholars such as Solom T. Kimball, Alfred L. Kroeber, Dorothy Lee, Margaret Mead, Felix M. Keesing, John Gillin, and Cora DuBois shared their concerns relating to the overall development of all children, the preparation of ethnically diverse children, and the need to pursue pedagogically appropriate methods of teaching (G. Spindler 1955). Why is critical ethnography a significant methodological tool, and what is its relationship to Vygotskian theories of cognitive development and adequate pedagogies for teaching Mexican immigrant children? The task of these pages is precisely to answer these questions, which are of critical importance in current national demographic, political, and economic contexts.

As Suárez-Orozco points out, the United States is experiencing national hardship. There exists a widespread job insecurity and a crisis in family values. Anxieties have focused on immigrants and refugees, who are blamed for our problems and our deep and "terrifying sense of home-less-ness" (Suárez-Orozco 1998: 283–319). How can critical ethnography help document the educational problems of Mexican children and the successes obtained, and how can teachers move from ethnographic accounts to constructive pedagogies that lead children to lasting empowerment. Indeed, to understand better the relationship between ethnographic research and pedagogical praxis, it is essential to examine the fundamental character of empowerment from a pedagogical standpoint as the successful acquisition of higher level cognitive skills that permit children to learn effectively in school. A pedagogy of hope is only possible if educators can go beyond the rhetoric of critical discourse into a deeper understanding of intellectual development (Vygotsky 1962, 1978) as the means to break the cycle of underachievement and oppression, away from hegemonic instructional structures.

In an age of rapid migration flows and a new postnational existence, Mexican immigrants explore economic and cultural survival strategies on both sides of the border in their continued pattern of binational existence. This strategy brings them a measure of stability and security (at least for a while) and provides them with the necessary emotional support to cement their characteristic long-term resiliency as immigrants. It can also give children the opportunity to receive some schooling, in spite of their nomadic residential patterns. The fact that so many of these children succeed in our schools may be linked to factors that enhance their successful binational adaptation.

In Mexican families, women have been stereotyped as passive followers of the male head of household, often depicted as victims, unable to organize themselves as a collective force. In reality, from my study in Migrant Town, I was confronted with an entirely different reality. I discovered women in the workplace as able and resilient as men. I met women in schools and found them capable of articulating their concerns and pursuing forcefully the fulfillment of their children's needs. When I examined specific cases of physical abuse by males, I also became aware of the assertive behavior and complete determination of women to demand respect and protection. As the year went by I came to realize that women held power in the most crucial areas of the life of the family. They controlled the budget (bank accounts, decisions on significant purchases—such as cars, a house, clothing, etc.) and controlled the moves to and from their village of origin. These decisions were crucial because they had consequences for the life of the entire family, especially schoolchildren. Given the insecurity of agricultural employment and other social and religious obligations, traveling back to Mexico was a very important decision for all. Finally, another area of women's power within the family was associated with their legal status and citizenship. It was the women who organized study groups to prepare for the examination to become a U.S. citizen. It was also the women who first became citizens and persuaded the males to do likewise. Women, however, had another very important role. They were responsible for maintaining the Spanish language and Mexican culture within the home and the community. This role, as in other communities, has been part of a long-term adaptive strategy of Mexican immigrant families (Hondagneu-Sotelo 1994; Trueba 1997). Many factors contribute to the retention of the Spanish language—the critical mass of immigrants who speak the language, the frequent visits to home towns and cities, and the interdependence among the families living on both sides of the border. To maintain the home language and culture women took a strong interest in the formation of extended networks. The organization of functional networks of family members and friends has been most instrumental in the survival of immigrant Mexican families during difficult economic times, but it has also served as a very strong emotional support system to retain an ethnic Mexican identity in the face of the traumas alluded to by the Suárez-Orozcos (1995a, 1995b, 1998). The substantial, although informal financial cooperative system can also become a powerful political base for demanding respect for their educational rights, as was the case in Central California (Trueba 1997). Organizations that had a religious character in the Mexican tradition become a strong political enclave and support system in immigrants' adaptation to this country (Trueba, Rodríguez, Zou, and Cintrón 1993). In fact, the only way for these families to engage in long-term economic ventures (buying land in Mexico, purchasing homes in the United States, and so on) is through the collective security of the family networks on both sides of the border, their collective savings, and their commitment to assist one another in times of crisis. The skills to survive emotionally and economically in the worst of situations continue to be a unique characteristic of many immigrant families, who strategically invest every possible resource they may find. These resources are often obtained through their binational networks. This "know-how" that Freire called "knowing the world," in contrast with literacy as "knowing the word," is often the key factor in the survival and adaptation of the immigrant family on both sides of the border. We, immigrants and children of immigrants, are now the ethnographers and must face the difficult task of coming to terms with our own identity crises as well as with conducting serious, scientific, and credible research. We have to deal with conflicts between our personal loyalties as members of ethnic communities and members of an elite of social scientists (see discussion of S. Villenas's ideas [1996] in Chapter 1). S. Villenas's most important insight regarding ethnic ethnographers is that we, the new generation of ethnic or native ethnographers, must learn to work within our own people and must face the ambiguities about our own collective histories and identities to make sure we do not perpetuate the hegemonic relationships of people in academia who have engaged in oppressive discourses of "othering" (1996, 729). Critical ethnographic practice demands a conscious realization of the risks and epistemological challenges all researchers, including ethnic researchers, must face.

What is Critical Ethnography?

A modern concept of critical ethnography as a research methodology stresses the notion that all education is intrinsically political (Freire 1973, 1995; Carspecken 1996), and consequently critical ethnography must advocate for the oppressed by (1) documenting the nature of oppression, (2) documenting the process of empowerment—a journey away from oppression, (3) accelerating the conscientization of the oppressed and the oppressors—without this reflective awareness of the rights and obligations of humans there is no way to conceptualize empowerment, equity, and a struggle of liberation, (4) sensitizing the research community to the implications of research for the quality of life—clearly linking intellectual work to real-life conditions, and (5) reaching a higher level of understanding of the historical, political, sociological, and economic factors supporting the abuse of power and oppression, of neglect and disregard for human rights, and of the mechanisms to learn and internalize rights and obligations. Ultimately, what this means is that there is an intimate relationship between the intellectual activity of research and the *praxis* of the daily life of researchers. Praxis (in Freire's sense of political commitment to struggle for liberation and in defense of human rights) is the ultimate goal of critical ethnography. Yes, this praxis must encompass a global and cross-cultural commitment to advocate for the rights of all humankind and, thus, to create human solidarity against oppression (Freire 1973, 1995). For most critical theorists, oppression is not only the result of class struggle but the result of structural elements perpetuated through cultural patterns leading to the perpetuation of economic, political, and other semiotic systems that violate human rights, especially the right to learn. Culture comes into the picture, not only from the standpoint of the oppressor's lifestyle, values, and the assumptions of "superiority" over "others" but as a socially structured set of relationships, expectations, and accepted practices. Ultimately, culture "justifies" the presumed "rights" of the oppressor to perpetuate his or her position of power over the oppressed and rationalizes the role of the oppressed in his or her own oppression. However, we must change our definitions of culture. What is culture? What is not culture?

In the early 1960s the classical definitions of culture included a complex set of values, traditions, lifestyle, and behavior patterns characterizing particular human groups and distinguishing them from one another; furthermore, culture was observable and transmitted from one generation to another. In the late 1960s and early 1970s culture became an integral part of the *cognitive revolution* that explored various conceptual configurations. Under the editorship of George Spindler the *American Anthropologist Journal* published a number of new methodological studies: *Ethnoscience, Ethno-Semantics, The Ethnography of Law, Ethno-Botany, Ethno-Linguistics,* and so forth. The new generation of linguist-ethnographers transformed ethnographic research into a very sophisticated instrument via discourse analysis in the study of diverse cultures. These studies became cross-cultural and more detached from any implications for praxis. Comparative cross-cultural ethnographic approaches are not all critical. They become "critical" only when their goal, ultimate purpose, direction, and expected outcomes are the *praxis* of the ethnographer, that is, a praxis of equity, a commitment for life to pursue equity and to struggle for the liberation of all humankind through ethnographic research. Yes, critical ethnography is advocacy oriented, but not all advocacy research is critical. This is one of the crucial elements of critical ethnography; one could say that its raison d'être is to transform society via conscientization and social change.

There are serious challenges involved in doing critical ethnographic research as a means of inquiry and as a means of transformation. In fact some view it as inherently "colonizing" and "exploitative." In some sense all social science research is suspected of being hegemonic, colonizing, and even of objectifying people while it attempts to understand them. "This contradiction (between ethnography's 'exemplary

status' and its 'colonial nature') instantiates the more generalized social division of intellectual and manual labor . . . [whereby] research is
posited only as the professional activity of the privileged minority"
(DeGenova 1997, 1). The historical changes in the concept of culture,
from something out there to observe to something in people's heads,
or cognitive configurations, affected anthropology, linguistics, and
psychology (Shweder 1996, 25). It moved the emphasis from observed
behavior to the study of language as a window for understanding cognitive structures. In other words, what Shweder calls "mental-state language" dealing with beliefs, desires, plans, wants, emotions, goals,
feelings, and so on, revealed a code and set of values that permitted
ethnographers to make inferences. Ethnographers had to use mental-
state language as accessible and public experiences (rather than inaccessible and private experiences) subject to external and intersubjective
interpretation (Shweder 1996, 26).

The two revolutions, the "cognitive revolution," which was "pro-
mentalistic," and the reaction against solipsism, which was antimen-
talistic, became compatible in the practice of ethnography conceptualized as an interpretive study of behavior sanctionable by members of
a community (a "moral community" according to Shweder). In other
words, ethnography is seen as the interpretive act of discourse and
praxis about beliefs, desires, and other mental-state language to render
observed behavior intelligible. This is clearly an effort to cross-cultural
(and cognitive) boundaries. Informants' reports about their own behavior are neither necessary nor sufficient to construct hypotheses
about observed behavior. We know that culture is acquired by doing,
acting, in praxis, and that it is through transmission that we manage
to change and recreate our configurations of culture and values. Ultimately, culture is the set of principles or norms of behavior exhibited
in everyday life and everyday evaluative discourse, beginning in the
small moral community of the family. The cohesiveness of a moral
community is maintained through "evaluative discourse," which reflects the agreed-upon norms of behavior. But in the context of several
moral communities in contact (as is the case of pluralistic societies),
there are many evaluative discourses and plural sets of principles,
norms, and value systems. The prevalence of one evaluative discourse
means oppression; freedom from evaluative discourses means liberation. Awareness of plural discourses is the start in the struggle for liberation because it facilitates the acquisition of "emancipatory knowledge." McLaren and da Silva feel that "emancipatory knowledge is
never realized fully, but is continually dreamed, continually revived,
and continually transformed in the heart of our memories, the flames
of our longing and the passion of our struggle" (1993, 59). Critical eth-

nography permits us to get into the emancipatory knowledge that motivates ethnic minority students' resistance to the dominant culture in America. By retaining their ethnic identity they feel empowered to resist racial and ethnic prejudicial policies and practices. Critical ethnography also permits us to reexamine cultural hegemony and the nature of cultural conflict as a drama taking place right in the classroom via reflection on historical factors of ethnic and racial legitimacy, reproduction of the social order, and the right to a voice in one's own language (Leistyna, Woodrum, and Sherblom 1996, 334).

The study of ethnic identity from a cultural perspective is central to critical ethnography and inherently problematic. The ethnographer is not only caught in between his own world of perceptions, assumptions, and biases about the "ethnic others" but involved in a complex process of making sense of rituals, routines, and actions that may have many possible interpretations and consequently many sociopolitical dimensions. An ethnographer does not discover and simply describe ethnic cultures from the outside. In order to make sense of an ethnic culture the ethnographer must enter this culture, or must enter the minds of those others to make appropriate inferences about meaning. This requires a great deal of reflection, experience, and analytical insightfulness. An ethnographer soon discovers that one's own reality is framing the perception of the "other" cultures and determining basic interpretations of peoples' behaviors. Therefore, one can argue that an ethnographer's membership in an ethnic group is an asset because it can help in the interpretation of peoples' behaviors, especially in the identification of strategies for survival and attributes of resilience often misleading even to trained observers.

Critical ethnography, however, requires the difficult task of documenting oppression or exploitation not only from the perspective of the victims but also from that of the oppressors. The complementarity of the roles and behaviors exhibited by both oppressors and oppressed can explain the organization of given structural settings in which oppressive conditions perpetuate inequities. By the same token, emancipatory roles and strategies of victims who acquire additional tools for breaking hegemonic relationships go beyond political processes and lead us to a better understanding of complex cultural and cognitive processes that require serious psychological analysis. Hence the need to interrelate critical ethnography as a tool for unraveling oppressive encounters with pedagogical approaches to facilitate development of higher mental functions (or the conditions in which such functions best develop, according to Vygotsky's developmental theories that link social and cognitive processes). In the end, the empowerment is cultural and cognitive, before it becomes political. These pages attempt to make the case for a complementary relationship between critical ethnography and a pedagogical approach to empowerment from the developmental perspective of Vygotsky's theory of assisted performance. But in order to focus on this relationship, it is necessary first to document what critical ethnography has revealed about oppression in the case of Mexican immigrants. Following this section, we will focus on the Vygotskian approach to empowerment, that is, a pedagogy of hope focused on the acquisition of higher mental functions of Mexican children in the classroom.

We have seen in Chapter 2 the magnitude of the educational problems faced by Mexican immigrant children as reflected in dropout rates, educational achievement, and segregation patterns. A brief historical account (Menchaca and Valencia 1990) reminds us of the historical character and biases that explain such neglect since the mid-nineteenth century. The work of these demographers suggests that Mexican immigration is here to stay, will continue growing at a rapid pace, and will lead to the "browning" of North America. For as long as the economic incentives continue, the stream of immigrants from Mexico—the single largest continental proportion of legal immigrants (38 percent) and other 80 percent of undocumented immigrants—will continue. These basic facts must be explained in the context of continued backlash against immigrants (Suárez-Orozco in press). Mexican immigrants will continue to hold on to a deceiving perception of progress without fully realizing the impact of exploitation. Their children will feel and perceive more accurately the impact of exploitation.

Indeed, immigrants' periodical visits to their villages of origin to celebrate the patron saints of *los hijos abandonados* ("the abandoned children"), or *los hijos olvidados* ("the forgotten children") as they are called in Mexico by their *paisanos* ("country men"), will confirm their fantasy of success by permitting them to display some wealth conspicuously, to show their new trucks and good clothes, and to spend money for their *paisanos*. M. Suárez-Orozco's suggestion that immigrants do not see their new life in terms of the ideals of the majority society but in terms of the "old culture" is very accurate (Suárez-Orozco and Suárez-Orozco 1995b, 325).

Adaptive Responses of Mexican Immigrants

A number of ethnographers have dealt with the adaptation problems of immigrant children in the context of the school environment (Trueba 1987; Trueba, Jacobs, and Kirton 1990; Delgado-Gaitan and Trueba 1991; Wilson 1991; Trueba, Cheng, and Ima 1993; Trueba, Rodríguez,

Zou, and Cintrón 1993; Patthey-Chavez 1993; Trueba and Zou 1994; Gutierrez 1994; Delgado-Gaitan 1994; Deyhle and Margonis 1995; Gutierrez, Larson, and Kreuter 1995; Bartolomé 1996; Bartolomé and Macedo 1997; Trueba 1997; Zou and Trueba 1998). Often these scholars use critical theory in an effort to design "transformative" strategies for teachers and students (based on Freire 1973, 1995, scholars such as Giroux and McLaren 1994; Freire and Macedo 1987, 1996; and McLaren 1995, 1997). The efforts, however, have not clarified the transition from an ethnographic or ethnohistorical account of oppression to a pedagogy of hope in the context of teaching and learning, and thus assisting children to acquire critical thinking skills that will prepare them to be fully in control of their lives, without forcing them to lose their ethnic and cultural identities. Some of the accounts of liberation in a culturally congruent way are genuinely Vygotskian in nature and open the door to what I have called a "Vygotskian pedagogy of hope" anchored in the research process.

Immigrants' adaptive responses vary according to their prearrival experiences. For example, the key factors determining the educational success of Mexican families are related to the prearrival socioeconomic, cultural, and political experiences that determine their skills for handling the traumas they face in the United States after their arrival. Let me be more specific. There is a process called marginalization often associated with conspicuous poverty and isolation in the new country. The lack of communication with individuals who speak their variety of Spanish and deal with issues similar to those the immigrants handled in Mexico creates a vacuum of support and a deep sense of anxiety over expectations and norms of appropriate behavior. Poverty is associated with the nature of the work, often inherently unstable and low-paying; another source of poverty is the family left behind in Mexico which, because of urgent needs, expects money to be sent regularly. Furthermore, immigrants often incur debts in order to pay the costs of going north to find employment.

Another factor affecting the adaptive strategies of Mexican immigrants is their degree of literacy (in a broad Freirean sense), that is, their understanding of complex social systems and their ability to handle text related to those systems (contracts, government documents, banks, hospitals, immigration office, etc.). The marginalization of many Mexican families started long before they arrived in this country. Their naive notions about the politics of employment, the organization of schools, and the demands of society reflect more a change from a rural to an urban setting, above and beyond the change from one country to another. Of course, the added dimension in this country is that in order to acquire the necessary sociopolitical knowledge of appropriate conduct in urban settings, immigrants must first acquire the communicative skills to do so in a second language. To compound the problem, immigrants often take jobs that are exhaustive and leave them little time to acquire communicative skills in English. The consequences for the children of immigrants is that soon they are forced to play adult rules in making momentous decisions for their parents, because the children know some English and understand the social system a bit better.

The political, economic, and educational consequences of this phenomenon require a massive, serious, and long-term interdisciplinary approach. California and Texas are the focus of intensive Mexican immigration, a population that is now more than ever segregated and neglected. As a consequence, Mexicans become rapidly marginalized and show their enduring high dropout rates. The ethnographer is not only an advocate for immigrant children but must discover the rich cultural and linguistic capital of the immigrant family and the optimal use of the cultural and linguistic resources available to children in their own home environments.

The marginalization of Mexican youth is related to their uprooting from their home communities and the rejection they feel in school. Consequently, for them to engage in learning relationships with teachers and more knowledgeable peers (in a Vygotskian sense) is culturally repugnant and the equivalent of siding with the oppressor. They see their parents being abused at work and they don't buy the notion that the family is better off in the United States. Whereas the point of reference for their parents is Mexico, the point of reference of the youth is not Mexico but what they see in this country. The marginalization and exploitation of their parents may have begun in Mexico, but the resistance to exploitation is an integral part of the self-definition of immigrant youth. Parents' naive notions about the politics of employment, organization and politics in schools, their perception of societal demands for cultural homogenization, and the acceptance of an inferior status are not shared by their children, who feel an ethical responsibility to react and fight back. Much of what happens in gang struggles is related to marginalization (Vigil 1989, 1997).

Furthermore, from a Vygotskian perspective, Mexican immigrant children who are socialized in a new linguistic and cultural environment cannot get the assistance that is congruent with their zones of proximal development and their linguistic and cognitive skills. Thus their development slows down considerably. This fact has important pedagogical implications for an educational reform that recognizes the need to prepare teachers capable of teaching culturally different children. In spite of the health problems of young mothers and children, most immigrant children adapt well in the United States and receive services that in their parents' villages are not readily available. However, in certain communities of the West Coast, pesticides and other toxic substances continue to cause serious problems in children's health and education. The most serious problem faced by the children of immigrants on the West Coast is the alienating experience of transitioning from the local Mexican community middle school to the mainstream high school in a nearby city. Schooling in that city brings a rapid marginalization of these children, and this adds to their confusion regarding personal identity, cultural values, social acceptance, their ability to achieve, and their overall self-worth. This is not surprising if we consider the recent research conducted by the Suárez-Orozcos (C. Suárez-Orozco and M. Suárez-Orozco 1995a and 1995b; M. Suárez-Orozco 1996) showing how immigrant children's learning ability and social skills deteriorate the longer they are exposed to American society's alienating environment. This environment seems to undermine their overall school achievement and adaptation to society. The traumatic experience of being uprooted and the confusion about family values, personal survival, and the need for peer support are bound to lead many youths to become affiliated with gangs and to disregard the codes of behavior prescribed by mainstream society. No wonder Mexican families frequently resort to the extreme decision of taking back their children to Mexico in an attempt to salvage their moral character. These families perceive their life in small rural villages to be a great deal safer, more peaceful and orderly. Life in a large metropolis in Mexico may be just as dangerous as in the United States. There are cases when the entire family returns to Mexico in order to reeducate teenagers in the family's values. In contrast with the alienation Mexican immigrant children experience in major cities such as Los Angeles, Chicago, New York, and Houston, those children who live in settings where they can retain their home language and culture and their familiar cultural institutions and networks seem to survive the trauma of schooling in the United States (Trueba 1997). This, of course, is the result of a carefully executed plan of education engineered primarily by the mothers, who monitor schooling and defend their language and culture by creating vast networks on both sides of the border, thus supporting their children's strong Mexican identity and their ability to live in a binational and bicultural world. It is also an example of the dual frame of reference enforced by the nature of the intermittent employment patterns in the United States, which has to be supplemented by either self-employment or temporary assistance from relatives and friends in Mexico. Needless to say, this binational pattern offers unique opportunities to renew social networks and cultural values. This pattern of binational adaptation fits the "postnational space" alluded to by M. Suárez-Orozco (1998), meaning "the vacuum that is created when social spaces are subverted, reconfigured, and reconstituted." As one of my colleagues in Colima stated, "the center of Comala [a small municipality of Colima] is in Pomona, California." That is, the political and economic power of Comala is vested in the individuals who reside permanently in Pomona, California, but maintain a very close communication with the town and municipality of Comala, own properties there, and exert considerable control over the major sociopolitical processes. Ethnicity and cultural identity are no longer grounded on a specific territory; they are as movable as the individuals that migrate from one place to another. On the one hand, Mexican immigrants no longer fit either in the United States or in Mexico, because they have become a permanent group of networks and relationships that extend on both sides of the border beyond any particular piece of land. Hence the difficulty faced by both Mexican and North American governments in attempting to formulate policies to control immigration and naturalization. It is not that U.S. immigration policy attempts to protect employers who oppress Mexicans, or that it condones the free flow of populations across the border without legal documents. It is a policy fundamentally based on one side of the border, without any recognition of the postnational space immigrants have created for themselves as the most effective adaptive strategy to economic instability and bicultural influences. Hence the insightful observation of Suárez-Orozco when he calls these immigrants "ghost workers," who are there when we need them as cheap laborers and ignored as mere phantoms when their needs and those of their children come to haunt us. "The ghost workers must at once 'be there' (to do the impossible jobs) but not be there (be voiceless and transparent)" (Suárez-Orozco 1998:301).

What is the role of schools in the face of such a crisis? What are the structural (economic, political, and educational) barriers behind school failure in Mexican children? Under what conditions is the academic achievement of Mexican children improving? What are the consequences of the increasing lack of cultural sensitivity and the cancellation of affirmative action efforts? These questions cannot be examined in detail here, but they provide additional incentives for looking into the education of Mexican children with a sense of urgency and commitment. There are, however, two important statistical facts that must be presented in advance: (1) the rapid growth of Mexican student enrollments over the last twenty-five years, and (2) Mexican students' increasing segregation.

Education and Empowerment of Mexican Immigrants

Immigrant families commit to educational excellence, because they believe that their economic survival ultimately depends on their children's education. They believe a good education in the United States will create future opportunities. In Chapter 4 we saw what Consuelo had to suffer in order to become a strong advocate for her children's education. Naturally, it is not enough to have parents like Consuelo. Schoolteachers also play a pivotal role in students' academic achievement. What is significant here is that students acquire, through very similar types of assisted performance on the one hand, the skills to cope with school (in interaction with their parents) and the motivation to achieve, and on the other hand, the knowledge and cognitive skills that translate into high achievement (in interaction with Mexican or Chicano teachers). The following is an example of this kind of interaction between children and their teacher, Mr. Villegas.

Mr. Villegas, the Fourth Grade Teacher

The elementary school in Migrant Town has 760 children (98 percent Mexican—about half of them born in Mexico and the other, children of recent immigrants from Mexico). The fourth grade teacher, Mr. Jorge Villegas, is at least six feet tall, dark brown, and perfectly fluent in Spanish and in English. His father a famous *matón* (literally translated "a killer" or a tough guy) came from Mexico during the 1960s and became one of the most feared and respected Mexicans in the region. He was known to be fair and quiet, but always armed and dangerous if attacked. Jorge was the youngest of three children, kind and given to poetry, math, and music. He likes teaching and does it well. He has received a number of awards, has been featured in the local papers, and is the most popular teacher in the elementary school. He opens his class with loud ranchero music, inviting all children to sing loud for a few minutes; then he makes them beg to start with math. Thus, the initial strategy is to involve all students in a group cultural activity, through rap music, banda, ranchera, hip/hop, R&B, and others. He creates a relaxed climate by using the children's Mexican nicknames *pulga* ("flee"—given to small children in an affectionate way), *mariposa* ("butterfly"), or in English, "Running Bear." Right after the music and initial greetings, he repeats as a mantra his daily "Nothing to it. Just do it," or its equivalent in Spanish, "*Orale, a darle.*" When the class is getting quiet and at certain occasions, Mr. Villegas uses his own poetry to inculcate in children the values of hard work, antidrug attitudes, antigang behavior, and of sacrifice for family and friends. In fact, if asked what he does (for example, in a social situation), Mr. Villegas may say half seriously, *Soy po-e-taaa* ("I am a po-e-t").

He is always proud of teaching at a level above the fourth grade and of doing it in his students' preferred language. He often gives his students the chance to go to the board and play with algebraic equations. The competition is tough, but he does not leave out a single student. The intensity of intellectual activity is the mark of his teaching. No one ever gets bored. His students excel not only in math but in writing and in most other subjects. Parents beg Mr. Villegas to take their children, putting pressure on the principal, if necessary. Jorge Villegas lives totally to teach and share with students. He retains control of the class at all times, although the classroom has the appearance of loud and free interaction. Two things become clear to all students: that "it is great to be in school" and "the use of either Spanish or English is equally acceptable as long as they know the subject."

During class, the intensity of the show and the strategically placed breaks to listen to music or to do other "fun" activities cannot distract a systematic observer from the seriousness of learning math, reading, and writing. Equally intense is the socialization of being proud to be Mexican. The theme in many of the songs Mr. Villegas plays is precisely this pride. The central topic in certain compositions is the pride of being Mexican, Chicano or Chicana, brown, and of being able to use two languages. Personally, Mr. Villegas is somewhat shy and distant. He is not close to his father, and he lives with his mother in a house whose mortgage he pays for. He describes himself as a *poeta*. Although he loves to perform in class (teach, sing, recite poems, act, etc.), he is a deeply sensitive person and often somewhat insecure and unsure of his talents. He is the best example I ever found of a teacher who can engage with children in learning transactions with absolute and profound knowledge of what the children know and how they function at every given minute. After an introduction to basic algebraic equations and a review of some procedures, he reviews negative numbers and replaces them with x and y as a transition to more difficult equations. He manages to select the people who are struggling with a concept, walk them through the concept, and set the stage for them to demonstrate their knowledge. Indeed, he uses the Vygotskian concept of assisted performance with unique mastery:

T: *A ver, ¿quién quiere pasar al pizarrón?* (Let's see, who is going to come to the blackboard? [The teacher scans the entire group as if he is looking for somebody in particular.] *A ver, a ver . . . Un calladito como . . . José, pasa al pizarrón* (Let me see, let me see . . . A quiet one like . . . José, go to the blackboard.) [José hesitantly gets up and goes to the blackboard.] *Escribe, $2x + 2x - 3y + y = 6$. ¿Puedes resolver esa ecuación?* (Write $2x + 2x - 3y + y = 6$. Can you solve that equation?) [José writes the ecuation and pauses.]

T: [Noticing some unrest among students who are anxious to go to the board, the Teacher says in a loud voice] *¡¡Callados todos!! Esperate José.* (Quiet all!! Wait José.) [The students are instantly quiet and wait.] *¿Puedes resolver la ecuación?* (Can you solve the equation?)

J: *Pos, no sé, pero . . . le haré la lucha.* (Well, I don't know, but . . . I will try.)

T: *Andale pues, puedes explicarlo en Español.* (Do it, then, you can explain it in Spanish.)

J: *$2x + 2x$ es $4x$. $-3y + y$ es $-2y$. Entónces, $4x - 2y = 6$.* ($2x + 2x$ is $4x$. $-3y + y$ is $-2y$. Then. $4x - 2y = 6$.)

T: *Explícalo y redúcelo más.* (Explain and reduce it further.)

J: *Puedo dividir por 2 los términos de la ecuación: $4x/2$ es $2x$; $-2y/2$ es $-y$. El resultado es: $2x - y = 3$.* (I can divide by 2 the terms of the equation: $4x/2$ is $2x$; $-2y/2$ is $-y$. The result is $2x - y = 3$.)

T: *Bien. ¿Si te digo que $x = 3$, cuál es valor de y?* (Good. If I tell you that $x = 3$, what is the value of y?)

J: *2 por 3, son 6, menos 3 son 3. $y = 3$.* (Two times 3 is 6, minus 3 is 3. $y = 3$.)

T: *¡Muy bien!* (Very good!) [The teacher smiles, proud of José's performance, and then announces]

T: *Siéntate, José* (sit down, José). I have a very difficult problem for all of you. If any of you can resolve it, you will receive *un premio grande* (a big prize). This is a math problem that nobody even in the fifth grade can resolve. But you are a very special class, and I know you will resolve it. [Then the teacher starts singing the mantra-type *"Cuarto año del 23, ¡gana siempre y otra vez!"* ("Fourth grade of room 23 always wins, and it will win once more!"), goes to the board, and writes the problem: $3y/ - 3x - 2y - 6x = ?$] You can work in teams. I will give you five minutes. [Students pick their groups as they have done before and start working individually within each group. The teacher walks around.]

Artemio, get to work. Help your group.

Alicia, ¿qué haces mi'jita? ¿Por qué no estás trabajando? (Alicia, what are you doing, my child? Why are you not working?)

A: *Me duele el estómago, Maestro, y la cabeza.* (My stomach hurts, Teacher, and my head.)

T: *Vete con la enfermera a que te de algo, ¡y no comas tantos chicharrones el domingo!* (Go the nurse so she can give you something, and don't eat so may *chicharrones* on Sunday.) [The students laugh, then they continue their intensive work, and Alicia goes out of class in the direction of the infirmary. Eventually, the students figure out the problem and compete loudly to present the solution on the board. Time for recreation, and the students don't want to go out as yet. They are so involved with their work that they would rather stay and share their progress with the teacher and friends. One leaves the classroom with a feeling that here, learning is a lot of fun and that although the penalties for making mistakes are rare, the rewards for learning are many.]

One of the basic cultural differences in the role of teachers among Mexicans, when compared with North American traditions, is that parents *entregan* "give away" their children to the teachers and clearly ask them to become surrogate parents. As a consequence, the relationship between a Mexican teacher and students is of a different quality. For example, in addition to the enormous respect students show Mr. Villegas, and in contrast with the collective behavior of submission and cooperation, in personal relationships the children hug Mr. Villegas and are playful as if they would challenge him in breaking small rules (regarding the use of space, leaving the classroom, stopping the use of the blackboard, becoming quiet, etc.). There is a conspicuous demonstration of love and affection. The *Maestro* is more than a regular teacher. In turn, Mr. Villegas can become jokingly sarcastic, or intimidating *te voy a castigar* ("I am going to punish you"), or *le voy a decir a tu mamá* ("I am going to tell your mother"). The response on the part of the children is an affectionate hug, laugh, or a gesture of a pretend "I don't care." What has happened, however, is that the teacher and children have created a unique bond that motivates children to learn. This is particularly congruent with a Vygotskian explanation of intellectual development, as we will see.

From Critical Ethnography to a Vygotskian Pedagogy of Hope

Critical ethnography, in order to document inequity, is a risky and painful type of research, the kind that, at times, ethnographers find frustrating and sterile, narcissistic and selfish, insightful but deprived of the social consequences of real life. It often leads researchers to the conviction that "[they] do not want to know too many of the details. They want to explain social inequality by blaming the victims or in any other way that leaves their accustomed identities intact. They are afraid of being wounded" (Carspecken 1996, 170–171). Because critical ethnography is a commitment to *praxis*, discourse alone is insufficient and even offensive if isolated from emancipatory action, from praxis. Research with Mexican immigrants was no exception to this pain, and the praxis associated with my inquiries about their resilience and their relative success in surviving culturally and psychologically did not take away my pain. I wanted to understand how relatively powerless Mexican immigrant people were to create a system of resistance to dominant beliefs, values, norms, and practices, which can be frightening to many people. But I also wanted to understand how children in school, assisted by their teachers and parents (especially their mothers), constructed for themselves a genuine *utopia* for a better future, perhaps as engineers, architects, businesspersons, and so on. Everyday, when middle and high school Mexican students saw their parents come home full of mud, smelly after working all day in the fields, burned by the sun and the wind, hungry, in pain with premature arthritis, and wearing a face of exhaustion, their motivation to pursue their utopic dreams became stronger. What was the role of teachers and mothers in the development of these dreams? What specific pedagogical strategies were followed by teachers who captured the opportunity and pushed students to their liberation? This is the central concern of this chapter.

Mothers, Mexican immigrant women who defend their cultural integrity in all arenas, especially in the schools, can be even more frightening. A pedagogy of hope based on Vygotskian principles establishes the relationship between culture, language, and cognition as the foundation for understanding the role of culture in meditating the transmission of knowledge and intellectual growth. The mediation through appropriate cultural symbols in the construction of academic knowledge (or via "assisted performance") must translate instruction into pedagogical practices that permit immigrant children to engage in their own development, to invest in their own culture and linguistic capital, and to advance without prejudice. The research in schools conducted by Kris Gutierrez and her colleagues (Gutierrez 1994; Gutierrez, Rymes, and Larson 1995; Gutierrez, Larson, and Kreuter 1995) is a clear example of critical ethnography with an understanding of the development principles that Vygotsky and neo-Vygotskians have established. This research not only disclosed teachers' hegemonic structures but introduced new interactional and curricular strategies for capitalizing on the linguistic and cultural richness of children's backgrounds through an intensive collaborative, joint construction of knowledge in the classroom.

In spite of the inherent challenges and difficulties faced by ethnographers, critical ethnography with a Vygotskian perspective continues to be one of the most promising fields in the hands of educational researchers committed to sound pedagogy and the full development of immigrant children, because it is a new avenue for creating a pedagogy of hope in actual instruction. This type of critical ethnography is based on the principles of assisted performance within the zone of proximal development (ZPD) established by Vygotsky (1962, 1978) and practiced today by neo-Vygotskians (Wertsch 1981, 1985, 1991; Cole 1990, 1996; Trueba 1991; Moll 1990). The combination of the principles of critical ethnography (consistent with Paulo Freire's pedagogy of hope) is compatible with, and complementary to, the principles of the sociohistorical school of psychology represented by the work Vygotsky (and neo-Vygotskians). More specifically, I suggest that in order to build an ethnographic research agenda with a relevant pedagogical praxis in schools, one could combine critical ethnography with Vygotsky's theory of human development.

One of Vygotsky's most important contributions to our understanding of immigrant children's intellectual development and school achievement, especially of those undergoing rapid sociocultural change, was his theory about the relationship between cognitive and social phenomena. Vygotsky states that the development of uniquely human higher-level mental functions, such as consciousness and the creation of taxonomic cognitive structures (required for academic learning), find their origin in day-to-day interaction. Vygotsky searches in our daily social lives for the origins of human consciousness and higher-level mental functions. According to Moll, if teachers follow Vygotskian principles, they will see literacy as "the understanding and communication of meaning" and will make efforts "to make classrooms literate environments in which many language experiences can take place and different types of literacies can be developed and learned" (1990, 8). Indeed, Moll stresses the following idea. "Teachers who follow this approach reject rote instruction or reducing reading and writing into skill sequences taught in isolation or a successive, stage like manner. Rather, they emphasize the creation of social contexts in which children actively learn to use, try, and manipulate language in the service of making sense or creating meaning" (Moll 1990, 8). Effective teachers who understand the process of internalization that permits students the transition from interpsychological experience to intrapsychological cognitive categories adopt culturally and linguistically meaningful teaching strategies (Vygotsky 1962, 1978), that is, strategies occurring within the zone of proximal development of children. The *zone of proximal development* was defined by Vygotsky as the distance between a child's "actual developmental level as determined by independent problem solving" and the higher level of "potential development as determined through problem solving under adult guidance or in collaboration with more capable peers" (1978, 86). Furthermore, if we accept the intimate relationship between language and thought proposed by Vygotsky (who sees language as a symbolic system mediating all social and cognitive functions), we must link the lower intellectual development and school achievement of some immigrant children with the abrupt transition from a familiar to an unfamiliar sociocultural environment, and therefore, the lack of both linguistic and cultural knowledge to interact meaningfully with adults and peers. Consequently, no suitable zones of proximal development are opened up for them by adults or more-informed peers, and the discourse and cognitive categories required to function in school are not readily available to them (Brown, Campione, Cole, Griffin, Mehan, and Riel 1982; Trueba 1991). In other words, it is impossible to create appropriate zones of proximal development in oppressive and unfamiliar learning environments that don't have the symbolic tools that allow a child to make sense of social transactions and to translate them into intrapsychological phenomena. However, a bilingual and bicultural teacher who understands the predicament of immigrant children can expand the zone of proximal development by creating a culturally familiar environment and establishing a personal relationship with immigrant students. That is what Mr. Villegas was doing in his class. The use of these zones of proximal development requires not only an awareness of the relationships among language, thought, and culture but also the appropriate pedagogical principles. A Vygotskian pedagogy requires that children become active engineers of their own learning and play a key role in determining the next intellectual challenge in their development. This pedagogy does not occur in a classroom where hegemonic discourse silences culturally and linguistically diverse children.

In a profoundly genuine sense, social life and intellectual life consist of *assisted performance* in one way or another, especially for children as they become acquainted with complex symbolic systems that form constellations of cognitive domains. If the basic Vygotskian tenet is kept in mind, that is, that children's intellectual development is measured by their ability to solve problems "unassisted," then effective teaching must prepare them to solve problems on their own. For this, it is important to identify the complex social systems surrounding children and consequently their ability to manipulate such systems. Special assistance (effective teaching) is needed by children who are in transition from one cultural and linguistic system to another. Immigrant children, by definition, are in transition and feel particularly vulnerable in instructional teaching settings that presuppose knowledge of symbolic and cognitive systems familiar only to local children who belong to a given culture and society. Effective teaching must take into consideration the unique zone of proximal development (ZPD) of culturally and linguistically different children. Teaching is defined by Tharp and Gallimore as follows:

> Distinguishing the *proximal zone* from the *developmental level* by contrasting assisted versus unassisted performance has profound implications for educational practice. It is in the proximal zone that teaching may be defined in terms of child development. In Vygotskian terms, teaching is good only when it *"awakens and rouses to life those functions which are in a stage of maturing, which lie in the zone of proximal development"* (Vygotsky 1956, 278; quoted in Sertsch and Stone 1985). We can therefore derive this general definition of teaching: *Teaching consists in assisting performance through the ZPD. Teaching can be said to occur when assistance is offered at points in the ZPD at which performance requires assistance.* (Tharp and Gallimore 1988, 31; italics in the original)

There are many ways to assist children, to teach children within their ZPD. A precondition, however, for teaching them effectively, is to establish a trusting relationship that permits an adult to model for the child, to engage in contingency managing, providing feedback, guiding, questioning, and organizing structurally cognitive domains. These important types of assistance must be calibrated to the children in ways that open up new avenues for intellectual growth. For a teacher to do this in a regular classroom is difficult enough; a teacher must be able to "read" the children and feel their grasping of ideas and their level of comprehension. But with children in transition, whose bilingual skills vary a great deal, a teacher must be prepared to be especially flexible, as Mr. Villegas was in Migrant Town.

Immigrant children's ability to learn is also contingent upon a minimum of continuity between the home learning environment and their school environment. Children must acquire a basic ability to understand their personal lives and their family struggle to defend their rights in a larger society. The vicarious experience of oppression must be understood, and education must be conceptualized by them as the way out of oppression for them as individuals and for their parents. In meetings with high school students I asked them how they handled the racism and verbal abuses from peers and even teachers. Their response was unanimous. "As our parents have taught us, we'll show them with our grades that we can succeed." This was pretty much the content of Consuelo's teaching to her children, and I am sure similar to the message inculcated by many other parents. The intimate relationship between the knowledge of the word (academic achievement) and the politics of success in school (the knowledge of the world) gives Mexican immigrant children and youth the basis for survival, for resilience. This is consistent with Vygotsky's theory of development (Vygotsky 1962, 1978; Wertsch 1981, 1985, 1991; Cole 1996) and Freire's broad concept of literacy (Freire 1973, 1995; Freire and Macedo 1987, 1996).

True empowerment of Mexican children was not obtained by preaching to them the rhetoric of liberation from hegemonic structures and the need to resist oppression, or even the just and fair demand for respect of their rights (which was taught to them by their parents). Beyond any abstract discourse on liberation, what made the difference was the teaching of the parents and teachers in very specific settings. When Consuelo came back from the cannery or the fields exhausted and muddy and tired, she still prepared a meal for her family and took the time to find out about schoolwork. That is a lesson never forgotten by her children. When Mr. Villegas asked José to go to the board and encouraged him to use his native language to explain difficult mathematical concepts, he pursued the assistance to give him feedback after each step of the operation and to question the possibility of further reduction of the algebraic equation:

T: Can you solve that equation? [Mr. Villegas is challenging José.] Quiet all!! Wait José. Can you solve the equation? [Mr. Villegas demands respect from all before he turns the floor to José.]

J: Well, I don't know, but . . . I will try.

T: Do it, then, you can explain it in Spanish. [Mr. Villegas encourages José. After José solves the equation, Mr. Villegas follows up.]

T: Explain and reduce it further. [Pursues the challenge and asks for an explanation.]

J: I can divide by 2 the terms of the equation: $4x/2$ is $2x$; $-2y/2$ is $-y$. The result is: $2x - y = 3$.

T: Good. If I tell you that $x = 3$, what is the value of y?

J: Two times 3 is 6, minus 3 is 3. $y = 3$.

T: Very good!

The messages sent to the entire class by Mr. Villegas are clear: (1) What is important is to acquire the knowledge. (2) You can use the language you know best to explain the concepts you have acquired. (3) You should be proud of who you are, and this pride should be reflected in your academic achievement. (4) The challenge is clearly above fourth-grade level, but he is confident in his students' ability. "Fourth grade of room 23 always wins, and it will win once more!" Modeling is not a task unique to the teacher. Often Mr. Villegas would permit a bright student to model for the others, without necessarily creating a stratification system in terms of performance. Some children would excel in some areas while their peers did well in others. In the end, the esprit de corps had priority over individual performance. The success of one student was the success of them all. Cognitive structuring occurred once in a while, as transitions from one general area to another demanded. Thus, for example, going from negative numbers to equations was explained in some detail in graphics and with specific problems. The more complex operations within equations (as one moves x or y from one side to another, or as one reduces more difficult equations) were not pursued for the entire class but were at times explained to some of the students who observed certain relationships between operations. In this sense, Mr. Villegas was adapting to different zones of proximal development, without neglecting the fundamental operations for all. What is remarkable is that the students' involvement was so intense and their motivation so high. In Vygotskian terms, the activity settings that were constructed in class or at home carried a strong motivational impetus, a commitment to acquire specific knowledge jointly (children and adult—teacher or parent). Tharp and Gallimore (1988, 77–78) observe that activity settings usually provide motivational impetus. Some children may join in because their friends are participating; some beginning readers may be unenthusiastic about the reading itself, but happy to follow their more powerful friends until they themselves incorporate the values and meanings of reading. Hence, the importance of belonging, of feeling a part of a class, regardless of their cultural and linguistic characteristics. That is what Mr. Villegas accomplished best. In contrast, for a Mexican immigrant child who is struggling to acquire English as a second language, not to be able to use Spanish in class is to be automatically reduced to a handicapped student. That is precisely what happens to many immigrant children in regular classrooms.

Concluding Thoughts

The challenge in the integration of critical ethnography within a Vygotskian pedagogical approach to instruction for empowerment is not only an intellectual or cognitive one, it is also a challenge of praxis, of commitment to the education of culturally different children. In a genuinely Freirean pedagogy ("knowing the word and knowing the world") literacy is an essential instrument to reclaim control of one's own life, full human rights, and dignity. In a Vygotskian theoretical framework, literacy is the essential link between the social and cognitive worlds that permits children to grow intellectually, to learn and develop their talents and capacity; but in order to acquire literacy, children need to enjoy full human rights and supportive relationships with "more-informed peers" and teachers. Both for Freire and Vygotsky, children need to know the world in order to learn the word. Higher mental functions cannot develop unless children enjoy positive social relationships and are not the victims of poverty, isolation, abuse, racism, neglect, or poor health. A Vygotskian pedagogy of hope presupposes a respect for human rights and more; the creation of a positive learning environment in which children become the engineers of their own intellectual destiny and coconstruct their future. For Freire there is no liberation or empowerment without active involvement in one's own liberation. Consequently, a Vygotskian pedagogy of hope is truly Freirean in substance, and, in turn, the logical sequel to Freirean critical pedagogy is a Vygotskian developmental approach to teaching and learning. Freedom from racism and oppression does not guarantee learning and development in children, but it is the necessary condition for both. Children's higher mental functions develop on the basis of an environment free of oppression but with the active engagement of joint social and cognitive relationships with those who can help children discover new worlds through new words. In brief, a Vygotskian theory of development picks up where a Freirean theory of equity and empowerment ends. The appropriate pedagogies developed on the basis of the zone of proximal development cannot produce the desired outcomes without Freire's principles and the abolition of hegemonic instructional structures. In the end, critical ethnographers must continue to ask themselves what their praxis is all about, what their genuine contribution is to the intellectual growth of children. Critical ethnographers must maintain a serious, consistent, and strong commitment to children's liberation from abuse, oppression, and misery; but such ethnographers must also commit to study further the use of appropriate strategies to maximize the intellectual development of children as they grow in schools and society. Pedagogy does not end in the school, it must continue in the homes, in society, and in all domains of life. Critical ethnographers are just beginning to open up doors and avenues for development. Their understanding of developmental theories is crucial to live their praxis as researchers.

Critical ethnography is no more a panacea than Vygotsky's theories are. But critical ethnography has fallen into a trap of competitive discourse with limited fieldwork and at times sterile discourse devoid of concern for the pedagogical needs of children, especially of immigrant children whose voices have been taken away by educational reform and backlash against the use of home languages. Indeed, the abuse of the rhetoric of racism and White supremacy in critical theory has obscured the fact that a genuine ethnography with serious grounding on the accounts obtained in the field, in the classroom, or in the homes of oppressed peoples can be married to a genuine Freirean pedagogy of hope, to action with passion in the classroom on behalf of silenced children. A genuine Freirean pedagogy must, however, be complemented by a clear understanding of the process of the intellectual empowerment of children. If cultural equity and familiar linguistic patterns open the door to better learning in immigrant children, the pursuit of higher developmental challenges must presuppose an understanding of the role children play in their own learning and their extraordinary capacity to learn and pursue creative strategies to survive intellectually, if we give them a chance. Teachers and children must jointly create new learning environments that suit their needs and match their cultural and linguistic skills and capital. All the discourse on oppression or on emancipation cannot substitute quality instruction, accountability, and assisted performance. Hegemonic classroom control must be denounced, but once that is done, the job of constructing appropriate pedagogies must start in earnest and must be based on three important principles: (1) children should determine the level of learning, the types of reasoning, the taxonomies, and cultural context of their own growth as well as the pace of transition into the teacher's planned instruction; (2) children need to participate fully and feel competent; and (3) school activities and the role of teachers must be supported by the children's family and larger community. How else can an immigrant child make sense of this new academic world and this new life; how else can a child have hope? And hope, as Freire often reminded us, is an ontological necessity; without hope we cannot exist (Freire 1995).

References

Bartolomé, L. "Beyond the Methods Fetish: Toward a Humanizing Pedagogy." In P. Leistyna, A. Woodrum, and S. Sherblom (eds.), *Breaking Free: The Transformative Power of Critical Pedagogy. Harvard Education Review, Reprint Series No. 27* (1996): 229–252.

Bartolomé, L, and D. Macedo. "Dancing with Bigotry: The Poisoning of Racial and Cultural Identities." *Harvard Educational Review* 67, no. 2 (1997): 222–242.

Brown, A., E. Campione, M. Cole, P. Griffin, H. Mehan, and M. Riel. "A Models System for the Study of Learning Difficulties." *The Quarterly Newsletter of the Laboratory of Comparative Human Cognition* 4, no. 3 (1982): 39–55.

Bureau of the Census. *Current Population Reports.* Published by the U.S. Department of Commerce, Economics and Statistics Administration, June 1996.

Carspecken, P. F. *Critical Ethnography in Educational Research: A Theoretical and Practical Guide.* New York: Routledge, 1996.

Cole, M. "Cognitive Development and Formal Schooling: The Evidence from Cross-Cultural Research." In L. Moll (ed.), *Vygotsky and Education: Instructional Implications and Applications of Sociohistorical Psychology.* Cambridge, Mass.: Cambridge University Press, 1990, 89–110.

———. *Cultural Psychology: A Once and Future Discipline.* Cambridge, Mass.: The Belknap Press of Harvard University, 1996.

DeGenova, N. "The Production of Language and the Language of Oppression: Mexican Labor and the Politics of ESL in Chicago Factories." University of California, Los Angeles, Spencer Foundation Winter Forum, February 14–15, 1997.

Delgado-Gaitan, C. "Russian Refugee Families: Accommodating Aspirations through Education. *Anthropology and Education Quarterly* 25, no. 2 (1994): 137–155.

Delgado-Gaitan, C., and H. T. Trueba. *Crossing Cultural Borders: Education for Immigrant Families in America.* London: Falmer Press, 1991.

Deyhle, D., and F. Margonis. "Navajo Mothers and Daughters: Schools, Jobs, and the Family. *Anthropology and Education Quarterly* 16, no. 2 (1995): 135–167.

Díaz Salcedo, S. "Successful Latino Students at the High School Level: A Case Study of Ten Students." An analytic paper presented to the Faculty of the Graduate School of Education of Harvard University, in partial fulfillment of the requirements for the degree of Doctor of Education, 1996.

Freire, P. *Pedagogy of the Oppressed.* New York: Seabury, 1973.

———. *Pedagogy of Hope: Reliving Pedagogy of the Oppressed.* Translated by Robert R. Barr. New York: Continuum, 1995.

Freire, P., and D. Macedo. *Literacy: Reading the Word and Reading the World.* Critical Studies in Education Series. Boston: Bergin and Garvey Publishers, 1987.

———. "A Dialogue: Culture, Language, and Race." In P. Leistyna, A. Woodrum, and S. Sherblom (eds.), *Breaking Free: The Transformative Power of Critical Pedagogy. Harvard Education Review, Reprint Series No. 27* (1996): 199–228.

Giroux, H., and P. McLaren. *Between Borders: Pedagogy and the Politics of Cultural Studies.* New York: Routledge, 1994.

Gutierrez, K. "How Talk, Context, and Script Shape Contexts for Learning: A Cross-Case Comparison of Journal Sharing." *Linguistics and Education* 5 (1994): 335–365.

Gutierrez, K., J. Larson, and B. Kreuter. "Cultural Tensions in the Scripted Classroom: The Value of the Subjugated Perspective." *Urban Education* 29, no. 4 (1995): 410–442.

Gutierrez, K., B. Rymes, and J. Larson. "Script, Counterscript, and Underlife in the Classroom: James Brown versus *Brown v. Board of Education." Harvard Educational Review* 65, no. 3 (1995): 445–471.

Health and Welfare Agency. *Mexican Service Study Area: Needs Indicators.* State of California, Department of Health Services, 1994.

Hondagneu-Sotelo, P. *Gendered Transitions: Mexican Experiences of Immigration.* Berkeley: University of California Press, 1994.

Leistyna, P., A. Woodrum, and S. A. Sherblom, eds. *Breaking Free: The Transformative Power of Critical Pedagogy.* Harvard Educational Review, Reprint Series No. 27, 1996.

León-Portilla, M. *La Flecha en el Blanco: Francisco Tenamaztle y Bartolomé de las Casa en la Lucha por los Derechos de los Indígenas 1541–1556.* Mexico City: Editorial Diana, México, 1995.

Martin, P., and E. Taylor. "Immigration and the Changing Face of Rural California: Summary Report of the Conference Held at Asilomar, June 12–14, 1995." Unpublished manuscript.

McLaren, P. *Critical Pedagogy and Predatory Culture.* New York: Routledge, 1995.

———. *Revolutionary Multiculturalism: Pedagogies of Dissent for the New Millennium.* Boulder: Westview Press, 1997.

McLaren, P., and T. da Silva. "Decentering Pedagogy: Critical Literacy, Resistance and the Politics of Memory." In Peter McLaren and Peter Leonard (eds.), *Paulo Freire: A Critical Encounter.* New York: Routledge, 1993, 47–89.

Menchaca, M., and R. R. Valencia. "Anglo-Saxon Ideologies in the 1920s–1930s: Their Impact on the Segregation of Mexican Students in California." *Anthropology and Education Quarterly* 21, no. 3 (1990): 222–249.

Moll, L. "Introduction." In L. Moll (ed.), *Vygotsky and Education: Instructional Implications and Applications of Sociohistorical Psychology.* Cambridge, Mass.: Cambridge University Press, 1990.

Portes, A. "Introduction: Immigration and Its Aftermath." In A. Portes (ed.), *The New Second Generation.* New York: Russell Sage Foundation, 1996, 1–7.

Shweder, R. A. "True Ethnography: The Lore, the Law, and the Lure." In R. Jessor, A. Colby, and R. A. Shweder (eds.), *Ethnography and Human Development: Context and Meaning in Social Inquiry.* Chicago: University of Chicago Press, 1996, 15–52.

Spindler, G. D., ed. *Anthropology and Education.* Stanford, Calif.: Stanford University Press, 1955.

Suárez-Orozco, C., and M. Suárez-Orozco. *Transformations: Immigration, Family Life and Achievement Motivation among Latino Adolescents.* Stanford, Calif.: Stanford University Press, 1995a.

———. "Migration: Generational Discontinuities and the Making of Latino Identities." In L. Romanucci-Ross and G. DeVos (eds.), *Ethnic Identity: Creation, Conflict, and Accommodation.* 3d ed. Walnut Creek, Calif.: Alta Mira Press, 1995b, 321–347.

Suárez-Orozco, M. M. "California Dreaming: Proposition 187 and the Cultural Psychology of Racial and Ethnic Exclusion." *Anthropology and Education Quarterly* 27, no. 2 (1996): 151–167.

———. "State Terrors: Immigrants and Refugees in the Post-National Space." In Y. Zou and H. T. Trueba (eds.), *Ethnic Identity and Power: Cultural Contexts of Political Action in School and Society.* New York: State University of New York Press, 1998, 283–319.

Tharp, R. G., and R. Gallimore. *Rousing Minds to Life: Teaching, Learning, and*

Schooling in Social Context. Cambridge, Mass.: Cambridge University Press, 1988.

Trueba, H. T. "The Ethnography of Schooling." In H. T. Trueba (ed.), *Success or Failure: Linguistic Minority Children at Home and in School.* New York: Harper and Row, 1987, 1–13.

———. "Linkages of Macro-Micro Analytical Levels." *Journal of Psychohistory* 18, no. 4 (1991): 457–468.

———. "A Mexican Immigrant Community in Central California." Unpublished manuscript. Harvard University, 1997.

Trueba, H. T., L. Cheng, and K. Ima. *Myth or Reality: Adaptive Strategies of Asian Americans in California.* London: Falmer Press, 1993.

Trueba, H. T., L. Jacobs, and E. Kirton. *Cultural Conflict and Adaptation: The Case of the Hmong Children in American Society.* London: Falmer Press, 1990.

Trueba, H. T., C. Rodríguez, Y. Zou, and J. Cintrón. *Healing Multicultural America: Mexican Immigrants Rise to Power in Rural California.* London: Falmer Press, 1993.

Trueba, H. T., and Y. Zou. *Power in Education: The Case of Miao University Students and Its Significance for American Culture.* London: Falmer Press, 1994.

Valencia, R. R. "The Plight of Chicano Students: An Overview of Schooling Conditions and Outcomes." In R. R. Valencia (ed.), *Chicano School Failure: An Analysis through Many Windows.* London: Falmer Press, 1991, 3–26.

Vigil, D. *Barrio Gangs.* Austin: University of Texas Press, 1989.

———. *Personas Mexicanas: Chicano High Schoolers in a Changing Los Angeles. Case Studies in Cultural Anthropology.* Series editors, George Spindler and Louise Spindler. Fort Worth, Philadelphia, San Diego: Harcourt Brace College Publishers, 1997.

Villenas, S. "The Colonizer/Colonized Chicana Ethnographer: Identity, Marginalization, and Co-Optation in the Field." *Harvard Educational Review* 66, no. 4 (1996): 711–731.

Vygotsky, L. S. *Thought and Language.* Cambridge: Massachusetts Institute of Technology Press, 1962.

———. "Interaction between Learning and Development." In L. Vygotsky, *Mind in Society: The Development of Higher Psychological Processes.* M. Cole, V. John-Teiner, S. Scribner, and E. Souberman (eds.). Cambridge, Mass.: Harvard University Press, 1978, 79–91.

Wertsch, J. *The Concept of Activity in Soviet Psychology.* New York: M. E. Sharpe, 1981.

———. "Beyond Vygotsky: Bakhtin's Contribution." In J. Wertsch, *Voices of the Mind: A Sociocultural Approach to Mediated Action.* Cambridge, Mass.: Harvard University Press, 1991, 46–66.

Wertsch, J., ed. *Culture, Communication, and Cognition: Vygotskian Perspectives.* Cambridge, Mass.: Cambridge University Press, 1985.

Wilson, P. "Trauma of Sioux Indian High School Students." *Anthropology and Education Quarterly* 22, no. 4 (1991): 367–383.

Zou, Y., and H. Trueba. *Ethnic Identity and Power: Cultural Contexts of Political Action in School and Society.* New York: State University of New York Press, 1998.

6

Latinos in the Twenty-First Century: The Components of Praxis for a Pedagogy of Hope

After reading the previous chapters the reader must have many questions. Some questions would be related to the theory of ethnic identity and resiliency as applied to Latinos, and other questions would be relative to a pedagogy of hope and the praxis of Latino educators. Specifically, what is the relationship of Latino identities to Latino resiliency? Another set of questions deals with the relationship of a pedagogy of hope and the required praxis of Latino educators. First, what are the consequences of a pedagogy of hope? What should be the concrete praxis of Latino educators? What are the ideological foundations and specific components and requirements of such a praxis? What are the logical consequences of a pedagogy of hope for educational reform? The last type of question refers to our need to peek into the next century and attempt to anticipate the fate of Latinos in this country. What do we anticipate will happen with Latinos in the next century? Will they increase their political and economic power? Will they change their collective cultural identity? Will they become strong advocates for all Latinos around the world? What will be their role in the United States and in the world? What are the dreams and concerns of contemporary Latino intellectuals? Although it will be impossible to answer adequately in one chapter any of these questions and totally impossible to answer all of them, it is important, at the very least, to point in the direction of some possible answers.

Resiliency and Latino Identities: A Theoretical Reflection

The moving targets of the concepts *identities* and *resiliency* and their complex interrelationship suggest that we distinguish three types of relationships between these concepts. Personal identities of Latinos, the most profound self-definition we give ourselves, most likely will not coincide with the definitions others give us. If we are "European" looking Latinos, and if we speak English fluently, and if we exhibit the expected gestures and kinesic characteristics of European Americans, people will never know our internal struggles in defining ourselves to ourselves. But if we are brown or black, and if we are conspicuously different in our interactional style, then other people's definitions of us will vary a great deal, and these definitions will have a greater impact on our own self-concept. Regardless of such perceptual differences of who we are, each of us must resolve the fundamental question of "Who am I?" and "How do I know that I am who I think I am?" Collectively, if we are close to Latino communities and interact with them often, we may think of ourselves as part of those communities, and in some way we share our identity with others. Insofar as we retain some measure of fluency in Spanish and some relationships with members of Latino organizations, we perpetuate the myth of our membership as Latinos. However, we will continue to pursue multiple memberships and multiple identities in response to the various groups that we must face every day. Consequently, we must face the following issues:

- the role of our multiple identities in developing resiliency as a foundation to cement various adaptive strategies
- the differential nature of each of the coexisting simultaneous identities and their interrelationships
- the temporary or permanent character of such identities and their relative autonomy

Multiple identities exist when we must interact with culturally and linguistically distinct groups on a regular basis, without the possibility of using the same cultural and linguistic forms to communicate with such groups. The need to adapt our communicative codes and competencies to each group creates a perception and experience of different selves in interaction, of alternative communicative codes with diverse cultural rules. At times, because of the social and economic differences of the groups with whom we interact, as well as because of the different domains that we must master in our communication with them, the coexistence of different personal identities is more functional and compartmentalized in clear categories. For example, a Latino working in the community as an activist will know many low-income families who are monolingual in rural forms of Spanish; fluency in such forms is essential to do one's work in the community. The same Latino may have to meet some executives from Mexico City doing business in this country. The etiquette, linguistic forms, and expected interactional patterns in these circumstances are totally different. This same Latino may have to work with Anglo populations of different social strata for other purposes: sports, art, social work, academia, volunteer organizations, church, and so forth. To a certain extent not only Latinos, but most people can develop the capability to communicate effectively with various audiences. Why do Latinos develop different coexistent identities? Because immigrant Latinos are in transition and need to interact with very different groups on a regular basis in order to survive. This is the reason why without an ability to identify with other groups of people, a Latino could not survive culturally and adapt to our society. The demands are such that multiple membership in the various groups ensures enough sources of information that permit Latinos to model adaptive strategies, to understand and construct meaning, to interpret and face risks, to secure a source of income, and to obtain safety. Immigrants are always afraid of making serious mistakes that can jeopardize their permanent status in the host country. The development of multiple identities is congruent with survival strategies at the reach of persons who have sacrificed a great deal in order to enter and remain in this country.

The different nature of the multiple identities becomes more understandable by looking at the lifestyle of immigrants. The case of farmworkers is perhaps the most clear because they are often confined to a clear routine, and they live in rural settings with clear boundaries. A farmworker must find work and be initiated into the agricultural field; he or she has to get experience and learn the ropes in order to work safely and retain a job. The main focus of the set of relationships is going to be with relatives and friends who got him or her the job. Personal loyalty, dependency on others (economically and emotionally) will reaffirm their village identity as *paisano* or as a countryman or countrywoman from a given Mexican village (for example, from Tangancícuaro). The town's local linguistic forms will be used and will serve as an indication of membership in that group. Very soon, however, the new worker will have to interact with *pochos*, or persons who no longer speak the same form of the language, don't eat the same things, have different interests, are fluent in English, and know the ropes with the boss. The association with the *pochos* is essential to retain one's job, and it is often a love–hate relationship that both native Mexicans and the *pochos* born in this country want to maintain for common benefits. The Mexicans have contacts in Mexico, and they can be instrumental in making binational deals, sending relatives home, looking after elderly parents, and so on. Those in this kind of relationship are vying for the same jobs, and, thus, hostility is also built in. One way of creating a friendly relationship is through the use of the *compadrazgo* system; by making your potential enemy a "sacred" member of your family, your *compadre* who will have a new and spiritual obligation to help you and your children, you become friends and allies for life. So you have now two clearly defined identities that have enormous differences yet are grounded in a common linguistic and cultural background. Code-switching from Spanish to English and from Spanish to "Spanglish" becomes the norm of interaction.

There are, however, other relationships that come to life in the host country. Religion is important, and often the need to belong in a new country, to belong economically and culturally, is greater than the spiritual need for worship. Therefore, many immigrants change their religion. They leave their Catholicism and become Protestants. Often the wife leads the movement because of the immediate behavioral payoffs. The husband will no longer drink, waste money, or become violent if he converts to Protestantism. If religious conversion happens, a new set of relationships with the Anglo-American world takes place. A very intensive religious, political, and cultural socialization takes place within the nuclear family, often carrying consequences to the extended family. New sets of relationships and networks with a church group create the need for a new identity, profoundly new in every single respect: ideologically, linguistically, culturally, economically, behaviorally, and so on. There are also other worlds of interaction that the immigrant will face as he or she moves up the social and economic ladder. As the children become educated and as the family finds economic security, participation in other middle-class (or lower–middle-class) groups becomes important for children and families. Often this new affiliation with an upwardly mobile group creates a clearer and more distinct set of requirements than any of the previous relationships. The question is: What is the relationship among all these coexisting identities? Not all are equally functional and they do not coexist for the same length of time. It seems that in the case of farmworkers the most important groups are of Latinos in the same type of job on both sides of the border. The endurance of these networks and relationships depends on the stability of the occupation and the relative interdependence of the members of the group. It is not unusual to have relatives and friends on both sides of the border depend on each other for several decades. These individuals can easily code-switch in a variety of forms of Spanish, even after they acquire some fluency in English.

What is relevant here is the fact that the instability in the lives of many Latino immigrants is compensated for by the stability of their networks and relationships as well as by their ability to adapt to new sets of relationships and to members of additional groups. It is not unusual to find individuals who keep those relationships beyond the immediate family for two or three decades. The nature of those networks, as well as the multiple memberships, should be pursued in order to explore the nature of the plural identity of Latinos and their ability to survive, or their resilience. *Resiliency* is a term that means different things to different people. In the context of our discussion on immigrants, I would conceive of resiliency as the capacity of immigrants to withstand pain, to survive physically and psychologically in circumstances that require enormous physical stamina and determination (such as crossing the border many times and doing farmwork for several years) as well as the psychological flexibility they need to adapt to a different lifestyle in the absence of their familiar environment. Resiliency is shown when a person persists in the face of serious problems and challenges, with a clarity of goals and serious intention to complete a task. At the heart of resiliency is motivation. People make rational choices with the information they have at the time. The resiliency of one individual can be the foolishness of another. I would characterize resiliency as the spiritual quality of Latinos that permits them to do the following:

- Select support systems and resources to survive physically, psychologically, and culturally; these would include the concerted effort to identify sources of self-esteem and persons offering moral support.
- Use such resources reciprocally so that the immigrant retains long-term support. Commitment to reciprocity is essential for the system to work.
- Create networks and the exchange of goods and services that permits the immigrant to meet his or her immediate needs and resolve immediate problems.
- Engage in social and cultural events that serve to maintain group identity and cohesiveness. At the same time such events enrich individuals' folklore, belief system, and a sense of satisfaction in life.

The relationship between identity and resiliency is, in the final analysis, one of interdependency. Without resiliency a person would not survive, and he or she would not internalize a self-identity in a host country. The reciprocal supportive relationships that feed the will to survive—those that create resiliency in individuals—also have the function of providing an identity to that individual. The need to depend on different groups for different needs allows the immigrant to develop a number of identities and a stronger resiliency, or a greater capacity to survive in times of crisis. There is no doubt that immigration is one of the most powerful intrapsychic experiences for many Latinos; one that creates intergenerational ripples and is vicariously transmitted to the second and third generations. It tends to shake the very foundations of our personality and the fundamental structure of personal relationships. It is so deep, profound, and personal that it takes years for it to be understood by the people who go through the experiences. Ainslie (1997) feels that immigrants become perpetual mourners and remain inconsolable because what they have lost can never be recovered. It is, however, more than individual mourning:

> It is the intimate connection between individual and collective experience that weds individual mourning to cultural mourning. When an immigrant leaves loved ones at home, he or she also leaves the cultural enclosures that have organized and sustained. The immigrant simultaneously must come to terms with the loss of family and friends on the one hand, and the cultural forms (food, music, art, for example) that have given the immigrant's native world a distinct and highly personal character. It is not only people who are mourned, but culture itself, which is inseparable from the loved ones whom it holds. (Ainslie 1997, 2)

The loss of the cultural forms that maintain one's identity are mourned by the immigrants who are aware that they are rapidly losing their personal identity before they acquire a new one. To decrease the impact of the loss, immigrants develop a deep connection with objects associated with their culture, thus providing an opportunity to express themselves emotionally in a new space and in new surrogate relationships. The new space lies between reality and fantasy, between inner psychological life and external interactive manifestations (Ainslie 1997, 4). The dislocation and separation, therefore, are faced with a new symbolic set of objects, rituals, and activities that gradually create a new ethnicity, a new lifestyle for the immigrant. The use of radio and television in the home language, the frequent social gatherings with various *paisanos,* and phone communication are also powerful stimuli that buffer the sense of loss and become part of the mourning process. Ainslie describes a conspicuous collective case of reconstitution of the lost culture and an attempt to recreate it in the host country. The flea market (called *La Pulga* by Latinos in Austin, Texas) offers fascinating examples of both mourning and adaptation strategies.

> Most of the immigrants are from rural Mexico, and La Pulga is very reminiscent of the *plazas* typical of the towns and villages they have left, both

in its form and in its relaxed, day-off atmosphere. A stage and dance floor are located in the very heart of the square that is formed by the arrangement of vendor's stalls. In front of the stage are metal tables and chairs, and concessions sell food, beer, and soft drinks. Originally, the music ranged from blues and rock and roll, to country western and Mexican Norteño and Tejano music. However, reading the tastes of their predominant clientele, the operators of the flea market now book Norteño and Tejano music almost exclusively. These *conjuntos* play Spanish language music characteristic of northern Mexico and Texas, but the lyrics closely parallel the motifs typical of American country western music: lost love, ill fate, and large doses of melancholy. The men sit at the metal tables, drinking imported Mexican beer by the six-pack, accompanied by fresh limes and salt, eating their roasted corn, tacos, gorditas, and other Mexican foods, while watching couples on the dance floor. Many of the women are dressed in their Sunday finest. (Ainslie 1997, 6)

This strategy of combining mourning with the re-creation of the familiar culture in the host country gradually takes a bicultural tone and becomes the grounds for taking up a new identity. Immigrants show their new clothes, T-shirts combining both Mexican and Texan lifestyle: *"¡Me Vale Madre!"* ("I don't give a shit"), or "Don't mess up with Texas," and even redneck jokes, "You know you're a redneck if your family tree is a straight line"), and the American and Texan flags next to each other (Ainslie, ibid.). Settings like La Pulga are an excellent buffer zone, allowing for a gradual adjustment and the fantasy that not everything is lost, that a little of Mexico is still with them.

I have met Mexican immigrants who have spent more than thirty years in the United States, who have married an Anglo-American person, and who have retained their Mexican citizenship. They have also re-created their "little Mexico" in their community of friends and relatives. Perhaps one of the reasons why some of them have delayed for decades taking citizenship in this country has to do with their mourning the culture they left and retaining a profound loyalty to their country of origin. It is like refusing to marry again after having lost a loved spouse. The permanence of undocumented workers and students may also have something to do with the mourning process just alluded to. These persons are willing to put up with the anxiety of deportation rather than symbolically reject their beloved country and culture. Remaining in this country for a "short period of time" or for a finite task (to complete a degree or to get some money) is more acceptable than facing the reality that they will never go back to live in Mexico, Central America, or South America. Dennis López has gathered some accounts of undocumented students and workers that give us insight into this dilemma between suffering anxiety about deportation or turning our back on our country of origin. A young woman, asked if she was aware of this anxiety, replies:

> I was very well aware. My parents constantly were afraid that if we were seen on the streets, that somehow [the authorities] would be suspicious and deport the entire family. So they constantly reminded us to not go into the streets and if we saw the police, to hide. . . . Something that happened that was very critical was when one of my best friends was deported. The Immigration Department or Immigration Service Officers were forewarned that immigrants were moving into that area, so they started raids in factories and elementary schools. And my father heard about it and so he pulled us out of school, and we had to stay at home for about a month until he felt that it was safe enough for us to go back to school. During that time my best friend Laura was deported with her family. . . . It was a very sad point, just because I felt that somehow I lost not only a friend but I also lost a feeling of being comfortable. I had a feeling of having to fear and I was in school. . . . I was in second grade in Juárez, and when I came here I was placed in the fourth grade. (López 1997, 21)

López feels that these immigrants who risk so much in order to get a better life and a better education for their children have an extraordinary resiliency, "Despite facing the disruption of relocation, the prospect of confronting a different culture and language and being subjected to discrimination, these families took the chance to come north. The parents knew they would have to work long hours for little pay and endure difficult conditions in order to provide for their families" (1997, 1). Where does that energy come from, the internal power to withstand pain and to continue to work under such difficult circumstances? The answer is not easy, but it does have to do with the extraordinary cohesive and complex force that is the Mexican culture: a combination of religious faith, kinship structure, folk belief systems, and personal investment in one another as a way of life. The observations are the basis of much of our hope, and they are our praxis for a pedagogy of hope.

Praxis for a Pedagogy of Hope

A pedagogy of hope does not exist in a cultural vacuum. Entering someone else's culture is somewhat comparable to the immigration experience without the risks and the mourning that immigrants have to suffer. A pedagogy of hope requires an emic, or insider's, view of the life of immigrant children in order to articulate instructional strategies and cognitive approaches that are suitable and effective. The praxis that accompanies a pedagogy of hope is clearly a conscious detachment from "whiteness" and from a rigid, dogmatic, and monolithic defense of a Western or North American way of life, schooling codes, and interactional patterns. A simple change of technique and a paternalistic response to "these poor immigrant children" will definitely not do. Educators who are serious about their praxis and committed to a pedagogy of hope must be prepared to take a long and hazardous psychological trip into lands and minds unknown before. Daily praxis through action and unbiased, open interaction with immigrant children starts from the assumption that these children can learn and they deserve to become empowered with knowledge. Consequently, the action that this praxis requires is ideologically moved by the basic assumption of children's ability to learn. This praxis is incompatible with despair, negligence, disrespect, and racism. This praxis is fully congruent with the strong belief in a utopia that extricates immigrant children from their temporary misery, poverty, marginality, isolation, negligence, and academic underachievement to a land of opportunity in which they can display their talents in their own cultural and linguistic terms and at their own pace. It is a utopia that not only accepts as possible the overall success of immigrant children, their intellectual development and academic achievement, but one that also counts on such success and builds a bright future on this assumption of success. Therefore, such praxis will create mechanisms to ensure that immigrant children have every possible opportunity for development without losing their cultural capital, personal identity, ethnic affiliation, or home culture.

The praxis of researchers and educators who work with Latino children must have the following characteristics:

- It should be a praxis not based on misleading stereotypes or failure or on misleading macrosociological pictures predicting the failure of Latinos across generations but on the judicious and prudent analysis of data—carefully disaggregated data of cohorts whose relative mobility is demonstrable.
- This praxis should welcome open discussion and debate on the political and economic contexts of education (the knowledge of politics and the politics of knowledge) and have a clear notion of the requirements for educational reform, the need to prepare new teachers and administrators, and new intellectual leaders who understand the educational problems of immigrant children and the importance of their role in our society.
- This praxis also must be deeply rooted in a profound confidence

that all immigrant children (especially Latino children) can acquire the knowledge to participate fully in the democratic process if taught in ways that capitalize on their language, culture, motivation, and values.

- This praxis should pursue long-term strategies to improve the quality of life of these immigrant children by ensuring their health and nutrition, their safety, and their fair share of the educational resources and cultural wealth of this country.
- This praxis ought to go beyond lip-service institutional commitment to a genuine respect for the immigrant family, the role of parents in children's education, and the commitment to help teachers work to help these children succeed. Indeed, this praxis must provide a new and more open space and the opportunity for these children to have a voice of their own in their future.

If educators' praxis, researchers' praxis, and the praxis of those in charge of policy are based on the above principles, then a pedagogy of hope can become a pedagogy of reality. The logical consequence of these principles for educational reform are sweeping and profound, well beyond the minimum of fairness and justice. It is not enough not to segregate immigrant children, not to isolate them, not to neglect them. It is not enough to decrease dropout rates and gang activity among the youth. There is a need for a collective encompassing commitment to facilitate the educational, social, and cultural development of Latino children (and of all immigrant children). Such commitment will generate more creative approaches as pathways to future success. We could open schools after school hours to enrich Latino children with new experiences of all kinds, including nonacademic, yet valuable, experiences for their future life. For example:

- Organize Japanese-style schooling with after-school hours to mentor children in special subjects.
- Establish predictable workshop activities in Spanish and English for writing exercises, reading poetry, journalistic activities, folk dancing, painting, theater plays, film festivals, health seminars, family therapy, and literacy activities with focus on specific needs (contracts, shopping, school documents, and so on).
- Offer weekly or monthly activities to engage in volunteer literacy efforts with adults, whereby skilled children work with community persons.
- Provide folklore and historical documentation seminars for children, whereby they gather original data on their families and their histories on both sides of the border.

- Arrange for economic seminars in which qualified local experts discuss banks, stocks and bonds, market principles, real estate, investments, and so on.
- Facilitate activities that parents and children request and desire to organize for their own benefit.

The notion behind these suggestions is that a praxis congruent with a pedagogy of hope does not leave any stone unturned, and it does not seek pretexts to cop out, to negate the responsibility we all have to the next generation. The intellectual enrichment of immigrant children and their families is the very best investment we can make for our own welfare and the welfare of this country. Furthermore, any investment in this country's harmonious pursuit of democracy is also an investment in what is an increasingly dangerous world where children continue to be neglected or abused. Because Latino children are among the poorest in this country, we must develop the economic infrastructure to provide them with the kinds of experiences previously listed. Also, the culturally congruent way of conducting these activities is through Latino networks. Using the existing networks of friends, relatives, and neighbors, these activities can enhance Latino children's sense of belonging to a community. Finally, in an increasingly more sophisticated technological world, we cannot implement any of the enriching strategies just discussed without a solid grasp of modern technology. That must be a sine qua non of each and every intellectual endeavor for the next generation. The organization of such activities should also have a measure of resocialization of teachers and counselors who, through the more personal engagement with Latino children and their families, will in time guide Latino children to a productive life, away from drugs, violence, and marginalization.

New Educational Leadership

Until we have a critical mass of Latino educators with a long-term vision of the potential of Latino children, we won't be able to implement enrichment policies and do away with the policies of exclusion and isolation. Latino intelligentsia, Latino educational leaders, and responsible educators agree that an effort beyond the call of duty is necessary to change the existing trends. A cadre of Latino leaders is indispensable to form a powerful and cohesive advocacy group on behalf of Latino children. Perhaps the route to form this cadre must first be explored and urged. Following are some of the minimum requirements for the formation of this cadre of Latino educational leaders as a single cohesive force in the United States.

- The creation of Latino educational organizations at various levels (elementary, secondary, and higher education) and of researchers in various disciplines, with national visibility and federal support (at least symbolic), and a national role as consultants for Latino affairs.
- The use of the above organizations as a resource to help school districts and higher education institutions to resolve conflicts and create a more effective pedagogy. Members of these organizations would serve as consultants and liaisons between more established authorities in a particular field and young scholars.
- These organizations could also serve as referral units to identity consultants, representatives of new initiatives, public offices, international Latino agencies, and so on, involved in immigration projects and prearrival and after-arrival assistance programs to immigrant and refugee families, as legal experts and support persons.
- National computer networks of Latino researchers and scholars to share the most current research findings.
- National computer networks of immigrant families to retain links across states and countries and to help in the adaptation of survival of newcomers.
- Job computer searches in Spanish and English to assist families in their economic survival.
- Counseling and other support systems for families in crisis, especially for families upon arrival.
- Health and education information networks to help immigrants with health and nutrition problems as well as with school problems, especially immediately after relocation or arrival.
- Latino college student networks to search for financial aid and information needed in order to complete college.
- National computer networks for information on the academic job market for Latinos and the support system necessary to reach promotion and tenure status.

Although some of these suggestions may prove helpful and may operationalize our praxis toward a pedagogy of hope, they are not the entire solution and they are not easy to implement. They are merely a direction toward a solution. As Freire states throughout his recent work (1995), hope is an ontological need that we cannot afford to neglect, but hope is also the beginning of a new utopia and a brighter future. We will, of course, continue to face serious dilemmas and raise questions difficult to answer, but we will, at least, know where the road to a better future starts.

Dreams, Worries, and Borders

What will happen to Latinos in the next century? Will they become diluted into the mainstream population? Will they become a powerful political force within the United States? Will they also become pivotal in the world economic equation and the United States' negotiation with the Spanish-speaking nations of the world? Will the *Raza Cósmica*, the mythical *Aztlán*, finally become a tangible reality with an even more impressive presence in the media, federal bureaucracy, professional ranks, elites of bankers, doctors, and scientists? And if this were to happen, would there be more Latino children in poverty, newcomers with new dreams, new needs, and new sufferings? Will the United States of North America get over the color line and engage frequently and naturally in interracial marriages? If so, it is likely that the United States may become a "brown country" faster than any European societies. I am sure that this very thought will crisp the hair of many people in the United States. The day the United States is more brown than White will be "doomsday" for White supremacists and racially prejudiced people. As new militias get organized across the country, as the old prejudice of White against "color" and "other" peoples becomes institutionalized and supported by some right-wing politicians advocating for new walls south of the border, quietly, patiently, and within the system, millions of Latinos are becoming the new Americans and are finding every corner of this country in which to work hard, raise their children, and dream about a better future. This is the United States, isn't it? The United States is the country in which we immigrants came to dream of great things, of a democracy and a political system that could accommodate us, no matter what our colors or accents are, no matter how low we were before we arrived! Yes and no. Yes, because that is the commitment of this new nation, and many of its people find immigrants necessary and even pleasant, if they work hard and help the country. No, because many of our citizens are terrified about the new wave of brown immigrants and consequently are now feeling marginalized, excluded, and dislocated by the sheer numbers of new immigrants of color. Are these Americans justified in their fears? Probably not, but their fears and anxiety are real nonetheless. The fact that Latinos assimilate rapidly and many of them disappear into the mainstream should give them a sense of relief, yet the pace of immigration from south of the border is fast and must be addressed

by policymakers. Is the solution to put up new walls and allow vigilantes to harass and murder undocumented Latinos? No, of course not; it
is not only cruel, illegal, and totally ineffective, it is also one of the
lowest forms of scapegoating and victimization of innocent people.

There is no way back. A country that invited low-skilled laborers of
color, that recruited (and continues to recruit aggressively) labor
hands, must accept the reality that hands do not come alone—they
come with families, children, cultures, and needs. In a capitalistic society where "labor is imported" we tend to think of people as objects
that can be discarded after we use them. Calling the *Migra* after we
take the poor migrants' work and terminating individuals who worked
in the fields for many years is unfair and is based on the theory that
business profits justify the use of "disposable" human beings and their
families. When we deny asylum to Indochinese refugees who were
abandoned in Vietnam or Thailand after working for us in the military
villages, or when we allow the enemy to destroy former allies, we are
"disposing" of human beings. This policy of "disposing" of human
beings has a way of catching up with us and forcing us to pay the
consequences. The price is that we have changed the texture of our
entire society, and if we have faith in our own democracy and our
nation as a powerful sociopolitical and economic superpower, we
should be true to our commitments. One of these commitments, perhaps the main dream of our democracy, is that education is for all and
that education can empower all peoples to participate in our democratic structures and make an important contribution to our society.
The time has come to test our own strength and our beliefs in the Constitution and the principles of our Founding Fathers. The Latino immigrants, especially the new generations, will prove worthy of their new
country and will undoubtedly play a very important role in the future
of the United States.

References

Ainslie, R. "Cultural Mourning, Immigration, and Engagement: Vignettes
from the Mexican Experience." Paper presented at the Conference on Immigration and Sociocultural Remaking of the North American Space, David
Rockefeller Center for Latin American Studies, Harvard University, April
11–12, 1997.

Freire, P. *Pedagogy of Hope. Reliving Pedagogy of the Oppressed.* New York: Continuum Press, 1995.

López, D. "Leticia A. Alumni: Two Case studies of Perseverance." Unpublished manuscript. Department of Human Development and Psychology.
Harvard University, 1997.

Index

About the Author

Enrique (Henry) T. Trueba is R. Hinojosa Regents Professor in the College of Education at the University of Texas, Austin.

DATE DUE